J. and C. HARRISON
The history of a family shipping venture
Malcolm Cooper

Ships in Focus Publications

Published in the UK by Ships in Focus Publications
18 Franklands, Longton
Preston PR4 5PD

© 2012 Malcolm Cooper and Ships in Focus Publications

Printed in the UK by Amadeus Press Ltd., Cleckheaton, West Yorkshire
ISBN 978-1-901703-23-8

Front cover: *Hartington* (3). *[Lucky Sinclair/Nigel Bowker]*
Harmattan (4) on trials. *[W. Ralston/Peter Harrison-Sleap]*
Title page: *Harpalion* (4) at Vancouver in 1959. *[Ships in Focus]*
Back cover: flag and funnel markings of J. and C. Harrison. *[J.L. Loughran]*
Harlingen (4) at Vancouver. *[J. and M. Clarkson]*
Harfleet at Hobart. *[Kingsley Barr/Russell Priest]*

Harlesden (2) running trials in 1932. *[J. and M. Clarkson collection]*

Preface

More than four decades have elapsed since J. and C. Harrison sold its last ship, bringing down the curtain on a successful family business which had purchased its first vessel in 1887. My father represented the fourth and last generation to manage the firm.

My first recollections of J. and C. Harrison were of my father taking me to the office on Saturday mornings in the mid-1950s. We would take the train from Sutton in Surrey to London Bridge Station, and then walk across the old London Bridge. We always walked on the downstream side, and if I was lucky one of our ships would be alongside discharging. Over the bridge, we would turn right past the Monument, past the fish market, through various buildings, and would arrive at 73-74 Mark Lane. The doorman would doff his cap and say 'Mornin' sir' to father, and up the stairs we would go to the first floor, through the doors on the left and round the corner to the left passing model after model of the company's ships. Passing various offices and receiving another 'Mornin sir' from the office boy (who was over 65), we would enter father's office.

The office was dominated by pictures of Uncle Charles and Uncle John, who had managed the company before my father. Their eyes used to stare down at me with a 'do not touch anything' look every time father left the room. Father's desk was huge and always covered in papers, all in piles about 12 inches high. If anyone came in and asked for a particular letter, father always went straight to it.

Father's Secretary would come in and ask if we would like a cup of tea and hand father the mail. This he would put on the board table (also in his office), open each letter carefully cutting out the foreign stamps, read each letter making comments in the margins with a red or yellow crayon and put each letter in a leather folder which had the various departments' names written on the cover. After tea we would go round to the various departments, provisioning, engineering, chartering and many more I cannot remember. As we entered each office the occupants would say 'good morning Mr Derek' and then add with surprise 'oh, we have Mr Peter in today'.

We now live in a very different world, and a modern shipping manager would probably find 73-74 Mark Lane positively Victorian, but it was the beating heart of an extremely successful company which had carried all types of cargo to the furthest corners of the globe, surviving two world wars and the great depression in an almost constant state of robust financial health. Throughout it remained very much a family business - one that set and maintained very high standards in everything it did.

I was delighted when I heard that Malcolm Cooper was writing a history of J. and C. Harrison and I believe he has done a masterful job of bringing a fascinating story back to life. I am very grateful to both Malcolm and Ships in Focus Publications for producing such a splendid monument to the achievements of my ancestors and to the ships and men of their company. I am sure you will find much to interest you in the pages that follow.

Peter Harrison-Sleap

Contents

Harmatris (2) of 1932 on a busy River Thames. *[Author's collection]*

J. AND C. HARRISON LTD.

Family, faith and industry

Most of Britain's great family shipping dynasties had their roots by the sea, either in the liner ports of London, Liverpool and Glasgow, or the coal ports of North East England, South West Scotland or South Wales. The firm of J. and C. Harrison Ltd., however, was very different. It sprang from the 2nd July 1838 marriage in the parish church of Pickering, Yorkshire of John Harrison, a Unitarian minister with roots stretching back to the Lancastrian Touchet aristocracy of the late Middle Ages, and Ann Elizabeth Gowland, the daughter of a prosperous Yorkshire landowning family.

John and Ann Harrison were to be blessed with no fewer than ten children, of whom nine survived to adulthood. They spent their early years together in Chowbent, a small Lancashire village near Atherton, where John led a Unitarian community. In late 1848, however, the family moved to Brixton in South London, where the Reverend Harrison became the minister of Effra Road Chapel. By this time, the couple had already produced five children, of whom four – three sons and a daughter – had survived. Five more children were born in Brixton between 1849 and 1858, three further sons and two daughters. Two of these younger sons would go on to found the firm of J. and C. Harrison Ltd., but almost all of the siblings would have a part to play in what was from the start very much a family enterprise.

	Born	Died
William Gowland Harrison	1839	1906
John Thomas Harrison	1841	1912
Ralph Harrison	1843	1843
Sarah Ann Harrison	1845	1910
Alfred Henry Harrison	1847	1874
Fanny Elizabeth Harrison	1849	1892
Frederick Angier Harrison	1851	1904
James Touchet Harrison	1853	1890
Charles Willis Harrison	1855	1937
Edith Agnes Harrison	1858	1891

The Reverend Harrison died of tuberculosis at his home in Kennington on 26th March 1866 aged only 51. Given what the family was to achieve, it is striking that few of his children actually lived long lives. Apart from poor little Ralph, three others died before they reached 40, and only John Thomas Harrison and Charles Willis Harrison lived past 70. By 1912, when he became the sole survivor of a family of ten, Charles had been present as an adult at the death beds of no fewer than six of his siblings. In their adult lives, however, Charles' brothers had achieved considerable commercial success, while his sisters, through marriage, were to exert an equally important influence over his career. The Reverend Harrison left his family with an important legacy made up in equal parts of a strong Unitarian faith, a deep work ethic, a broad education and a spirit of industry. All were to play their part in shaping the Harrison shipping dynasty.

A business based on coal

The two eldest Harrison boys were already making their way in the business world when their father passed away. William had become a colonial merchant and would eventually set up a chemicals business of his own. John became involved in the coastal coal trade and was himself a ship owner. Neither man would ever be directly associated with the partnership of J. and C. Harrison, although both would play an important part in shaping its destiny in its early years. The most influential part played by the older children was actually that of the eldest daughter Sarah, who on 15th August 1866 married Thomas Henry Lambert, a London solicitor. Her husband himself played no significant part in our story, but his family did – Thomas was one of the sons of Francis Devereux Lambert, founder of the large firm of coal merchants later to be known as Lambert Brothers.

The marriage directly affected the careers of three of the younger Harrison brothers. Alfred joined Lamberts as a clerk, a move which was to prove fatal for him as he died of cholera at Constantinople in 1874, where the firm had sent him to establish an office. The next brother down in age, Frederick, went to sea and gained his master's certificate in the late 1870s, but the two youngest, James and Charles, both started work as clerks in Lambert's London offices, where they were both employed at the time of the 1871 census.

Their association with the firm was brief but extremely important in shaping their business futures. James left first to earn a chartered accountancy qualification, Charles followed him in 1873 when the two entered the coal trade on their own account as J. and C. Harrison.

At the time they formed their partnership, James was 20 and Charles only 18. By any stretch, they were making an early start but, beyond their own ambition, energy and intelligence, they could draw on strong education in both the basic and business senses of the word, an excellent network of contacts within the industry, and the financial backing of a relatively wealthy family. Fifteen years were to elapse before the brothers branched into ship ownership, during which time their older brother Frederick returned from the sea to join the business (but not the partnership). In that time, the Harrisons became a significant player in the huge UK coal trade.

The history of J. and C. Harrison as coal merchants is beyond the scope of this book, but a measure of the size and success of the business can be gleaned from its office network. The company was based on the second and third floors of 66 Mark Lane in the City of London. It had other offices at 102 Bute Street, Cardiff; 122 Dock Street, Newport; 12 Cambrian Place, Swansea; Baltic Chambers, Newcastle-upon-Tyne; and 134 Rue du Faubourg Poissonniere, Paris. It also owned four steam tugs, two steam launches and the coal hulks *Mark Lane* and *Leopard* moored at Gravesend. By the time the brothers took the decision to enter ship owning in the late 1880s, they were already experienced and successful businessmen, both still in their mid-thirties.

Ship ownership and family tragedy
With the London coal trade almost totally dependent on steam colliers operating between the capital and the great coal fields of the North East, it was a logical move for coal merchants to seek vertical integration, eliminate dependence on independent ship owners, and purchase vessels of their own. Most of the large London coal firms made just such a move between 1870 and 1900 – the Harrison brothers took their first tentative step into the new business in late 1887.

On 9th December 1887, James, Frederick and Charles Harrison purchased 8/64th shares in the 34-year-old, 700-ton steam collier *James Southern* from the London coastal shipping firm Harris and Dixon. Before the end of the year they acquired a further 7/64th shares, and the company's formal entry into ship owning was confirmed on 12th January 1888, when they became managing owners. By March 1889 they had built their shareholding up to 32/64th shares, which were then split formally between James (11), Frederick (10) and Charles (12). On 22nd May 1890 they renamed the vessel *Harlow* (1), thus beginning a naming tradition which the company would maintain through its entire existence.

While the brothers were still accumulating shares in their first purchase, they made a second, acquiring 16/64th shares in the slightly newer and slightly larger *Cannel* on 23rd December 1887, once again from Harris and Dixon. Management of this vessel was transferred on the same day as that of the *James Southern*. The brothers moved far more quickly to rename this acquisition, and she became the *Clapton* on 17th November 1888. They also moved more quickly to acquire full ownership of the ship, buying all of the outstanding 64th shares on 31st May 1889.

The choice of name for the second acquisition might appear strange, but the reason was actually quite simple. Their elder brother, John Harrison, was running a coastal collier business of his own from an office on Great Tower Street, and the name fitted perfectly into his own fleet's nomenclature. The younger trio had obviously already agreed to sell the vessel on to John before they bought out Harris and Dixon, and on 5th July 1889 the vessel was sold outright to him. One of the fascinating aspects of the Harrison family's venture into shipping was that it spawned two separate companies. In the early days, they were operating in very similar businesses, but as we will see later, they diverged dramatically in 1896. J. and C. Harrison would actually retain a holding in what was first John Harrison Ltd. and later H. Harrison (Shipping) Ltd. into the 1960s, but the relationship was basically arm's length in the very early years of both enterprises.

A third acquisition followed the same course as the second. On 17th November 1888 James Harrison, using only his own capital, purchased the small 10-year-old Aberdeen-built coaster *Benamain* from J. and A. Davidson of the same port. In the following July he sold her on to John Harrison. Three months later he made a far more significant acquisition. The *Godrevy*, purchased from Thomas Briggs of Manchester, was not a coaster, but an ocean-going tramp steamer. Only five years old, she had a carrying capacity equivalent to the three previous purchases combined. Her purchase was the first indication that the brothers' shipping aspirations were now aiming far higher than the horizon of the coastal shipping trade. Two months after the initial purchase, the brothers re-balanced their individual holdings, with Charles buying 24/64th shares, and Frederick 16, leaving James with 24.

At this stage fate intervened to deal the family a series of heavy blows. The widowed Ann Elizabeth Harrison passed away at her home in Brixton on 19th October 1890 aged 72. She was followed in less than a week by one of her sons. On 24th October 1890 James Touchet Harrison died at his home at 30 Amhurst Park, Hackney. He was only 37, and through his 24 shares in the *Godrevy* controlled a significant part of the family capital invested in the shipping business. Such a blow would have meant the end for most family enterprises. Charles, who was himself just a month past his 36th birthday, was now the sole partner of J. and C. Harrison. While he had already proved himself a resourceful business man, it is questionable that even he would have been able to continue to build the enterprise on his own.

One of the founders, James Touchet Harrison.
[Peter Harrison-Sleap]

5

Charles, however, was anything but alone. His elder brother Frederick was now a well-established coal merchant in his own right, and could also offer a decade's sea-going experience. He did not become a partner, but henceforth became an active contributor to the management of the business and a significant source of capital. The oldest of the Harrison brothers, William, was also drawn into the business, albeit in a more passive fashion. James left a family of young children, including three sons who would play an important role in the later history of the business. His will charged his eldest brother to act as trustee until these boys came of age. While William never took a direct role in running the business, there can be little doubt that his wisdom and business acumen supported Frederick and Charles in facing up to the challenge ahead of them.

Death, sadly, had not finished with the Harrison family. Before 1892 was out, Charles, who had been at the death bed of both his mother and his brother, had also watched two of his sisters pass away. The sad death of Fanny Elizabeth Harrison, twice-widowed and still several years short of her fiftieth birthday, was a blow to the family, but was to have no consequences for any of the family businesses. The far more tragic demise of her young sister Edith was by contrast to shape the entire future direction of both family shipping ventures. Edith Agnes Harrison had married Joseph Pooley, a wine merchant in 1880. The couple subsequently moved to Brighton, where Edith gave birth to three sons, Francis Joseph, Harold and Paul Adrian. Any prospects of a happy family life were quickly shattered. In the late 1880s Joseph Pooley lost his mind and subsequently died in an asylum, leaving Edith a widow before she was 30. The poor girl herself did not last much longer. Having moved with her sons back into the supporting arms of the family in London, she contracted a liver infection and died after a short illness on 3rd December 1891.

Once again the family stood strong in the face of adversity. John Harrison had been happily married to his wife Elizabeth since 1865, but the couple had produced no children. He now stepped in to adopt all three of his youngest sister's sons. He also changed their name by deed poll to Harrison. All three would play an important future role in the family shipping businesses, both of which were now beginning to grow.

The foundations of fortune
It is striking testimony to the business ability and sheer doggedness of Charles Willis Harrison that within a few months of the loss of the man who was both his senior partner and older brother he was moving the shipping enterprise up to a new level. In no more than a couple of years, he would take the key steps to transform a shipping business which owned nothing more than one superannuated coastal collier and one smallish second-hand tramp steamer into a fleet of substance. It takes more than individual ability and will to grow a business – it also takes capital. One of the key ingredients of the rapid growth of J. and C. Harrison's shipping enterprise was the fact that Charles and Frederick were already running a large and profitable coal business, and had spent the previous decade building up significant financial reserves.

The year 1891 was a climacteric one for the shipping business. On 2nd March, Charles bought out the shares (11/64th shares of the *Harlow* (1) and 32/64th shares

of the *Godrevy*) which William was holding in trust for their recently deceased brother's young children. This transaction was no doubt driven by a fraternal agreement to give William the liquid funds to provide for his sister-in-law and nephews. Far more significantly, in the early months of 1891 Charles Harrison ordered his first new vessel from a shipbuilder. The yard chosen was the small Newcastle firm of Edward's Shipbuilding Co. Ltd. The vessel specification was a slightly smaller, but otherwise very similar version of the *Godrevy* – a 1,450-ton, 245-feet long, engine-amidships steamer that could function in any of the short sea and European tramp trades around the UK.

The new vessel was named *Harlyn* (1) when she slipped into the waters of the Tyne and, after fitting out and builder's trials, she was formally registered in London on 30th November in the names of Charles and Frederick Harrison. At the time of register, the brothers nominally held all 64 of the 64th shares, but on the same day 54 of them were 'sold' back to the ship builder. In reality, the 'sale' was a purely paper transaction. The Harrisons had taken possession of the *Harlyn* by making a down-payment of roughly 15.6% of her contract price. They had almost certainly already agreed the terms of future payments with the builder. In modern parlance the transaction might be described as a hire-purchase scheme. The brothers would purchase back 10/64th shares at the end of 1892; 11/64th shares at the end of 1893 and the remaining 33 in November 1894.

This was a highly advantageous arrangement for J. and C. Harrison. The firm would earn the full management fee for the vessel (normally charged at 5 to 6% of gross freight revenues) from the start. They would have to pay the builder only a share of net voyage profits in proportion to the percentage of the ship's residual capital in the builder's hands. After a period of three years, they would end up with complete ownership of the vessel, having only taken on the financing of roughly 52% of her cost at the end of the 'hire-purchase' period. The Harrisons were to use this system to finance a fair proportion of their early fleet expansion. To understand how they were able to acquire what were effectively a series of low interest loans from shipbuilders, it is necessary to pause briefly and explain the inter-dependent but highly unstable relationship which bound owners and builders together.

A shipyard is a very large, capital-intensive asset. It needs to operate at or near full capacity to cover its capital costs. In addition, it requires a staff (depending on size) of hundreds or even thousands of highly skilled workers. While these can be laid-off in times of low demand, yard owners are only likely to do so as a last resort, as the workers can take their skills elsewhere, and there is no guarantee that they will be available to hire back on when business picks up.

A ship is also a large, capital intensive asset, but the capital itself is much lower, and the ship itself is highly vendible. A ship owner, facing poor market conditions, can lay his vessel up at relatively low cost, or in buoyant times sell it for a capital gain. A shipbuilder has no such flexibility. This imbalance is equally as pronounced on the employment front. Ship owners need experienced and professionally qualified deck and engineer officers and a small number of experienced seamen for the bridge, the engine room and the stokehold. Most of a ship's crew in the low technology conditions prevailing before the mid-20th century, however, were low skilled, and hired on only on a voyage by voyage basis. When times were bad, a ship owner need only pay the wages of a few very senior seagoing staff and, if the vessel is laid up, a watchman.

The factor that makes this imbalance so important is the volatility of the shipping market – a volatility which originates in cargo rates and feeds quickly through to ship values, both new and second-hand. When the market is booming, the shipbuilder can capitalize on these conditions to take on orders at premium prices. The market, however, does not move in a smooth fashion – it is normally characterized by short sharp upward spikes, followed by long downwards troughs. In these conditions, a ship owner, as long as he has a strong underlying franchise and an adequate capital base, holds most of the cards in his hands when dealing with the builder. He also, if he calls the market right, has the ability to enhance its profits by expanding his fleet when prices are low, and selling vessels when prices are high. All of the really profitable tramp operators, men such as Runciman, Maclay and Burrell, made the bulk of their fortunes this way. Charles Harrison was to prove as adept as any of them in running his business along these lines.

Between 1892 and 1896 the Harrison brothers built what was only a trio of vessels into a medium-sized tramp-collier fleet. They started slowly. The only event of note in 1892 was the renaming of *Godrevy* as *Harbury* (1), an event significant simply because it indicated that the company had made up its mind for good about how it ships would be named. In early 1893, however, it took delivery of the 1,150-ton collier *Harbourne* from S.P. Austin and Son Ltd. of Sunderland. The connection with Austins was to prove a strong one, and over the next decade most of the Harrison brothers' new ships would be launched from their Wearside yard.

Before fleet expansion could proceed much further, J. and C. Harrison suffered its first marine losses almost back to back. On 11th March 1894 the *Harbury* (1) was wrecked off Algiers. On the 29th of the same month, the *Harbourne*, only just over a year old, went down off Flamborough Head with a cargo of coal after colliding with another British steamer. These losses, however, would be balanced before the end of the year by the arrival of three ships, two new from the builder's yard and one purchased second hand. The company stuck with the builders it knew, signing one contract each with Austins and Edwards. The new ships were a completely mismatched pair. The *Harberton* (1), delivered by Austins in July, was a 1,450-ton collier; the *Harden*, delivered a month later, was a 1,950-ton tramp designed for the well-established coal out/grain home trade to the Mediterranean and Black Sea. At this stage, it seems clear that the brothers were seeking to establish a position in both the British coastal coal trade and the wider European tramp business. What is not immediately clear is the motivation for the second hand acquisition they squeezed in between the arrival of their two new ships. The 22-year-old *Glenfinlas* had been built for the Glen Line's express cargo service to the Far East. She was designed for speed, not carrying capacity, and had been sold off by her owners as obsolete in 1890. She had been run by a small Newcastle firm for four years when Harrisons purchased her in July 1894. They cannot have entertained any hope of extracting a profit from a vessel equipped with a powerful but inefficient compound engine which had already given more than two decades of hard service. The most likely explanation is that they picked her up at something close to her scrap value to meet the requirements of a single time charter. Within less than a year they had sold her on to a Swedish owner – almost certainly at a profit.

1895 also saw the disposal of the company's two oldest ships. The veteran *Harlow* (1), in which the brothers still held only 31/64th shares, was sold in July in a straightforward transaction with an Essex-based owner. The disposal of the *Harlyn* (1), a four-year old vessel built to the company's own specifications, was a more complex transaction – one which hinted that the Harrison brothers were beginning to build a network of shipping contacts independent of their original coal business. As we have seen, the brothers had only bought the outstanding 33/64th shares in the vessel in November 1894. In February 1895 they sold 16/64ths to Thomas Mann of West Hartlepool and in July they sold all the remaining shares to the same person. Mann's ships were managed by Julius E. Guthe, and the two were working together with a consortium of other Teeside investors to form what in 1899 would become the West Hartlepool Steam Navigation Co. Ltd. The brothers had obviously formed a link with Guthe, because several other J. and C. Harrison vessels would be sold to the same company in future years.

The 1895 disposals were not a matter of retrenchment. In fact the brothers were raising capital for accelerated investment. In 1895 they took delivery of three new vessels from three different builders: the 1,000-ton collier *Harlington* from Austins, the 1,450-ton collier *Harpalus* from J.L. Thompson and Sons Ltd. of Sunderland, and the 2,400-ton tramp *Harcalo* (1) from William Pickersgill and Sons, also of Sunderland. The brothers appear to have decided that the *Harlington* (1) was simply too small, and she was sold to P&O for £14,272 in mid-January 1896. The acquisition of the *Harpalus* introduced a new dynamic into the firm's investment strategy – the short-term involvement of a significant outside investor. While all vessels acquired before had been registered under the

Harlington of 1895 seen in Harrisons' colours during the brief period before her sale to P&O. *[Nigel Farrell collection]*

names of Charles and Frederick Harrison, the *Harpalus* was registered under the names of Charles Harrison and Sir Christopher Furness, with all 64/64th shares held jointly. The younger Harrison was moving in very august company – Furness controlled one of the largest shipping empires in Britain; an empire which included his own shipyard on the Tees. No records survive to document exactly what arrangement the two men had come to, but they had probably come together to purchase a vessel for which Thompsons had lost their original buyer. Once again, Charles Harrison was using an outside source of capital to help finance the expansion of his fleet.

The pace of new building was maintained in 1896. Austin and Son delivered three vessels of completely different sizes: the 1,800-ton *Harbury* (2) in August, the 1,300-ton *Harborne* in October and the 3,100-ton *Harpenden* (1) in December. The brothers brought the year to an end with another apparently idiosyncratic second-hand acquisition, the 16-year-old, 640-ton coaster *Mandarin* of Glasgow. As with the earlier purchase of the *Glenfinlas*, there was more to the transaction than met the eye. Although the vessel was registered in the names of James and Alexander Wyllie of Troon, the original seller of 32/64th shares was their mortgagee James Dickie. This suggests a distressed sale and a bargain price. In addition, although the ship was renamed *Hardy* in May 1897, she was sold to John Harrison in July. John was almost certainly the intended owner all along, and his younger brothers were simply using their greater liquidity to facilitate the purchase. One way, or the other, J. and C. Harrison should have ended 1896 with a medium-sized fleet of new vessels, half designed for the coastal coal trade and half for high seas tramping. In fact, by the end of the year, the fleet size had halved and the coastal coal business was gone for good. The Harrisons had completed a transaction which would set the company's course for the remainder of its commercial existence.

The years of decision

By the mid-1890s the British coastal coal trade had spawned a large number of specialist shipping companies, most of them relatively small. The time was ripe for consolidation – for the creation of larger companies able to deal on an even footing with the increasingly concentrated coal industry on the one hand, and large customers like the London coal wholesalers on the other. The lead was taken in London by the firm of William Cory and Son Ltd., which persuaded five separate owners to sell them their coastal collier businesses. Four of the sellers, D. Radford and Co., Beadle Brothers Ltd., Green Holland and Son, and Mann George had relatively small fleets – the fifth was J. and C. Harrison.

The transaction between Cory and J. and C. Harrison was both large and complex, but its underlying principle was a simple one. The Harrison brothers sold their collier business to Cory and agreed to an undertaking that effectively stated that they would take no further interest in the business of coastal coal shipping. The core assets sold were the fully-owned steam colliers: *Harberton*

(1), *Harpalus*, *Harbury* (1) and *Harborne*. The vessels were more or less brand new – indeed the last named was registered in Harrison ownership on 1st October and sold on 7th November. With them, the Harrisons also disposed of four steam tugs, two steam launches, and minority 64th shares in no fewer than 28 other steamers. They also disposed of an impressive portfolio of shares in 29 limited liability shipping companies with a combined value of £37,536 10s.

The most striking thing about this transaction is its sheer size. J. and C. Harrison had built up a considerable portfolio of shipping assets in a fairly short time, and obviously made the sale of the shares portfolio a condition of the disposal of the collier business and the undertaking not to re-enter the trade. The brothers were thus able to arm themselves with a significant cash chest with which to invest in deep sea tramping – the business to which they would now devote their entire attention.

Having made such a momentous business decision, one which left them with a fleet of only three vessels (leaving aside the soon-to-be-disposed-of *Hardy*), it might have been expected that the Harrisons would embark on a policy of slowly building up a medium-sized fleet of deep-sea tramps. What actually transpired was completely different – the guiding principle for J. and C. Harrison over the next decade was not to be fleet expansion, but rather further capital growth.

At the beginning of 1897 the deep-sea fleet was composed of the *Harden* of 1894, the *Harcalo* (1) of 1895 and the *Harpenden* (1) of 1896, all good-sized modern vessels ideally suited to the demands of the trade. The *Harden* unfortunately was wrecked in January near Cape Passero while carrying grain and wood from the Black Sea to Rotterdam. Her loss was more than compensated for by the arrival of no fewer than five new vessels in the fleet. They were very much a mixed bag in terms of size, and it is difficult to come to any other conclusion than that the brothers were still experimenting to find the vessels best suited to their newly defined business.

The first arrival was the Austin-built, 1,200-ton *Harlech* (1) in April 1897. She remained in the fleet only for just over a year before being sold to the US Navy. She was followed by the 2,875-ton tramp *Harmonic*, launched by Austins exactly two months after her smaller predecessor. The third and smallest Austin contribution arrived in August, the 1,100-ton *Harmony*. The next two acquisitions provided

Harcalo (1) built in 1895.*[Nigel Farrell collection]*

8

another example of the Harrisons' ability to deploy their financial resources to profit from the misfortunes of other ship owners and acquire new tonnage at a discount from shipbuilders left with vessels whose would-be owners had defaulted. The London partnership of Smith and Scaramanga had placed an order for two tramps with William Gray of West Hartlepool. The first was launched as the 2,600-ton *Saint Helen* in August. However, Smith and Scaramanga had overstretched themselves and, although she was registered at London in their names on 16th September, Frederick Harrison was appointed as ship's husband. On the same day 55/64th shares were sold back to the builder and 9/64th shares to the Harrison brothers. They subsequently increased their holding to 32/64th shares in September 1898, but took no steps to rename the ship to fit in with her fleet mates. At the same time as they took over management of the *Saint Helen*, the brothers took over the contract for the second, larger vessel which was still on the slips. She was launched in December as the *Harlingen* (1), but never joined the fleet, being resold before completion to Harrowing of Whitby who registered her as the *Ethelbrytha* in March of the following year. The last acquisition of 1897 was equally unconventional, although not without precedent. The 2,500-ton *Harperley* (1) came from the Middlesbrough yard of R. Craggs and Sons Ltd. and, as with the *Harpalus* of 1895, she was acquired jointly with the Furness family, in this case the name on the register being that of Stephen Furness, Sir Christopher's son.

1898 was to produce another batch of new vessels, but before describing these, it is best and stop to consider why the Harrisons, who had only a decade of ship owning experience behind them (and the first half of that decidedly small scale) were lavishing so many orders on the shipbuilders of the North East. After a brief rally at the beginning of the decade, freight rates spent most of the 1890s in the doldrums. This was reflected in a slowdown in the flow of new orders to shipbuilders. From the mid-1890s on, these builders were quoting lower and lower prices to keep their berths full. This was the business environment in which the Harrison brothers were building up their fleet. The fact that the bulk of their business went to one yard suggests that Austin was giving them particularly favourable terms to secure a dependable flow of business.

Austin and Son delivered three vessels to the Harrisons in 1898: the 1,700-ton near-sisters *Harrington* and *Harport* (1), and the 1,200-ton *Harlech* (2). On 6th July of the same year, J. and C. Harrison, which had hitherto traded only as a partnership, was incorporated as a private limited liability company under the name of J. and C. Harrison Ltd. Authorized capital was set at £400,000, divided into 30,000 Cumulative Preference Shares of £5 each, and 50,000 Ordinary Shares of £5 each, all fully paid-up.

The preference shares were entirely in the hands of the four surviving Harrison brothers, who also held the bulk of the ordinary share capital. Caroline Harrison was their mother, and Kathleen and Jeannie were the wives of Frederick and Charles respectively. The bulk of the remaining shares were held by business associates, of whom the most notable was Charles Palmer, the Jarrow shipbuilder. Bryden was the firm's lawyer, and Turkentine the firm's accountant. It was very much a private family affair, with Charles holding the bulk of the capital. The initial allocation of shares was as follows:

	Preference Shares	Ordinary Shares
William Gowland Harrison	200	201
Charles Willis Harrison	26,000	37,794
Frederick Harrison	3,600	8,001
Caroline Harrison		1
Kathleen Elizabeth Harrison		1
Jeannie Isabella Harrison		1
John Thomas Harrison	200	201
Peter Young		700
Roland Thomas Tidswell		600
Charles Douglas Palmer		400
Walter Horseley		400
George Harris		400
John Cleland Napier		1,200
John Bryden		50
Thomas Turkentine		50

The actual transfer of assets from the original investors to the company was a two-stage process. First, the joint shareholders (either Charles and Frederick, or Charles and a member of the Furness family) sold all 64/64th shares to Charles. Frederick was paid with shares in the new company and Sir Christopher and Stephen Furness presumably in cash. Charles then sold all the assets to J. and C. Harrison Ltd. At the time, neither the *Harport* (1) nor the *Harlech* (2) had been delivered. The total schedule of assets was nonetheless extensive.

Property

1. The tenancy of the second and third floors of 66 Mark Lane, City of London.
2. The tenancy of two front rooms on the first floor of 102 Bute Street, Cardiff.
3. The tenancy of one large front room on the first floor of 122 Dock Street, Newport.
4. The tenancy of the 1st floor of 12 Cambrian Place, Swansea.
5. The leasehold of six rooms on the second floor of Baltic Chambers, Newcastle-upon-Tyne.
6. The tenancy of 134 Rue du Faubourg Poissonniere, Paris.

Steamers

Harcalo	(1)	64/64th shares
Brator		8/64th shares
Harpenden	(1)	64/64th shares
Sportsman		8/64th shares
Harmonic	(1)	64/64th shares
Umgeni		4/64th shares
Harmony	(1)	64/64th shares
Birchtor		5/64th shares
Harperley	(1)	64/64th shares
Archtor		5/64th shares
Harrington	(1)	64/64th shares
Plastor		4/64th shares
Saint Helen		32/64th shares
Edenhall		32/64th shares

Ship and other companies

194	£50 shares	Manin Steam Ship Co. Ltd.
3	£100 shares	Falkirk Steam Ship Co. Ltd.
20	£100 shares	Steam Ship Royston Grange Ltd.
20	£100 shares	Steam Ship Beacon Grange Ltd.
5	£100 shares	Sutton Steam Ship Co. Ltd.
5	£100 shares	Frederick Knight Steam Ship Co. Ltd.
150	£10 6% preference shares	Ceres Steam Ship Co. Ltd.
5	£100 shares	Steam Ship Ulverston Co. Ltd.
10	£100 shares	Steam Ship Rippingham Grange Ltd.
10	£100 shares	Steam Ship Labuan Co. Ltd.
8	£100 shares	Steam Ship Mainstay Co. Ltd.
10	£10 shares	Steam Ship Rock Channel Co. Ltd.
10	£100 shares	Cuban Steam Ship Co. Ltd.
40	£10 shares	Durham Steam Ship Co. Ltd.
50	£100 shares	Furness Withy and Co. Ltd.
500	5% preference shares	Houlder Brothers and Co. Ltd.
4½%	£2,500 debenture bond	Houlder Brothers and Co. Ltd.
50	£10 shares	London Exchange Steam Ship Co. Ltd.

The vendors' interest in the Ante Breakage Co., Cardiff

There were a number of interesting features of this extensive portfolio of assets. The first and most important was that its components had been transferred into J. and C. Harrison Ltd. at their acquisition cost, and the aggregate market value of the holdings must have been far higher than the company's initial capital of £400,000. The second was the impressive spread of assets across the entire shipping industry, ranging from single-ship tramp ventures to the massive Furness Withy liner business. Thirdly, there was the half share in the *Edenhall*, which actually represented another joint venture with J.E. Guthe of West Hartlepool, who would shortly purchase the vessel outright for the West Hartlepool Steam Navigation Co. Ltd. Finally, there were two concentrations of assets in very different shipping businesses. J. and C. Harrison Ltd. held preference shares and a debenture bond in Houlder Brothers' South American liner business, as well as shares in three of the group's single ship companies. This early connection with the trade between Europe and South America was to prove the foundation of a business that the Harrison fleet would enter directly in the 1930s. The second was the company's significant interest in the London tramping business of John Holman and Sons, in four of whose ships (*Archtor, Birchtor, Brator* and *Plastor*) it held a stake.

Beyond the company's holdings, the most important aspect of the formation of J. and C. Harrison Ltd. was its confirmation of Charles Willis Harrison as the arbiter of its fortunes. This was not simply a matter of him holding a huge majority of the ordinary and preference share capital. The company's Articles of Associations gave him sole control of the business as Managing Director. While he could, and no doubt did, consult with his fellow shareholders in general and his brothers in particular, all key business decisions were his to make. The principle of complete corporate power concentrated in the hands of one man was to remain in place until his death. Even after that, when the number of managing directors increased to two, the principle remained in place. J. and C. Harrison Ltd. was always to be very much a private family business, with decision-taking entrusted to that family's elders. There is one oddity about the whole transaction. While all the company's vessels were

re-registered in the name of the new corporate entity, the principals reverted to the practice of registering ships directly under their own names in the following decade. Beyond the normal corporate objectives of limited liability, and the establishment of Charles Harrison's position of power, the new company appears to have been created with another object in mind – a second, and far more dramatic sale of tonnage.

Genius unleashed

The newly created J. and C. Harrison Ltd. entered the last year of the 19th century in a state of robust good health. With the delivery of the *Harport* (1) and the *Harlech* (2) in late 1898, it owned outright a fleet of eight steamers, the oldest of which had been built as recently as 1895. In March the number grew to nine when the company bought the remaining 32/64th shares in the *Saint Helen* from her builder. Most tramp owners in this situation would have been looking forward to reaping the long-term benefits of operating a modern fleet acquired at a low capital cost in a business environment in which it would be normal to expect a cyclical upswing in freight rates and ship values. The business environment, however, was not to be normal, and Charles Harrison was about to prove once and for all that he was not a typical tramp owner.

The shipping market was transformed by the outbreak of war in South Africa. What at first might have seemed like another brief colonial skirmish, rapidly developed into a long war of attrition against a well-armed, highly motivated and elusive enemy. Vast resources of men and material were mobilized in Britain, the Empire and the Dominions, and the resulting large field army had to be supplied from a chain which stretched from North America to New Zealand. The British government chartered hundreds of mercantile vessels, most of them from large British liner companies. These companies in turn had to find replacement tonnage to keep their regular services running. Freight rates and ship values soared in the tramping industry, and Charles Harrison moved quickly to take advantage of the opportunity to realize sizeable capital gains.

Harrison sold his first vessel, the *Harmony* (1), to the Red Cross Iquitos Steamship Co. Ltd. of Liverpool in early January. He then made two disposals in February and March, the *Harpenden* (1) and the *Harperley* (1). Both went to the same London ship broker who subsequently sold them to the rapidly expanding fleet of Frank C. Strick. In April, the only non-British disposal took place when *Harcalo* (1) went to Bilbao owners. With almost half of the fleet already sold at a profit, there was now a lull, while the remaining ships were employed on what should have been highly rewarding charters.

By the end of the year, however, all five of these vessels had also been sold. The *Harport* (1) went to Australian owners in September and in October the *Harlech* (2) became the second sale to Red Cross Iquitos. The other three ships were sold in December. The *Harmonic*

The clipper-bowed *Archtor* (3,414/1895) of J. Holman and Sons in which J. and C. Harrison held 5/64 shares. She had been built by R. Thompson and Sons, Sunderland as *Whetstone* for Culliford and Clark, also of Sunderland, and acquired by Holman in 1898. *Archtor* went missing after passing Cape Henry on 3rd January 1912 whilst on a voyage from Norfolk, Virginia to Rotterdam with a cargo of phosphate rock. *[Roy Fenton collection]*

(1) and *Saint Helen* were both purchased by Strick, who had acquired two of their fleet mates earlier in the year via an intermediary. Finally, the *Harrington* was sold to the Liverpool tramp owner W.R. Rea. The last three sales agreements were all signed on 11th December 1899. The ship owning firm of J. and C. Harrison Ltd. had disposed of its entire fleet less than a year and a half after coming into being.

Charles Harrison was not unique in taking such dramatic advantage of soaring asset values. The Glasgow ship owner William Burrell was involved in an even larger sale of assets at exactly the same time. Unlike Burrell, however, Harrison was dealing almost entirely with his own private capital (the Burrell fleet was organized as a series of single ship companies with multiple small minority shareholders). In addition, Burrell did not remove his house flag entirely from the seven seas, but retained several vessels to keep his ship management business ticking over. As no detailed business records survive, it is impossible to be certain of the extent of Harrison's involvement in the shipping industry after the disposal of the fleet. Given his reputation, his family connections with the coal trade, and his representative offices in the major coal exporting ports, it seems highly likely that he was active as a freight broker, and perhaps also as a third-party ship manager. With regard to his company's capital, it is fairly easy to work out what he must have done. He did not order any new vessels of his own, and with market values where they were it is unlikely that he was an active buyer of shares in other vessels or companies. The money was almost certainly invested in short-term government bonds where it could earn a steady dividend until the time came to invest again.

The Boer War dragged on until 1902 keeping shipping tied up on government service and freight rates at inflated levels. With the return of peace, the market slumped sharply. Not only was the government's need for shipping brought to an end, but the return of government-chartered vessels to the market produced an immediate glut of tonnage, a glut made all the larger by a three-year surge in new vessel orders. By 1903 the shipping industry was locked in what would prove to be a decade-long period of depressed rates, collapsing second-hand values and serial business failures. After staying out of the market for four years, Charles Harrison returned in 1904. His return was every bit as dramatic as the whirlwind investments of 1895-98. In a weak market, J. and C. Harrison Ltd. was expanding rapidly when shipbuilding prices were low.

Re-inventing the business

The *Harcalo* (2), a 2,800-ton tramp, was launched for the Harrison brothers by Furness, Withy and Co. Ltd., West Hartlepool on 11th August 1904. It seems obvious that Charles Harrison had maintained his connections with the Furness family, as he had not used their shipyard before. When the vessel was registered on 28th September, however, it was not in the names of the new limited company, but rather in the names of the brothers themselves. As has already been mentioned, this practice was to be maintained until 1920, and in the absence of published accounts for J. and C. Harrison Ltd. it is impossible to understand how the brothers arranged financial transactions between themselves and the limited company they controlled.

The *Harcalo* (2) was followed into service by two sisters, both built by Furness, Withy and Co. Ltd. – the *Harmonic* (2) joining the fleet in January 1905 and the *Harmony* (2) a month later, both also registered in the joint names of the brothers. They were joined in the second half of the year by a trio of significantly larger vessels: the 3,470-ton twins *Harlingen* (2) and *Harlech* (3) from William Gray and Co. Ltd., West Hartlepool, and the slightly bigger 3,500-ton *Harley* (1) from Furness. This latest round of acquisitions was supported by the same sort of financing from the shipbuilder that had been employed in the 1890s. The *Harley* was registered in the joint names of Frederick Harrison and Stephen Furness. In the case of the two Gray-built vessels, the ships were registered in the sole name of Frederick Harrison, and 33/64th shares in the *Harlingen* (2), and 32/64th shares in the *Harlech* (3) were re-sold to the builder immediately after registration.

1906 was to prove a momentous year, even by the standards of what had already been an incident-filled company history. In February, William Gray delivered the 4,000-ton *Harperley* (2) (again registered only in the name of Frederick Harrison) and he was re-sold 40/64th shares in the vessel several days after she was registered. In April, 15/64th shares in the *Harlech* (3) were re-purchased by Frederick Harrison, bring his holding up to 48/64th shares. At the end of May, all 64/64th shares in the *Harley* (1) were 'sold' by Frederick Harrison and Stephen Furness to William G. Harrison. This was merely the prelude to the immediate sale of the vessel to Belgian owners. The ship had been in the fleet for less than nine months, and the purchasers, the large shipping concern of A. Deppe, must have been offering a healthy premium to her building cost to persuade the Harrisons to sell so quickly. This rapid sale was more than compensated for by the addition of three more new steamers, all launched at West Hartlepool between 2nd August and 3rd September. William Gray produced the 3,500-ton *Harlyn* (2), while Furness was responsible for the 3,500-ton *Harpenden* (2) and the 4,170-ton *Harley* (2). There cannot have been many other cases of the same builder producing two ships of the same name for the same owner within one 12-month period.

Even before any of the autumn order was launched, the company had been hit hard by yet another family tragedy. On 1st June 1906 Frederick Angier Harrison died at his home in Sydenham after a brief illness. While he had never been a partner in the shipping business, and had carried on trading as a coal merchant, his contribution to the firm was enormous in terms of capital, time and market knowledge. With his brother's demise, Charles Harrison was very much on his own, even though elder brother William held Frederick's shares in trust for his wife and eight children, and John remained a minority shareholder in the parent limited company. Before the year was out, Charles suffered a further blow with the loss of the *Harlingen* (2), wrecked on the coast of Brazil in November.

As Frederick had actually held most of the family-controlled 64th shares in the newly built fleet, the granting of probate for his will on 14th September produced a series of linked share transactions, most of which involved either Charles purchasing shares from his deceased brother's estate or William taking ownership of them as Trustee. Rather than untangle these, it is better to summarize the ownership structure as it stood at the end of 1906.

Harcalo (2)	Charles W. Harrison 64/64th shares
Harmonic (2)	Charles W. Harrison and Stephen W. Furness 64/64th shares
Harmony (2)	Charles W. Harrison 64/64th shares
Harlech (3)	Charles W. Harrison 17/64th shares; William G. Harrison 47/64th shares
Harperley (2)	Charles W. Harrison 30/64th shares; William Gray and Co. Ltd. 34/64th shares
Harpenden (2)	Charles W. Harrison and Sir Christopher Furness 64/64th shares
Harlyn (2)	Charles W. Harrison 64/64th shares
Harley (2)	Charles W. Harrison and Stephen W Furness 64/64th shares

Charles thus was at least part owner of all eight vessels in the J. and C. Harrison fleet, but only financing 100% of the capital cost of three of them. One other was shared with his elder brother acting as Trustee, but the other half of the fleet was still being significantly underwritten by shipbuilders, particular the Furness family.

After the vicissitudes of 1906, it might have been expected that Charles Harrison, now running the shipping business entirely on his own, would have paused to take stock and consolidate. This, however, was not his way, and 1907 saw another burst of activity. The *Harcalo* (2) was sold in July to a Cardiff tramp owner. Her departure was more than matched by the delivery of a trio of new arrivals. The first of these, the 4,000-ton *Hartington* (1), was another product of William Gray and Co. Ltd., who in line with previous practice re-purchased 36/64th shares in the vessel a few days after she was registered. The other two acquisitions were steps in new directions. The first was one of the company's few second-hand purchases. Although built as recently as 1902, the ship in question had already passed through two pairs of hands, having been launched by Short Brothers of Sunderland as the *Sagami* for the New York and Oriental Steam Ship Co. Ltd. of Liverpool, but sold before completion to the Hindustan Steam Shipping Co. Ltd. of Newcastle. Harrison purchased her in October and renamed her *Harlow* (2). For some reason none of her owners had her registered in their own home port, and she remained registered at Sunderland, the place where she had been built, for her entire 10-year career under the red ensign. The last arrival of the year was a new vessel, but in her case the company strayed away from the Tees for the first time since the re-entry into ship ownership. The builder of the 3,985-ton *Harport* (2) was John Readhead and Sons Ltd., South Shields. While Harrison might have moved builders, he had not changed his financing model – 40/64th shares were taken back on the books of the builder; in this case the bill of sale actually being dated a day prior to the vessel's entry on to the London register.

In contrast to the four before, 1908 was a fairly quiet year by Harrison standards. Only one vessel joined the fleet, and she was a second-hand purchase. The 4,000-ton *Incharran* had been built at Sunderland for Liverpool owners in 1904. Charles Harrison purchased her outright in July and renamed her *Harcroft*. A week after

the purchase, and before the name change had actually been registered, he sold 32/64th shares to a fellow London ship owner John Holman and Sons Ltd. This was a new departure in fleet financing – Harrison retained a 50% interest in the ship and earned the normal managing fees for running her, but the vessel was functionally a joint venture with another ship owner. This arrangement was to stay in place until April 1912, when Harrison bought Holman's share back from him.

The pace of activity returned to more normal levels in 1909 with no fewer than four vessels joining the fleet, all of them new buildings. William Gray and Co. Ltd. contributed two 4,600-ton sisters, the *Harfleur* (1) which joined the fleet on the second day of the new year and the *Harpeake* which appeared in August. John Readhead and Sons Ltd. delivered the 4,400-ton *Harford* a few days after the *Harfleur* (1), and the 4,300-ton *Harlesden* (1) in March. In every case, some form of outside financing was involved. Gray bought back 50/64th shares in each of the vessels it delivered, and Readhead bought back 34/64th shares in the *Harford*. In the case of the *Harlesden* (1), the vessel was simply registered in the joint names of Charles W. Harrison and John B. Adam – the latter being another London ship owner. One of the new vessels served less than a year with the fleet, her departure being caused not by sale but by misfortune. On 6th November the *Harford* was badly damaged by fire in her bunkers while loading a cargo of timber at Barracouta. She was subsequently abandoned to the underwriters as a constructive total loss. She was to be repaired and sold to a Japanese firm before returning to the red ensign in 1915. She would be owned by four different companies and carry three different names before she was lost in collision in 1924.

Fleet expansion continued at a more modest pace in 1910, with William Gray and Co. Ltd. delivering two new 5,865 sisters, the *Harpagus* (1) and the *Harpalion* (1). In both cases, the builder once again bought back 50/64th shares. Beyond this, the most striking aspect of the expansion was the considerable increase in vessel size. Harrison had begun in business operating vessels very much at the lower end of the size scale for ocean-going tramps. By 1910, he had moved to the opposite end, building ships which were considerably larger than most competing vessels, which tended to range in size between 3,000 and 4,500 tons. This, however, was to prove a short-lived phenomenon. After 1911, only one ship topped the 5,000 ton mark, and she was sold out of the fleet

Harlesden (1) of 1909 in a US ship yard. *[Kevin O'Donoghue collection]*

in less than a year. Having experimented with larger ships, Charles Harrison appears to have decided that the optimal size range for his business was between 4,500 and 5,000 tons.

1911 was more or less a repeat of 1910, with two more new ships joining the fleet. Gray supplied one of these, the 5,950-ton *Harpalyce* (1), effectively the last of three sisters. The other ship, the 4,800-ton *Harmattan* (1) came from one of the company's less commonly used builders, Swan, Hunter and Wigham Richardson Ltd. of Wallsend-on-Tyne. Although it would not be clear until the following year, the long slump in freight rates and the related era of low building costs was about to come to an end. While Charles Harrison would add new ships to his fleet in both 1912 and 1913, he was a net seller of tonnage over the period between January 1912 and the outbreak of war in August 1914. While there was no question of him selling his entire fleet as he had done in 1899, he was as ready as ever to realize a capital gain when market conditions permitted.

Before moving on to discuss the fortunes of the business in the years immediately preceding the outbreak of the First World War, it is worth pausing to consider two aspects of the way Charles Harrison was running his business. The first is the extent to which he used shipbuilders' capital to finance fleet expansion. Only a minority of vessels were actually under full ownership, these dating entirely from the period 1905-06 when the death of Frederick Harrison produced a consolidation of existing shareholdings in the hands of Charles and William, the latter in his role as Trustee. The remaining vessels were all partly financed from outside. This financing came in a variety of forms, but the bulk of it came from the company's shipbuilders. Much of the early finance came from Furness, Withy and Co. Ltd., but after the company concentrated most of its order book with William Gray and Co. Ltd. and John Readhead and Sons Ltd., it was these two firms that carried most of the burden. To get an idea of just how extensive this support was, the table below summarizes the extent and duration of their support. In effect, the two firms, particularly Gray, provided loans for well in excess of half of the capital cost of each vessel until Harrison was in a position to repay them as he began to sell off tonnage, mostly in 1912.

William Gray and Co. Ltd.

Hartington (1)	36/64th shares	25.7.1907 – 30.7.1910
Harfleur (1)	50/64th shares	4.1.1909 – 22.4.1912
Harpeake	50/64th shares	11.8.1909 – 27.4.1912
Harpagus (1)	50/64th shares	10.6.1910 – 30.4.1912
Harpalion (1)	50/64th shares	15.11.1910 – 19.6.1912
Harpalyce (1)	50/64th shares	17.6.1911 – 1.7.1912

John Readhead and Sons Ltd.

Harport (2)	40/64th shares	15.11.1907 – 23.8.1911
Harford	34/64th shares	1.1.1909 – 24.8.1910*

*Date of formal closure of register following vessel being abandoned to the underwriters.

After Frederick's death in 1906, Charles Harrison ran the business very much on his own, with William involved only as a trustee. He would actually remain the sole Managing Director until his own death three decades later, but in the years leading up to 1914 he found assistants among the sons of his deceased siblings. Over time, two would emerge as his firm successors: John Harrison, the son of James

Touchet Harrison, and Francis A. Harrison (known in the family as Frank), one of the three sons of Edith who had all been adopted by John Harrison the elder. Most of the other boys worked for one of the Harrison shipping companies in the early parts of their career. Harold Harrison was brought up to inherit John Harrison the elder's coastal shipping business. One of his brothers, Alfred Harrison (always known in the family as Paul), went to work for J. and C. Harrison Ltd. in 1901. He wrote a memorial about his remarkable set of uncles shortly before his own death in the 1970s, which gives us a glimpse of working life in the early days of the business.

My career began as a clerk in the firm in 1901 and I sat in a small office in 66 Mark Lane with only Uncle Charles and Uncle Frederick. At that time the firm owned no ships, but I do know that whatever ships they owned previously had been sold, as prices were very high consequent upon the Boer War. I was the only clerk, with a Miss Hope, the typist, and my two uncles, but presumably there were other clerks in other rooms.

Charles' two older brothers died after long and successful business careers, William in March 1910 and John in June 1912. William had no children of his own but had two stepsons to whom he left his business. He also made generous bequests to his orphaned nephews who had been brought up by John. The only involvement with J. and C. Harrison had concerned shares in individual vessels which he had held as a Trustee, but these had all been purchased back by Charles several years earlier. John's death was to cause some disruption. The major part of his estate was made up of the £50,000 share capital of his coastal shipping company, John Harrison Ltd. He left a £25,000 stake in the business to Harold, the step son who he had trained to take over the company; and £16,750 to one trusted business associate, and £1,330 to a business partner in Paris. He left £3,500 each to his other two step sons, Francis (Frank) and Arthur (Paul). Both of these young men had been taken into the employ of J. and C. Harrison Ltd. and, despite the fact that his dead brother left him a £1,500 cash bequest, Charles took severe exception to the two nephews in his employ being given shares in the other family shipping business, describing the bequests as 'the greatest disservice John could have done him'. Paul's memoirs suggest that he nursed the grievance for some time. Such a reaction is hard to understand – the coaster company did not compete in any way with J. and C. Harrison, and the boys had simply become sleeping minority shareholders. In addition, John had held shares in J. and C. Harrison Ltd., and the latter was to maintain a cross-shareholding in the coaster company for years. The episode hints at what might have been a slightly dark side to Charles character – he was perhaps a man who had with time grown use to exercising absolute and unchallenged power within a company which had grown up very much as a joint venture between brothers.

As mentioned before, the shipping market began to rally in 1912, and the company entered a three-year period of extensive buying and selling. Two vessels joined the fleet in 1912. The first arrived as a result of Charles Harrison acting himself as a ship financier. The *Harfield* had been built in 1904 as the *Hillgrove* for Liverpool owners. They had sold her in 1907 to the Phoenix Steamship Co. Ltd. of London who renamed her *Calyx*. The purchase was financed by Charles W. Harrison and Francis A. Beane, acting as joint mortgagees. By 1911 the owners were in trouble – management of the vessel was transferred to J. and C. Harrison Ltd. in November of that year, and on 3rd January 1912 the mortgagees formally sold the vessel to Charles Harrison, who renamed her *Harfield* later in the year. Harrison was basically getting the vessel back in exchange for the money he had loaned – as the loan will not have been for the full acquisition cost of the ship, he would have got a good bargain. The second addition was a new vessel, the 4,860-ton *Harmatris* (1). The only thing unusual about her arrival was that she came from a builder, the Northumberland Shipbuilding Co. Ltd. of Sunderland, with which Harrison had never before carried out any business.

There were no fewer than four disposals on the other side of the balance sheet. Two ships were sold in June to very different owners. The *Harport* (2) of 1907 went to the Deutsch-Amerikanische Petroleum Company of Hamburg for conversion into an oil tanker; while the *Harfleur* (1) of 1909 was sold to the Union Navigation Co. Ltd. of Toronto, Canada for use as a conventional cargo steamer. The second pair of disposals came in December when the *Harmony* (2) of 1905 was sold to the Union Steamship Co. of New Zealand Ltd. for use as a collier, and the *Harlow* (2) of 1907 went to S.A. Lloyd del Pacifico to become part of their Europe-Pacific cargo fleet.

1913 witnessed a total of seven transactions, in this case split between four new-built vessels and three disposals. The four new vessels came from three different Sunderland shipbuilders. The Sunderland Shipbuilding Co. Ltd. delivered the 4,900-ton *Harpathian* (1) in February; William Doxford and Sons Ltd. the 6,550-ton *Harlow* (3) in May; Bartram and Sons Ltd. the 4,800 ton *Harflete* later in the same month; and finally the 4,570-ton *Harbury* (3), the second Sunderland Shipbuilding product, arrived in October. The first disposal was the *Harley* (2), sold in January to the same Canadian owners who had bought the *Harfleur* (1) the year before. The second disposal, which took place in the same month, was a more complicated transaction. Harrison sold the *Harcroft* of 1908 to the Guarantee Insurance and Investment Co. Ltd. of London – this company was just an intermediary,

as the vessel was sold on within four months to the Taconic Steamship Co. Ltd. of Toronto; the same London-based man appears as ship manager for both the investment and the shipping company, and the vessel remained on the London register. The third sale was very straightforward, but was the first case since 1899 in which the purchaser was a British liner company; the *Harpeake* of 1909 going to the Moss Steamship Co. Ltd. of Liverpool in July.

The cost of tonnage rose steadily from the middle of 1912 to the outbreak of the war two years later. It was highly significant that the *Harbury* (3), which would have been ordered around the end of 1912, was to be the last new ship to join the fleet for what was to become a period of almost two decades. Charles Harrison simply did not build ships when prices were high. He did, however, sell them aggressively, and in the first five months of 1914 he disposed of no fewer than four steamers, one of them less than a year old. The *Harlow* (3), which had only entered the fleet in the previous May, was the first to go, sold to the German Roland Linie A.G. of Bremen in January. The *Harlech* (3) of 1905 and the *Harpenden* (2) of 1906 both went in April to Greek and French owners respectively. Finally the second-hand *Harfield*, built in 1904 and acquired in 1912 was sold to an Italian concern in May.

It is unlikely that Charles Harrison was reducing his fleet or building up his capital reserves in anticipation of war. There was no general expectation of war until several months later and, acute though his business senses were, Harrison did not have a crystal ball. He was simply following an adapted version of the business model he had developed in the 1890s. He was selling and not building when prices were high, but the critical difference this time was that he was also retaining a medium-sized fleet of modern steamers. The result would be that J. and C. Harrison would enter the conflict itself in a very strong position with both the ships ready to reap the benefits of war-inflated freight rates, and the capital reserves to invest in the high-yield gilts which the Government would need to issue to finance Britain's war effort.

One of four new vessels delivered in 1911, *Harpathian* (1) ran trials in February. *[Nigel Farrell collection]*

Profit, loss and war

When Britain went to war on 4th August 1914, J. and C. Harrison Ltd. was operating a fleet of 13 large, modern steamers totalling just under 60,000 tons in a tramping business that quite literally embraced the entire maritime world. The average age of the ships was under five years, and no fewer than eight of them had been delivered from 1910 on. By the time the war ended on 11th November 1918, this fine fleet had shrunk to only two ships. The company took advantage of soaring second-hand values to sell several ships, but the main agent of the fleet's decline was the German submarine fleet. It is often argued that Germany came far closer to winning the First World War through submarine warfare than it did the Second. While this is open to conjecture, it is undoubtedly true that, on a comparative basis, the smaller submarine force of 1914-1918 sank significantly more merchant ships per U-boat than its far bigger equivalent two and a half decades later. Some British shipping companies experienced extremely high levels of losses. Harrison was not in this category in terms of the number of ships lost, but it certainly was in terms of losses relative to the size of its fleet.

The fleet in August 1914

Harmonic (2)	1905	2,827 grt
Harperley (2)	1906	3,990 grt
Harlyn (2)	1906	3,459 grt
Hartington (1)	1907	4,043 grt
Harlesden (1)	1909	4,334 grt
Harpagus (1)	1910	5,866 grt
Harpalion (1)	1910	5,867 grt
Harmattan (1)	1911	4,791 grt
Harpalyce (1)	1911	5,940 grt
Harmatris (1)	1912	4,863 grt
Harpathian (1)	1913	4,588 grt
Harflete	1913	4,814 grt
Harbury (3)	1913	4,572 grt

The first war-time departure from the fleet had nothing to do with the enemy and simply provided further evidence of Charles Harrison's willingness to sell a vessel at almost any time as long as the price was sufficiently attractive. Thus the relative veteran *Harlyn* (2), the third oldest and second smallest member of the fleet was sold to another London owner in November 1914 to be given the distinctly non-British name *Ioanna*. It was, however, to be only a few months before German U-boats made their presence felt.

Before it committed itself fully to unrestricted submarine warfare in the spring of 1917, Germany experimented with a limited version of it once in 1915 and once in 1916, in both cases calling the experiment off when international condemnation gave the German Foreign Ministry the strength to rein in an Admiralty which was fully prepared to use its still small submarine fleet as a weapon of economic warfare. The 1915 campaign lasted from 4th February to 20th September and was largely restricted to the waters around the British Isles. Losses were relatively light compared to what would come later in the war. Only about 75,000 tons of Allied shipping were lost to U-boats up to January 1915; the figure rose to 130,000 tons from January to April and to over 250,000 tons from then until July. J. and C. Harrison was thus extremely unlucky to lose two of their biggest ships in a two month period in the early stages of the campaign.

The first victim was the *Harpalion* (1), torpedoed without warning by *U 8* on 24th February 1915 in the English Channel. Readers versed in the later horrors of the submarine war might easily be amused by the loss reports submitted after such early attacks. That for the *Harpalion* devotes more space to the location of the Captain (in his cabin), the activities of the Chief Engineer (about to say Grace), and every other officer apart from the man on the bridge (waiting to have their lunch) than it does to the attack itself. There was also a contrast in behaviour after the attack. The crew abandoned ship immediately although she was in no danger of sinking, and did not return from the rescue vessels that quickly picked them up. Another vessel then appeared and put a party on board to rig a tow to bring the ship into harbour. Two days later bad weather forced them to give up the fight and the *Harpalion* foundered, but there can be little doubt that even two years later she would almost certainly have been saved.

A second U-boat, the tiny coastal submarine *UB 4*, struck on 10th April 1915, torpedoing the *Harpalyce* (1) near the North Hinder Light Vessel. This was an altogether more fatal attack – the ship sank quickly and 15 men were lost. The loss report, however, still reflected the naivety of sea warfare at a time when land warfare had already accounted for hundreds of thousands of lives. The sinking is described in some detail, but more space is devoted to an outraged description of the size, lettering and colouring of the Belgian Relief Commission canvas sign that the vessel was displaying on her hull. The sinking of the *Harpalyce* caused outrage in the United States, whence she was ultimately bound to collect food, but this was swiftly drowned out by the far greater controversy triggered by the sinking of the *Lusitania* a month later.

1916 saw the fleet shrink by a further three vessels. The enemy was only responsible for the first of these departures. On 8th March *Harmatris* (1) was torpedoed

Photographed in a US port, the unfortunate *Harpalyce* (1) is identified as carrying supplies for the Belgian Relief Commission, but the size of the sign means that it would be hardly legible to a U-boat captain. *[Kevin O'Donoghue collection]*

and sunk just off the Boulogne breakwater by another small coastal submarine *UB 18* while in sight of the final destination for her cargo of Canadian oats and hay. There were only four casualties, caused by the initial explosion, and the remainder of the crew was quickly rescued. Later in the spring, however, Charles Harrison took advantage of further increases in second-hand values to sell two of the older ships in his fleet. The *Harlesden* (1) was sold on 17th April and the *Harmonic* (2) on 22nd May, in both cases to other British tramp owners.

In January 1917, the German Chancellor, Bethmann-Hollweg finally lost his argument with the combined forces of the Army and Navy General Staffs, and on 1st February Germany announced full unrestricted submarine warfare in an area stretching out 400 miles into the Atlantic, with no concessions to neutrals save narrow access channels for Spain and Greece, and an allowance of two ships a week into Falmouth for the United States. The German submarine fleet had expanded considerably during 1916, and U-boats were soon sinking Allied and neutral tonnage at hitherto unprecedented rates. In April 1917 alone they sank just over 800 Allied merchant vessels of an aggregate tonnage of 860,000 – equivalent to roughly 800 tons per U-boat per day. Losses remained very high until a reluctant Admiralty introduced a convoy system in the summer. By that time, however, the damage had already been done to J. and C. Harrison, the company losing four ships within a period of less than two months.

The first casualty was the *Harflete*, inbound from Cuba with a cargo of sugar. A U-boat surfaced and attacked the vessel with long-range gunfire in the early afternoon of 26 April some 200 miles west north west of the Fastnet. This attack was beaten off with the ship's own 12-pounder gun. At 11 in the same evening, however, two submarines attacked the vessel simultaneously with torpedoes. One submarine missed with two torpedoes, but her compatriot, subsequently identified as the *U 70*, fired one which exploded in number 2 hold. The ship was promptly abandoned, although one man fell in the sea and was drowned. The survivors were picked up in the following morning by Royal Navy vessels and the *Harflete* was last seen at 9.30am in a sinking condition.

The second loss was by far the most serious in terms of lives lost. The *Harmattan* (1) had sailed from Gibraltar for the Eastern Mediterranean on 1st May with a military cargo and 30 soldiers travelling as passengers. At 7.30 on the morning of 5th May she struck a mine laid by *UC 37* north of Cape Rosa, Algeria. The explosion took place amidships and triggered a secondary explosion of part of the cargo. The vessel foundered immediately, taking with her the Master and 35 of the 41-man crew, as well as 16 soldiers.

A third ship was lost in the Mediterranean just four days later. The *Harpagus* (1) was nearing the end of a voyage from New York to Marseilles when she was hit in number 1 hold by a torpedo fired by *U 34*. Three crewmen were lost, two Chinese and one Japanese, while the Master and Chief Engineer were taken prisoner by the submarine. The ship herself sank in 15 minutes and the survivors were rescued by a Spanish steamer.

The last loss occurred back in the Atlantic and caused a heavy loss of life. In the early hours of 9th June the *Harbury* (3) was torpedoed abaft number 2 hatch by *U 70*, the same submarine which had accounted for the *Harflete* in April. The crew attempted to abandon ship while the vessel was still underway and all the lifeboats capsized. The submarine then surfaced and opened fire, causing those still aboard to jump overboard. The vessel sank some time before dawn and 13 men including the Master had drowned before the survivors were picked up by a Japanese vessel and landed at Gibraltar.

Thus by the summer of 1917, the J. and C. Harrison fleet had been reduced from 13 ships to only three. The losses had fallen most heavily on the more modern ships in the fleet. Only one of the survivors had been built after 1907, and she was to become the company's last war loss, just under a year after the *Harbury* (3) had gone down. The loss of the *Harpathian* (1) was atypical of most First World War U-boat successes. She was torpedoed on 5th June 1918 some 80 miles off the coast of Virginia by the U-cruiser *U 151*. The torpedo struck between numbers 4 and 5 holds, but despite the ship going down in six minutes, the entire crew was able to get away in the boats. In a curious echo of a way of warfare that had ended four years before, the sinking report praised the U-boat captain for his courtesy and for giving the men in the boats water and tobacco.

When the war ended five months later, Charles Harrison owned only two ships, the *Harperley* (2) of 1906 and the *Hartington* (1) of 1907. The firm did manage two war standard freighters for the Shipping Controller in the immediate post-war period, but otherwise it simply traded its two ships. Freight rates were booming and vessel values soaring due to a combination of euphoria over the end of hostilities, and artificial shortages of tonnage due to the long time it took dislocated trade routes to return to their normal patterns. Speculation was rife, and fortunes were both won and lost. Given his past record, shipping commentators must have been keeping an eye on 66 Mark Lane to see what Charles Harrison would do. If they expected something dramatic, he was to disappoint them.

Consolidation for growth
The three years between 1919 and 1921 produced the wildest fluctuations in business conditions which the shipping industry would ever experience in times of peace. The period began with freight rates and vessel values soaring;

Harmattan (1) of 1911 was mined off Algeria in May 1917 with serious loss of life amongst the crew and soldiers on board. *[Kevin O'Donoghue collection]*

and with ship owners scrambling to take advantage of the bonanza. The British merchant marine had been decimated by the U-boat offensive as had most of its pre-1914 competitors, and the need to find replacement tonnage was uppermost in most company managers' minds. A bounty of new tonnage, however, was entering the market, first as the British, Japanese and later US authorities sold off the hundreds of standard design cargo vessels they had ordered from early 1917 on. Most of these ships had not even been launched when hostilities ceased, and in some cases the vessels were purchased off the slips. One way or the other, each government did its taxpayers proud, selling at prices far higher than could possibly have been realised in normal times. In 1920 this armada of brand new ships was augmented by the arrival on the market of the fleets of the defeated Central Powers. One of the requirements of the Versailles peace treaty was that the vanquished surrender all commercial vessels of more than 1,500 tons in compensation for other nations' shipping losses. These ships – mostly German, and many very modern – were then allocated to the respective governments in proportion to the losses they had suffered. Almost all of these ships were also sold directly to commercial owners at high prices.

The market was operating under highly artificial conditions, while simultaneously adjusting to the disappearance of one large merchant fleet (German) and the arrival of another (that of the USA). Boom conditions continued into 1920 but before the year was out, the bubble had burst, and the shipping market went through a sharp downwards adjustment. Many fortunes were won and lost during this stage, particularly through selling or buying vessels, both new and second-hand. Charles Harrison, already a master of this form of business, might have been expected to become involved. In fact, he did not enter the market in any way. On the face of things this might not have looked surprising. Charles turned 65 in 1919. A normal ship owner, with his fleet down to two vessels and the firm's profits safely invested in government bonds, would probably have been considering selling his remaining ships while prices were high and looking forward to a comfortable retirement. Charles Willis Harrison, however, was anything but a normal ship owner.

Untroubled by the near-mania sweeping the shipping world, Charles and his by now well-experienced nephews spent 1919 planning a complete re-structuring of the family business. This re-structuring would have two main objectives: first, to establish a corporate framework to allow the directors to re-invest in shipping when market conditions were right; and second to establish a tax-efficient shareholding structure, built around a series of inter-related trusts and investment companies, to preserve the family wealth and ensure that family members and trusted employees could reap the benefits of the business's progress.

Before describing this complex operation, it is best to summarize the state of Charles Harrison's shipping venture as it stood in January 1920. The sole registered corporate entity was J. and C. Harrison Ltd. with a share capital of £150,000 cumulative preference shares and £250,000 ordinary shares – just under £20,000 of the latter had not been issued. Charles owned £132,000 of the preference stock; the remainder being held in trust for the children of his deceased brother Frederick. Charles also owned £178,740 of the ordinary stock while Frederick's Trustees held another £40,010. Three of Charles's nephews working for the company, John, Frank and

Paul, each held £10,000 of ordinary stock. The remainder of the issued stock was distributed between a handful of outside minority shareholders, and three Harrison employees, Thomas Turketine, John Bryden and Edgar Nash. The company was only managing two of its own vessels: the 14-year-old *Harperley* (2) and the 13-year-old *Hartington* (1) – both of which were registered in the name of Charles Harrison himself.

In March 1920, corporate structure was changed completely. The existing company, J. and C. Harrison Ltd., was wound up, and its assets transferred to a new entity, J. and C. Harrison (1920) Ltd. The new entity (which dropped the '(1920)' from its name in 1928) was capitalized at £500,000, and would for the time being remain a management company. Simultaneously, a second new company – the Willis Steamship Co. Ltd. – was formed with a share capital of £350,000, specifically to acquire Charles Harrison's two remaining ships, which were each 'sold' at a nominal price of £150,000. In both cases, the sum was about three times the original acquisition cost and roughly five times what the ships would have been worth under normal market circumstances. The market, however, was anything but normal, and as Charles was effectively selling to himself, the device created the potential for significant tax-reducing depreciation charges over the vessels' remaining lives. Unlike the family's first venture into limited liability company ship ownership, this move was to prove permanent. Henceforth, all Harrison ships would be owned via a corporate entity.

Charles held £100,200 of Willis stock. John, Frank and Paul Harrison each held £50,200, as did a younger Charles Harrison, the son and inheritor of Frederick Harrison. The remaining £50,000 of the stock was held by another new foundation, the Harrison Trust Ltd. The creation of the Harrison Trust was the first in a series of such formations. The guiding hand was that of Charles Willis Harrison, and his guiding principle was the gradual transfer of revenues paid in the form of dividends to trusts which would in turn provide income for qualifying family members. The directors of the new Trust were the same family members who held shares in the shipping companies: Charles Willis Harrison himself, as well as his nephews John, Frank, Paul and Charles, and the group's trusted accountant Thomas Turketine. The beneficiaries of the Trust were the children of James, Frederick and Charles Harrison (their two older brothers, John and William, had fathered no children of their own), the children of Edith Pooley (nee Harrison) and those of the other two sisters not otherwise provided for. The Trust was as tightly controlled as the shipping companies – during the lifetime of Charles Willis Harrison, he remained in complete control.

There was one feature of the structure of the trust, and similar parallel trusts set up by the family, which was unique. All of the Reverend Harrison's children had been brought up in line with strict Unitarian principles, and these stayed with them through their business lives. These principles manifested themselves in what today might seem to be blatant discrimination, but was far from unusual among families raised in the religious and moral climate of the Victorian era. The deeds of all the trusts specifically excluded Roman Catholics from being beneficiaries, and automatically removed beneficial status from any family member who subsequently converted to that faith. Over time, this provision was to exclude several descendent lines from what would prove a source of considerable income.

The creation of the new trust was followed by a memorandum of agreement between it and J. and C. Harrison Ltd. by which the latter sold a portfolio of bonds and shares to the former for a consideration of £1,600,000 in fully-paid-up ordinary shares in the Trust. The resulting holdings are reproduced below. The sum involved was huge, particularly when it is remembered that the company's fleet was greatly reduced by the time freight rates soared in the second half of the war, and that even these profits would have been subject to high excess war profits tax. The schedule itself shows that Charles Harrison had been carefully setting aside money generated from capital gains and investing it in no risk, medium to long-term sovereign bonds. The Trust itself had obviously been in his mind for some time.

Bond portfolio

£844,000	5%	War Loan Bonds	1929/47
£250,000	5%	National War Bonds	1st October 1927
£176,000	5%	National War Bonds	1st April 1928
£250,000	4%	National war Bonds	1st October 1927
£50,000	4%	Victory Bonds	
£100,000	4%	Funding Loan Bonds	1960/90

Shareholders

Charles Willis Harrison	£1,034,960
John Harrison	£40,000
Francis Joseph (Frank) Harrison	£50,000
Alfred (Paul) Harrison	£40,000
Charles Harrison	£40,000
Thomas Turketine	£500
Charles Douglas Palmer	£1,000
John Bryden	£1,000
Helen Elizabeth Turketine	£200
Thomas Leslie Turketine	£150
Allan William Henry Turketine	£150
The Atherton Investment Corporation Ltd.	£392,040

The Atherton Investment Corporation Ltd. was the second of the two family investment companies formed in 1920. It differed from the Harrison Investment Trust in being registered as a company rather than a trust, although in practice it performed the same function as an investment vehicle between the various corporate entities of the Harrison Group and the family beneficiaries. Its initial issued capital was just in excess of £790,000, of which just over £750,000 was held by Charles Willis Henderson. The other significant holders were his wife Jeannie with £10,000, his nephew John Harrison with £5,000, and three members of the Turketine family (the father and two sons) all of whom were now employed by the Groups as accountants, each with between £5,000 and £5,101. His daughter Adeline held £1,000, as did a number of senior clerks in the shipping office. Even the three office juniors, including the typist, held £100 each. While J. and C. Harrison Ltd. was now at the centre of a significant business empire, it was still very much a family business, and provided for its employees in a similar fashion. A third and far smaller investment company, Chowbent Ltd., was formed in 1924, but the year in question was more significant for a seemingly inconsequential event which took place it December – an event which marked the beginning of the expansion of J. and C. Harrison's commitment to ship ownership.

Tramping through the twenties

As trading conditions returned to normal in 1921-22, many British ship owners who had built up fleets during the boom conditions of 1916-1920 found themselves struggling to survive. Using the Chamber of Shipping Tramp Freight Index for 1913 (itself a year of relatively high rates) as 100, the corresponding figure for 1920 was 427.35 – by 1929 it had fallen to 106.26. A similar pattern emerges from the index of vessel values constructed by the shipping journal 'Fairplay'. This index was based on a theoretical 'standard' ship with dimensions of 380 x 49 x 29 feet, with a deadweight capacity of 7,500 tons, with a triple-expansion engine and three boilers capable of steaming at nine knots on 25 tons of coal per day. While the 'standard' ship was presumed to be second-hand, new-building costs were factored in. The table below shows the estimated price of such a vessel for selected year-ends between 1914 and 1929.

1914	£54,375
1916	£172,500
1920	£225,000
1921	£97,500
1925	£60,000
1929	£67,750

With British tramp owners struggling to face heavy competition from large Norwegian, Italian, Japanese and Greek fleets, as well as a rapidly recovering German merchant marine, and some large state-supported US ventures, an increasing number struggled to cover the financing costs of their expensive new tonnage. Many were dependent on banks for mortgage finance, and there was a steady stream of defaulters, whose assets were seized by their mortgagees and sold into the market at prevailing prices.

J. and C. Harrison pursued a fairly cautious strategy throughout the 1920s. While it was certainly possible to pick up large numbers of relatively new ships at a fraction of their construction cost, market conditions were fragile, and Charles Harrison must have judged that the scope for anything more than modest returns did not justify any significant rebuilding of his war-ravaged fleet. In 1925, the year in which the Fairplay Index hit its lowest level of the decade, he did make a modest acquisition. It was entirely typical of the times that the ships he bought came from the mortgagees of a failed British tramp concern.

The Adams family had started a shipping business on the Tyne as far back as the 1860s. After a variety of ups and downs, the family embraced limited liability in 1916 as D. and T. G. Adams and Co. Ltd. The new company built up a mid-sized fleet of modern tramp steamers, most of them second-hand purchases. Despite the fact that the fleet totalled only seven vessels in 1921, it was actually operated through three separate subsidiaries: the Mede Line Ltd.; the Brands-Adams Steamship Co. Ltd.; and the Canute Steamship Co. Ltd. Within only a few years the business was in trouble, and in 1924 the Midland Bank, which owned mortgages on the entire fleet, seized all the vessels.

In December 1924, Midland Bank appointed J. and C. Harrison Ltd. as managers of four of the former Adams tramps: the *Avonmede*, *Shannonmede* and *Clydemede* of 1917, and the *Nilemede* of 1918. The first three were near sisters of 4,250 to 4,275 tons, all built by Pickersgill of Sunderland for tramp owners, but acquired by the Johnston

Clydemede was one of four ships from the fleet of D. and T.G. Adams placed in Harrison's management in 1924. She was later acquired and renamed *Harpagus* (2). *[Roy Fenton collection]*

Line almost immediately, and subsequently sold on to the Adams companies in 1920. The 4,450-ton *Nilemede* was the former standard ship *War Fantail*, acquired from the Shipping Controller in 1919. The Midland almost certainly appointed the company to manage the vessels as the prelude to selling them to Harrisons. This is exactly what happened on 2nd April 1925; the formal buyer being the Willis Steamship Co. Ltd., the owner of the existing two ships in the Harrison fleet. The combined cost of the four is likely to have been significantly under £250,000 – roughly what it would have cost to build one vessel in early 1921.

The four new acquisitions, all of which were significantly more modern that the two pre-war survivors, were each given new names in line with normal fleet nomenclature. The *Avonmede* became the *Harpalion* (2); the *Shannonmede*, the *Harpalyce* (2); the *Clydemede*, the *Harpagus* (2); and the *Nilemede* the *Harmattan* (2). J. and C. Harrison Ltd. now had a fleet of six tramp steamers – even the oldest pair was not yet 20-years-old, while the remainder were less than half that age. Trading conditions, however, remained relatively tough, and while Charles Harrison cannot possibly have foreseen the economic cataclysm which was to hit the world in 1929, he was sufficiently wary to take advantage of gradually improving market conditions between 1926 and 1929 to dispose of part of his fleet at a profit.

The second-hand ship market staged a brief rally between the spring and winter of 1928. Charles Harrison sold no fewer than four of his six ships during this period, including three of the relatively new vessels he had acquired only in 1925. The first vessel to go was the war standard *Harmattan* (2), sold to Swansea owners in May 1928. The other three were all sold between December 1928 and January 1929: the pre-war *Harperley* (2) and the 1917-built *Harpagus* (2) going to Greek owners in December, and the latter's sister *Harpalyce* (2) to London buyers in January. This left the company trading only two ships – the veteran *Hartington* (1) and the last of the ex-Adams acquisitions the *Harpalion* (2).

J. and C. Harrison Ltd., however, was to acquire additional tonnage through taking over the management of another shipping company. The London firm of Fisher, Alimonda and Co. Ltd. had acquired the long dormant National Steamship Company Ltd., originally a North

Atlantic passenger firm, in 1915, and had started building up a tramp fleet. The firm proved a fairly typical victim of the post-war boom/bust cycle. It expanded rapidly during the war, buying, for example, five ships at high prices from the Glasgow ship owner William Burrell, but it was forced to sell almost all of its ships in 1921 just to survive. The company struggled through the 1920s, but at the end of the decade it too fell into the hands of its mortgagee, in this case the London and South Western Bank Ltd. At the time, the company's capital had been written down to only £10,000 and it owned just two vessels: the *Lamington* of 1907 and the *Fotinia* of 1913. These remained under Harrison control for several years, but they were never given *Har-* names – a clear sign that they would be sold on when suitable buyers could be found. J. and C. Harrison Ltd. took over the mortgages on 23rd May 1929. The original mortgages had totalled a staggering £357,500, but these had already been either partially paid or written-down and it seems unlikely that Charles Harrison would have taken on a combined mortgage of much above the two ships' break-up value. J. and C. Harrison Ltd. was formally appointed manager in place of Fisher, Alimonda and Co. Ltd. at the beginning of June with an annual remuneration of £500.

The Great Depression had an immediate impact on world shipping and, even by the end of 1929, the estuaries around Britain were becoming crowded with laid-up vessels. No ship owner could survive unscathed, but few were better placed to ride out the storm than Charles Harrison. His four ships would be kept on the seas as long as possible. More importantly, he had built up huge capital reserves. He was to begin deploying these within a year, and was to continue to do so on a scale which would amaze a shipping world otherwise locked in near total recession.

Building against the tide

By 1930, Charles Harrison had been a ship owner for just over four decades. Although a large number of ships had passed through his hands during this long career, he had actually only run a fleet of more than a dozen vessels very briefly between 1913 and 1915. For most of his ship owning career, the fleet had numbered less than ten, often significantly so, and for several years he had actually owned no ships at all. He was therefore an unlikely candidate to begin building a large fleet in the depths of the Great Depression. The proposition becomes even more unlikely when one considers that 1930 marked his 75th birthday. Build a large fleet, however, was exactly what he started to do. In fact it was to become the largest fleet by a comfortable margin ever to carry the J. and C. Harrison Ltd. company colours, and one of the largest tramp fleets flying the red ensign in the late 1930s.

The initial investment decision must have been taken in 1929 soon after the Wall Street Crash tipped the world into the Great Depression. Between June and October 1930, the company took delivery of no fewer than eight new vessels from five different builders. Bartram of Sunderland contributed the *Harpathian* (2) and the *Harpenden* (3); Robert Thompson of the same port, the *Harmattan* (3) and the *Harmonic* (3); and John Readhead of South Shields, the *Harpagus* (3) and *Harpalyce* (3). In addition, Short Brothers of Sunderland delivered the *Harberton* (2), and William Gray of West Hartlepool the *Harperley* (3). Although there were minor differences in size and horsepower, all eight vessels were effectively sisters of 4,550 to 4,700 tons, 395 to 400 feet in length, and capable of 10½ to 10¾ knots. Few British tramp owners had yet to experiment with oil engines, and Harrison stuck with the well-proven triple expansion, coal-fired steam engine. The vessels themselves were all built with a distinctive long bridge-deck.

The sheer size of Charles Harrison's venture produced considerable comment and criticism in British shipping circles. Owners and brokers who were struggling to find cargoes for even a fraction of existing tonnage thought that he was taking a wild gamble. He had in fact only started on what would be an even larger building programme, but this was not to become clear until 1932. In the meantime, he began to dispose of the older ships in his fleet. The *Harpalion* (2), the last of the four vessels acquired from the Midland Bank in 1925, was sold to Greek owners in October 1931. He also disposed of the *Lamington* and *Fotinia*, acquired from Fisher and Alimonda. Interestingly enough, the last ship to be sold was the *Hartington* (1), which was ten years older than the *Harpalion* (2), but stayed in the fleet until June 1933. There is nothing in Charles Harrison's record as a ship owner to suggest that he allowed sentimentality to cloud his judgment, so the choice was more likely driven by lower capital costs than any favouritism towards a vessel that had been built to his own design.

After a stop for breath in 1931, Charles Harrison's fleet expansion resumed. Seven new vessels were delivered in 1932, six more in 1933, and another two in 1934 before the programme finally came to an end in 1935 with the arrival of a final three. Only three builders were involved in producing a total of 18 ships. Hawthorn Leslie of Hebburn-on-Tyne and William Gray of West Hartlepool were each responsible for three vessels. The other 12 all came from the Port Glasgow shipyard of Lithgows Ltd. – the name under which William Lithgow had consolidated the well-known yards of Russell and Co. earlier in the century. We will return to the business relationship between J. and C. Harrison Ltd., which had hitherto built all of its ships in the North East of England and Lithgows, easily the largest builder of cargo tonnage on the Clyde, later. First, however, we will look at the vessels themselves. They were all essentially larger versions of the 1930 ships, but they fell into three distinct groups, and are listed below in the order they were registered.

First batch, 5,420 to 5,490 tons, 425 to 428 feet, 11 knots*

Harpalion (3)	May 1932	Hawthorn Leslie
Harmatris (2)	May 1932	Lithgows
Hartington (2)	June 1932	William Gray
Harmanteh	June 1932	Lithgows
Harlesden (2)	July 1932	Hawthorn Leslie
Harborough (1)	August 1932	Lithgows
Hartlepool	September 1932	William Gray
Harlingen (4)	January 1933	Lithgows
Hartismere (1)	January 1933	William Gray
Hardingham (1)	January 1933	Lithgows
Harbledown	April 1933	Lithgows

Second batch, 5,080 tons, 418 feet, 11 knots

Harbury (4)	October 1933	Lithgows
Harcalo (3)	November 1933	Lithgows
Harpasa	January 1934	Lithgows
Hartlebury	February 1934	Lithgows

Third batch, 5,630 to 5,730 tons, 428 to 434 feet, 11 knots*

Harpagon (1)	June 1935	Lithgows
Harmala	September 1935	Lithgows
Harpalycus (1)	November 1935	Hawthorn Leslie

*The three Hawthorn Leslie vessels were rated at 10½ knots.

As already mentioned, the company disposed of its remaining old ships in the midst of this wave of new acquisitions, all of them to Greek owners. The last to go, the veteran *Hartington* (1), built in 1907, would ironically outlast almost all of the vessels built between 1930 and 1935, soldiering on under the unlikely name *Fred* until going to the breakers in 1952. In the meantime, the wisdom of Charles Harrison's huge building programme had not yet become apparent to the shipping community at large. The situation is summed up in the words of his nephew Paul:

When Uncle Charles built the 26 coal burners in 1933 [sic] onwards, it was said of him on the Baltic Exchange that the general opinion was, that for the first time in his life, he had made a serious error of judgement. How wrong these critics were was very soon manifest as the impending war drew nearer. He never went on the Baltic Exchange and so never heard these criticisms. His right-hand man was my eldest brother Frank who every day went on the Baltic but never mentioned the criticisms to my uncle. I am only sorry Charles did not live long enough to prove how right he was.

Two factors will have driven Charles Harrison in his decision to invest so heavily. The first would have been the belief that he should be prepared to take full advantage of rising freight rates when the world economy began to recover – as it did just as the last new ships were being delivered. The second would have been his long-established practice of placing new orders when shipbuilders were starved of business and only too happy to offer low prices and favourable terms of payment. The last point can be illustrated by looking at J. and C. Harrison Ltd.'s contracts with its single largest supplier of new vessels, Lithgows Ltd. of Port Glasgow.

James Lithgow was undoubtedly the dominant Clyde shipbuilder of his age. He had inherited the firm of Russell and Co. owned by his father William Tod Lithgow when the latter died in 1908 and had rapidly moved to build it into a large integrated shipbuilding concern – he re-purchased the breakaway firm of A. Rodger and Co. in 1911 following the death of its owner, and then added the neighbouring yards of Robert Duncan and Co. Ltd. (purchased in 1915), William Hamilton and Co. Ltd. and Dunlop, Bremner and Co. Ltd. (both purchased in 1919), as well as a controlling interest in the Glasgow firm of marine engineers, David Rowan and Co. (purchased in 1917). Finally, to ensure a supply of steel, he acquired the well-established firm of James Dunlop and Co. in 1919. The original Russell and Co. yards were renamed Lithgows Ltd. in 1919, but the other firms all operated as separate businesses within the group. Lithgow Senior had been a pioneer of mass production in the shipbuilding industry, beginning with large sailing vessels in the late 1880s

Three examples
of ships from the
rebuilding programme
of the 1930s.
Top: The South
Shields-built
Harpalyce (3) at
Cardiff. *[National
Museum of Wales
379/677]*
Middle: *Harpagus* (3)
seen at Avonmouth
was also from the yard
of John Readhead and
Sons Ltd. at South
Shields.
Lower: *Harmonic*
(3), built by Robert
Thompson and Sons
Ltd, Sunderland, again
at Avonmouth. *[Both:
Kevin O'Donoghue
collection]*

and moving progressively into steam from the mid-1890s. He built primarily for the tramp shipping industry. Young James would continue with this business model, but operated it on a far larger scale and in a vertically integrated fashion. The growth through acquisition during the wartime years was all the more impressive in that James engineered most of it at long distance. He had, quite literally, been proving his manhood elsewhere, serving first at the Front with the 40th Battery of the Royal Siege Artillery and then in London as Director of Merchant Shipbuilding. He returned to his inheritance as a Lieutenant-Colonel.

Although Lithgows was better funded and better organized than most British shipyards, it faced the common problem of finding business to service its high capital costs and retain its skilled labour force at a time when new orders slowed down abruptly from 1930. The drop in business was so dramatic that the yard, which had launched 19 ships in 1929, and still managed nine in 1930, launched only two vessels in 1931. He was thus an ideal counterparty for Charles Harrison when he embarked on the second and more ambitious phase of his expansion programme towards the end of 1931.

Between 1932 and 1933 in particular, J. and C. Harrison Ltd. quite literally kept Lithgows in business. Charles Harrison was the buyer of five of the eight ships launched in 1932; and four of the five launched in 1933. Overall, he ordered 12 of the 26 ships Lithgows launched between 1932 and 1935. The orders for the first two vessels, the future *Harmatris* (2) and *Harmanteh* were placed on 30th July 1931. These were followed by the future *Harborough* (1) on 13th October of the same year, and another two, the future *Harlingen* (4) and *Hardingham* (1) on 27th October. The order was rounded off with the contract for the future *Harbledown* on 10th June 1932. As described before, these vessels were all sister ships of the first batch of vessels, similar to another five built by Hawthorn Leslie and William Gray. Lithgows built all four vessels of the slightly smaller second batch, the agreements being signed on 25th November for *Harbury* (4) and *Harcalo* (3); and for *Harpasa* and *Hartlebury* on 24th December. Finally, Lithgows contributed two vessels to the third batch, contracts being signed for *Harpagon* (1) on 25th May 1934 and *Harmala* on 5th September of the same year.

Charles Harrison's position relative to his shipbuilders had changed considerably since his early years in the business. It was common practice for ship owners to make payments in instalments as the building work was carried out. In every Lithgow contract, Harrison only contracted to pay for the vessel in full and in cash upon successful completion of trials – up until that time, the builder had to shoulder the full burden of providing working capital. He was also able to obtain highly favourable prices, as summarised below:

30th July 1931	*Harmatris* (2) and *Harmanteh* £78,500 per vessel
13th October 1931	*Harborough* (1) £77,000
27th October 1931	*Harlingen* (4) and *Hardingham* (1) £76,750 per vessel
10th June 1932	*Harbledown* £74,000
25th November 1932	*Harbury* (4) and *Harcalo* (3) £75,000
24th December 1932	*Harpasa* and *Hartlebury* £74,250
25th May 1934	*Harpagon* (1) £83,500
5th September 1934	*Harmala* £83,500

A number of changes in the corporate structure of the Harrison group of companies were undertaken to support the fleet expansion programme. In 1931 the capital of the National Steamship Co. Ltd. was increased from £10,000 to £600,000 through the issue of £440,000 ordinary shares and £150,000 4% preference shares, the latter held entirely by Harrison Trust Ltd. In 1933, its capital was increased again with the issue of another £300,000 4% preference shares.

In addition, Harrison floated an entirely new company, the Gowland Steamship Co. Ltd., in 1935 with an initial capital of £300,000. In 1939, this company's capital was increased to £500,000, all of which was held by J. and C. Harrison Ltd., of which it was a solely-owned subsidiary.

Finally, Harrison created a third investment trust, Chowbent Ltd., to provide another vehicle for harnessing the Group's wealth, financing the purchase of new vessels, and providing income for family beneficiaries.

All the 1930-built ships were registered in the name of the National subsidiary. With subsequent vessels, registration was spread across all four shipping companies, National, Willis, Gowland and, for the first time, the parent company J. and C. Harrison and Co. Ltd. itself.

The launch of the *Harmala* at Port Glasgow on 15th August 1935 (left) brought to a temporary end to Harrison's massive rebuilding programme. She is also seen fitting out at Lithgow's yard. *[Both Kevin O'Donoghue collection]*

Assuming an overall average cost per vessel of £77,500 for the entire new fleet, J. and C. Harrison had spent the huge sum of £2,015,000 at a time when most of the shipping industry was on its knees. It had acquired, however, a fleet of 26 modern, cost-efficient steamers, at prices some £10,000 lower than those subsequently paid by other tramp companies with the assistance of Government loans under the 'Scrap and Build' scheme. The Harrison fleet was already carrying freights on the ocean sea lanes when most of the latter were still being laid down. It was quite simply, a brilliant achievement, and the crowning glory of Charles Willis Harrison's long career.

Changing the guard

Charles Harrison celebrated his 80th birthday as the last of his 26-strong new fleet entered service. For most of its existence, the firm had only managed a modest fleet, but now it was in control of one more than twice the size of anything it had owned before. There never seems to have been any thought of Charles retiring, indeed after he lost his wife Jeannie he appears to have treated the office almost as a second home. He was no longer overseeing a tiny staff. His two oldest nephews, John and Frank, had long been groomed to take over and were by now handling the bulk of the day to day decision making. They were supported by a growing staff, the senior members of which had been with the firm for decades. Charles Harrison, however, was still the Managing Director and the final arbiter of anything of business importance. Paul Harrison provides a poignant view of the twilight years of his career.

Uncle Charles lived in a large house in Cadogan Place SW1 and walked each day to the Underground station in Sloane Street. The last two or three years of his life were lonely for him as Aunt Jeannie had predeceased him, nevertheless he carried on and was always in his office in Mark Lane at 8.30 am. Uncle Charles was rather autocratic in his ways but very highly respected for his remarkable achievements as a ship owner. During the last six months of his very active life, his general health declined and he was deeply grieved to give up his office duties.

Charles Willis Harrison died at his home at 49 Cadogan Place on 20th July 1937 aged 82. He was buried in Norwood Cemetery along with many other members of the family. His only child, his daughter Jeannette, lived a long a fruitful life and was finally buried near him when she died in 1972 aged 88. Charles had already made provision through the various trusts he had set up for his daughter, nephews, nieces and employees. His will left Jeannette his house in Cadogan Place. He charged his trustees (his daughter, John and Frank

Charles Harrison (1855-1937)
[Peter Harrison-Sleap]

Harrison, and Thomas Turketine and the latter's two sons) with realizing funds on all real and personal property not subject to specific bequests, to retain all his personal debentures and shares in the Harrison Trust Ltd., the Atherton Investment Corporation Ltd., Chowbent Ltd., and the National Steamship Co Ltd. Charles holdings in the three investment trusts totalled £1,750,000, and he instructed that the dividends from them should be lent free of interest to the shipping companies to pay for new tonnage as required. He also gave his Trustees full authority to make any changes to the corporate structure of the four shipping companies that might be required in the future. A codicil to the will bequeathed specific portions of the overall estate to the trustees for the benefit of his daughter, his nephew Frank and his wife.

While J. and C. Harrison Ltd. lost an irreplaceable streak of genius with the passing of its co-founder, the company was not left short of the managerial and financial experience necessary to run what was now a large shipping company. Charles' two senior nephews, John (the son of his co-founder James) and Frank (the son of his sister Edith, and stepson of his brother John) were now experienced ship managers in their early fifties and well capable of taking on the shared mantle of Managing Directors. They were supported by the financial acumen of Thomas Turketine and his two sons, and by a loyal and experienced office staff, some of whom had already been with the company for several decades.

The new directors faced a shipping world redolent with opportunities. They had a fleet of 28 modern steamers at their disposal, freight rates - which had begun to creep upwards in 1934 - were rising rapidly by the time of their uncle's death, and most of their competitors were struggling to add modern tonnage to fleets which had in many cases received no new ships since the early 1920s. The Harrison fleet could be deployed to profitable effect in the tramping trades all over the world. The company, however, added to its business portfolio by making a bold entry into the liner trade.

Harmanteh was wrecked off the coast of Chile on 22nd May 1938 whilst on a voyage to San Francisco. *[Roy Fenton collection]*

Liner companies, which had been forced to replace First World War losses at exorbitant cost in order to meet their scheduled conference commitments, were often in an even weaker state than their tramping compatriots. The largest British liner combine, the Royal Mail Group, had collapsed spectacularly in the early 1930s, and its liquidators spent the middle years of the decade trying to restructure it, and find buyers for its constituent companies. P&O, the other titan of the British liner sector also had trouble, and historical research has revealed that its owners had only avoided a Royal Mail style collapse by subsidizing its main operations from the cash reserves of the Union Steam Ship Company of New Zealand Ltd., and by hiding these transfers in its published accounts. Large liner operators in Germany, Holland and Japan had also had their share of problems, and been forced to retrench.

J. and C. Harrison Ltd. took advantage of this situation to launch a cargo liner service from southern Baltic ports to the River Plate. The company had long experience of the South American grain trade and was all but assured of homewards cargoes. Outwards it carried general cargo, much of it heavy machinery for Argentina's developing industrial and transportation network.

While the new management were heavily committed to operating vessels rather than selling them for capital gain, within several years of the completion of the fleet rebuilding programme, the company was making a small number of disposals to take advantage of rising second values. In late 1937, J. and C. Harrison sold two of the vessels from its 1930 building programme. The *Harpalyce* (3) went to Dutch owners in October and the *Harpagus* (3) to German ones in the following month. The fleet was further depleted in 1938, but this time not as a result of a sale but of a marine casualty. The *Harmanteh* was wrecked off the southern Chilean coast in May 1938 while on a ballast trip round the Horn from Santos to San Francisco.

To make good these losses to the fleet, the company placed an order for two new vessels with Bartrams of Sunderland in 1939. The two 5,190-ton sisters were to be called *Harpalyce* (4) and *Harpagus* (4), the names given to the ships sold in 1937. Their hull structure was somewhat different from the older vessels, but Harrison's continued to depend on the triple-expansion steam engine. The world, however, was heading inexorably towards another global conflict, and neither ship would have left the slipway before Britain became involved in the Second World War with its commencement of hostilities against Nazi Germany on 3rd September 1939.

Ordeal by fire

J. and C. Harrison Ltd. had suffered the loss of a significant proportion of its ships during the First World War, but the fleet itself had been relatively small, and in its absolute numbers its losses were dwarfed by those of bigger companies. It entered the Second World War with a fleet double the size of that of 1914, and in this case it was absolutely devastated in both numerical and relative terms. The war at sea between 1939 and 1945 was far more all-embracing than its predecessor. Merchant ships had to contend with a whole new range of menaces, and with enemies which from the very start saw an attack on Britain's commerce as one of the major strategic tools at its disposal to attain victory. Merchant ships also encountered the enemy over a far greater area of the globe, from the Indian Ocean to the Arctic Sea, and from the North Atlantic convoy routes to the lonely waters of the great southern oceans.

The crews of Harrison vessels put their lives at risk not only on company-owned ships, but also in a number of other ships managed on behalf first of the Ministry of Shipping and then of the Ministry of War Transport, some of them taken over from foreign powers, and some of them built in war emergency programmes by the governments of the UK, Canada and USA. The result was that the total number of ships and lives lost was far higher, and that some company stalwarts survived having more than one ship sunk under them.

The company entered the war with 25 ships in commission and another two under construction. During the war it would take delivery of another four new vessels, but would sell them before the war was over. It managed a total of 20 ships for the Ministry of Shipping and its successor the Ministry of War Transport. A total of 19 of the company's own ships were lost, and one more abandoned to the government as a constructive total loss. In addition, eight of the ships managed for the government were also lost. At the end of the war, the fleet that Charles Harrison had built was reduced to only five vessels.

Photographed at Melbourne, *Hardingham* (1) was mined in the Thames Estuary in June 1940. *[Warwick Foote collection]*

While the disposition of its ships was increasingly affected by government control of shipping and the early introduction of convoys, the closing months of 1939 did not result in any fatal brushes with the enemy. Indeed, the only event of note from a company history point of view was the launch on 27th November of the new *Harpagus* (4), the first of the Bartram-built pair ordered to replace the ships sold in 1937. She would enter service in early April 1940, just a few weeks after the launch of her sister the *Harpalyce* (4). Before the company experienced any casualties, it had also taken on the management of its first two ships for the British government. Both were Yugoslav-owned, and were transferred and registered in the name of a British-based subsidiary upon requisition as *Oakcrest* and *Fircrest*. Neither was to survive the year.

Little historical attention has been paid to German offensive mine-laying operations in British coastal waters by a combination of submarines, surface warships and aircraft. In the early years of the war, before the Royal Navy was able to assemble an adequate fleet of coastal minesweepers, these mines claimed a substantial number of victims, particularly in the outer estuaries of major east coast ports. The first two Harrison ships to be sunk in the war would fall victim to mines within two days of each other in the approaches to the Thames.

The first casualty was the *Harcalo* (3), inward-bound to London with a cargo of iron ore. She picked up her pilot at 11 am on 6th June and was proceeding up the channel to the examination vessel at Southend when she exploded a mine at about noon. The detonation took place under the after end of number 2 hold, bulging out both sides of the ship and fracturing the deck in line with the after end of the cross bunker hatch. The full force of the blast vented through the engine room, and the engines and lights failed. With the ship's back clearly broken, Captain Dyer ordered the ship abandoned, and all aboard got away safely, save the three men missing and presumed killed in the engine room. Shortly afterwards a tug appeared, and the Master, officers

and several other volunteers returned to the ship to secure a tow. After some effort the derelict was beached in a semi-submerged condition near the Gull Buoy, but quickly broke in two. Her wreck was subsequently dispersed to clear the way for other shipping.

The loss of the *Hardingham* (1) on 8th June was almost a carbon copy of that of her sister. Under the command of Captain C.L. Doughty, she was near the South Knock Buoy heading for Southend with a cargo of coal when she detonated a mine amidships at 10 minutes past noon. The ship's back was broken and the crew, less two men killed by the explosion, took to the lifeboats from where they were shortly rescued by an armed trawler. Once again the Master led a small party back aboard to attempt to organise a tow, but with the ship sagging badly and no tug in the offing, they quickly had to abandon the attempt and return to the trawler. Shortly afterwards the tow rope broke as the tide caught the derelict. The crew returned safely to Harwich, but a naval submarine chaser stayed with the vessel until she sank.

The next Harrison vessel to fall foul of the enemy survived the experience, but only just. The early British practice had been to route ships from east coast ports to the Atlantic via the English Channel. The practice worked reasonably well at the beginning, but after the fall of France it became next to suicidal. The *Hartlepool* was on her way from the Tyne to Sydney, Nova Scotia as part of convoy OA.178 which was first subjected to prolonged air attack by day and then to E-boat attack at night. A total of five ships was sunk and another 11 damaged. The *Hartlepool* was one of the victims of the E-boats, *S26* had already damaged the tanker *British Corporal* (6,972/1922) during the night of 4th/5th July before she turned her attention to the Harrison tramp. Some 16 miles south by west from Portland Bill she scored one hit dead aft, which blew off the propeller and exploded the stern magazine, killing three men. Captain Rogerson did not believe that his ship was in any danger of sinking, and only abandoned ship after repeated prodding by naval escorts. The vessel was almost certainly saved because

Hartlepool in Australian waters. She was to become a victim of an E-boat on the UK's east coast. *[Russell Priest collection]*

it seems likely that *S26* had expended all of her torpedoes. In the morning tugs came out and towed the *Hartlepool* into Weymouth where she was beached. Eventually the wrecked stern was cut away and the remainder of the vessel towed to Southampton, where a new after-part was fitted.

The German U-boat offensive finally made its first mark on the company in August. The brand new *Harpalyce* (4), which had entered the British register only on 19th June, had made a safe westward crossing of the Atlantic. For her homeward passage she carried the Commodore of convoy HX.65, having loaded steel and iron at Baltimore before arriving at the convoy departure port of Halifax. Wolf pack attacks were still largely a thing of the future, but after the convoy split in two with one part heading for the Mersey, what had now become HX.65A, in which the Harrison-managed *Fircrest* was also sailing, lost two ships to one U-boat on the night of 24/25th August, and was then attacked just before

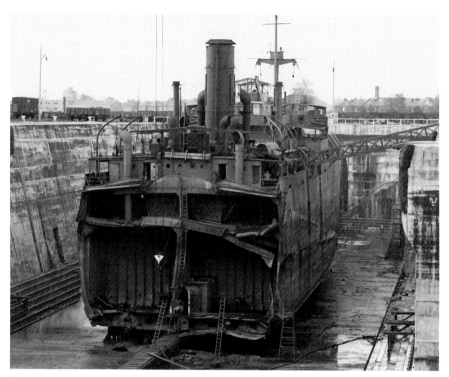

Hartlepool of 1932 in dry dock at Southampton during 1941 awaiting a new stern after being torpedoed in July 1940. *[Roy Fenton collection]*

midnight on the next evening when it had almost reached the safety of home waters, some 20 miles north west of the Butt of Lewis. The attacking submarine, Kapitanleutnant Wilhelm Schulz's *U 124*, was not only on her first patrol, but was also making her first attack. This notwithstanding, she hit three ships in a matter of minutes, the first vessel struck, the Ropner tramp *Stakesby* (3,900/1930), survived to limp into port. The *Harpalyce* was not so fortunate, taking a torpedo on the port side aft which must have flooded both holds. By the time the Third Officer reached number 3 hatch between the funnel and the bridge, the boat deck was already under water. He and the helmsman were struggling to release a raft from the fore rigging when the ship sank underneath them, the shifting steel cargo causing a tremendous roar and the boilers exploding in the process. In all only ten men were pulled from the water, and Mr Young, the Third Officer, was the senior survivor. A total of 37 men were lost including both the Master and the Commodore. There was no survivor's report from the third ship lost, the Harrison-managed *Fircrest*. She was carrying a full cargo of iron ore and the 36 year-old vessel must have gone down just as quickly as her brand new counterpart, taking all 40 of her crew with her.

Within a matter of days, the company almost lost another ship to a U-boat. On this occasion the assailant was no novice. While *U 100* was on her first patrol, her captain, Kapitänleutnant Joachim Schepke was on his ninth and had already sunk 11 ships in earlier commands. He had already sunk two independents when he encountered convoy OA.204 south east of Rockall late on the evening of 28th August. In the early hours of the 29th he launched two attacks sinking one vessel in each, and in the first attack also put one torpedo into the *Hartismere* (1), which was outward bound from Hull in ballast. Schepke rounded off his performance by despatching two stragglers, but luckily he did not re-encounter the Harrison vessel, which was able to make her way back to the Clyde under her own power, arriving safely there for repairs on the 31st.

Less than two weeks later another company ship had a near-fatal brush with a U-boat. On 11th September, the *Harpenden* (3) was hit in the stern by a torpedo from the *U 28* while outward bound in ballast in convoy OA.210. The ship was not in danger of sinking and was successfully towed into the Clyde for repairs. Her damage, however, was severe, and as was the practice in such cases, the Ministry of War Transport took her over and funded her reconstruction. Her engine was removed and used in another vessel, and she eventually re-emerged in 1941 with a new stern and engine as the *Empire Stour*. She was placed under Harrison management, but never returned to their ownership.

U-boats were not the only threat to merchant vessels in British waters. Up until the bulk of its strength was deployed elsewhere from early 1941 on, anti-shipping units of the Luftwaffe patrolled the Northern Aproaches and the North Sea itself in an aggressive fashion. On 6th November 1940 the *Harborough* (1), having survived all the perils of a voyage from Bahia Blanca to UK waters with a cargo of wheat destined for Hull was caught and bombed in position 58.35 north, 02.53 west. The vessel caught fire and had to be abandoned, but assistance arrived, allowing the fires to be extinguished and the ship taken first into Scapa Flow and then down to the Tyne for discharge and repairs.

Before the year ended, the second of the ill-fated ex-Yugoslav managed vessels was also lost to submarine attack. The westbound convoy OB.244 lost two ships to *U 103* in the early morning of 21st November and was then harried for two days by *U 123* which sank a total of six ships in four separate attacks. The *Oakcrest* fell victim to the second of these, being torpedoed at 4.00 am on the 23rd. By this time the convoy was in disarray and the escort sparse – only six were saved of her crew of 41.

Apart from the re-born *Empire Stour*, the company took on the management of another five vessels in the course of 1941. They were a very mixed bag. The first was a Romanian vessel requisitioned while under repair in London. She was registered under Ministry of War Transport

Harpenden (3), taken over by the Ministry of War Transport, rebuilt and renamed *Empire Stour*, at Durban in August 1943. *[National Maritime Museum P22473]*

ownership as the *Hampton Lodge*, the fifth name she had carried since her launch in 1911. She was followed by two ex-Yugoslavian tramps, taken over and renamed *Radhurst* and *Radport* – the second of these was a mid-1920s built vessel of similar size to the ships in Harrison's own fleet, but the *Radhurst* was significantly smaller and already 25 years old. She was one of a number of small, obsolescent vessels which would struggle to keep up with even slow convoys in difficult weather conditions, and two years later she would straggle with fatal consequences. The other two vessels were both new products of the Government's war emergency building programme, but were completely different vessel types. The *Empire Carey* was of the 'Scandinavian' type, of some 2,800 tons and designed for the carriage of large deck cargoes, particularly timber. The *Empire Byron*, on the other hand, was a standard tramp ship with very similar dimensions to those in the Harrison fleet, her high gross tonnage of 6,645 being simply the product of her being fitted with a shelter deck.

The most dramatic episodes of the war at sea in the first half of 1941 were the destruction of HMS *Hood* by the German battleship *Bismarck*, and the latter's subsequent sinking by other British naval forces. The death ride of the *Bismarck*, however, was preceded by a successful raid into the North Atlantic by the battlecruisers *Scharnhorst* and *Gneisenau*, which between them sank over 100,000 tons of Allied shipping. At this stage of the war, only eastbound convoys were escorted all the way across the Atlantic. Westbound convoys only received protection for less than half of their journey, after which they dispersed to their individual destinations. The two German raiders found most of their victims among clusters of ships from recently dispersed convoys. One of these was the *Harlesden* (2), which had sailed in ballast with convoy OB.285 and set an independent course for Halifax when the convoy dispersed on 15th February. All went well until the morning of the

22nd when a signal was intercepted reporting that raiders were attacking ships in the vicinity. Captain Parry ordered a 180-degree turn away from the area, but at two in the afternoon a seaplane appeared. The aircraft, an Arado 196 from the *Gneisenau*, first used her floats to tear down the ship's wireless aerial and then flew low over the ship to drop a brown paper parcel tied with red ribbon on number 2 hatch. The Master, fearing it might be an explosive device, had it thrown overboard. It was to prove an unwise decision.

The German seaplane then began to machine-gun the *Harlesden* to some effect. The ship's sole Lewis gun was put out of action and its operator wounded, while the Chief Officer, Second Officer and Third Officer were also hit; the Second Officer subsequently dying from his wounds. After an hour and a half of intermittent attacks, the seaplane dropped two small bombs, both of which missed and then flew off. Captain Parry did the only sensible thing he could. The boiler fires were double banked and, working the ship up to 12 knots, he steered in the opposite direction to where he thought the raider was operating. Hopes of escaping in the dark were shattered at 21.00 hours when a searchlight was turned on the ship and the startled crew saw the *Gneisenau* on the starboard side. The raider opened fire immediately – one six-shot broadside from part of her 11-inch main armament and a hail of shells from her 5.9-inch secondary battery

Harlesden (2) was a victim of the German battlecruiser *Gneisenau* in February 1941. *[Nigel Farrell collection]*

lasting roughly 15 minutes. The radio room was destroyed by the first shot, which killed the Third Radio Officer and blew the officer of the watch onto the deck. As the shelling continued, the Quartermaster had both legs blown off and the starboard lifeboat destroyed. By the time the Germans stopped firing, the *Harlesden* was already sinking and abandon ship was ordered by the Master who had somehow survived the storm of shells and splinters. At roughly 21.30 the ship rolled over to starboard and sank by the stern. The German captain, to his credit, did everything he could to rescue the survivors, searching the area until 22.00 when it was clear all the survivors were aboard. From a total crew of 32, three were killed, three wounded and four missing – an amazingly low cost considering the battering the *Harlesden* had taken. The toll would have been lower had the Master opened the air-dropped parcel, which was simply a warning to surrender or face the consequences.

The spring of 1941 was to prove one of the worst times of the war for the company, with two ships being sunk within days of each other in early April, and another in mid-May. The first victim was the *Harbledown*, which had sailed from Halifax with convoy SC.26 on 20th March with a cargo of wheat. The slower SC convoys were always more vulnerable to Wolf pack attack, and SC.26 had the misfortune to run into a patrol line of eight U-boats, which sank a total of ten ships over three nights, during one of which the convoy had no anti-submarine escort whatsoever. The *Harbledown* almost survived, but at 1.45 on the morning of 4th April while steaming with a group of seven survivors of the earlier attacks and two destroyers, she was struck by two torpedoes from *U 94* on the port side, one in number 2 hold and one in the fore part of the engine room. The effects were catastrophic; the hatch covers were blown off, the bridge collapsed, the wireless room was wrecked and the vessel broke in two almost exactly amidships. The port boat had been destroyed, and only part of the crew got away in the starboard boat. The other survivors, including Captain Jones, who had been knocked unconscious by the first blast, managed to get away on a raft which floated off as the ship foundered. As it turned out, they were the lucky ones, as the starboard lifeboat capsized in rough seas before the destroyer HMS *Veteran* could bring her alongside, and most of its occupants were drowned. The destroyer found the raft at 5.00 am and saved those on board, but the total loss of life in the sinking came to 16.

The loss of *Harpathian* (2) on 8th April was also due to U-boat attack, but in this case not in the North Atlantic. She had sailed for Freetown with convoy OG.57, but these convoys also dispersed, in this case south of Gibraltar. She was thus proceeding alone when she was intercepted west of Madeira by *U 107*. It was the vessel's double misfortune that the enemy submarine was commanded by the U-boat ace Gunter Hessler, who was in the early stages of what would prove to be the single most successful U-boat sortie of the war, sinking 14 ships totalling 86,699 tons. Hessler's torpedo hit the port side towards the aft of number 1 hold, rupturing the bulkhead with number 2 hold with the result that the ship began to settle very rapidly by the head. The crew managed to get the two after lifeboats into the water, but the ship settled so quickly that some men had to jump overboard, and the boats themselves were blown sideways when the boilers exploded soon after. The ship went vertically down by the head and had disappeared entirely within four minutes of being hit. Hessler surfaced and gave the lifeboats directions, but they were hundreds of miles from land and faced a very long voyage. The two boats became separated on the first night, but both made epic journeys to safety, the Master's landing in the Canary Islands on 18th April, and the First Officer's boat, having been blown south by a gale, was finally picked up 30 miles from the African coast by a Spanish fishing boat. Four men did not survive the ordeal, three of them dying in the lifeboats. The Master, Captain John Wharton, was eventually awarded an MBE for his 380-mile, 11-day journey. We will hear of him again.

The last casualty of the spring was the company's other new vessel, the *Harpagus* (4), which had only just survived a year in service. She was sailing with convoy HX.126, which lost nine ships over two nights in the mid-Atlantic. The *Harpagus* was sailing as the rear ship in the three ship starboard outer column when the *Norman Monarch* at the head of the column was hit by a torpedo from *U 94* just before 5 on the morning of 20th May and fell out of line. Captain Steward dropped back to render assistance. The Master of the *Norman Monarch* initially believed that his ship might be saved, but his hopes were misplaced and, after what was to prove a fatal delay of some four hours, the *Harpagus* took aboard the stricken vessel's entire complement of 48 just before she foundered. The *Harpagus* made her best speed to rejoin the convoy throughout the day but, apart from one brief appearance, could not be afforded any escort, as the main body of the convoy was under continuous attack from a wolf pack. She had almost reached the convoy by 23.20, when the inevitable happened and she was struck by two torpedoes from *U 109* on the starboard side in Number 3 hold and Number 4 hold, just abaft the engine room. The vessel listed rapidly and sank in about three minutes. Only two boats which had been picked up from the *Norman Monarch* got away safely, and most aboard had to jump into the sea. Given that the *Harpagus* had effectively been carrying two full crews, casualties were heavy, even although HMS *Burnham* arrived on the scene to pick up survivors less than three hours after the sinking. A total of 55 lives were lost, 26 each from the crews of the two ships, and an entire family of three travelling as passengers aboard the *Harpagus*.

The company lost one final ship in 1941. Like the *Harpathian* (2) in the spring, the *Harlingen* (4) was operating on the West African convoy route, on this occasion homewards bound, but by the time SL.81 was attacked by a small pack of U-boats in the early hours of 5 August, the convoy was nearing home waters and was effectively ensnared in the Battle of the Atlantic. A total of five ships were lost to the enemy. The *Harlingen* had just taken up a position at the head of the third column to replace a vessel already sunk, when she and the ship astern were hit on the port side by torpedoes from the same spread fired by *U 75*. The *Harlingen* was struck in the engine room just slightly abaft of the amidships line. The Master, Captain Willingham, got everybody except two men killed in the explosion safely into the starboard lifeboat before exploring the damage. He found that the water was already up to the top of the engine room, and the ship subsequently settled quickly until the after well deck was awash. Rejoining the boat he laid off as the ship seemed to stabilize, but after about an hour she finally foundered. The survivors were picked up shortly afterwards by a corvette and landed at Gourock. By the standards of a bloody year, they were the most fortunate of the crews whose ships had been sunk.

Harpasa was sunk by Japanese bombers in April 1942 and her name was not used again. [Ships in Focus]

1942 was to prove the turning point of the war on land in the West. At sea, however, the situation was very different, and the year witnessed the highest level of Allied merchant shipping losses of the entire conflict. By the end of 1941, the company had lost nine of its pre-war fleet (including the now-government owned *Harpenden*) as well as two ships it was managing for the Government. While the Ministry of War Transport allocated almost all UK shipbuilding capacity to the construction of standard types for government ownership, it did grant special permission to some owners to build a small number of ships to replace particularly heavy losses. J. and C. Harrison Ltd. was granted yard space for the construction of four new vessels at the end of 1941, and placed its order with William Doxford and Sons Ltd. of Pallion. The new vessels represented a revolution in Harrison design policy. While their basic hull dimensions were similar to the last of the pre-war steam tramps, these vessels introduced a shelter deck, and, far more importantly, the marine diesel engine. With a gross tonnage of 7,300 and a design speed of 12 knots, they were a generation ahead of anything else in the fleet.

The four new vessels would begin to enter the fleet in the autumn of 1942; the first pair – *Hardingham* (2) and *Harpalyce* (5) – were launched in June and delivered in September and October respectively. The *Harpagus* (5) followed in November, but the *Harlesden* (3) was held up awaiting a building berth and was only delivered in March 1943. The company relinquished management of the *Empire Carey*, which had been sold to the Norwegian Government, but also took over management of four war standard vessels built in North America to British design – the *Fort Maurepas* and *Fort La Montee* from Canadian yards, and the *Ocean Gypsy* and *Ocean Glory* from the massive Todd-Bath yard at Portland, Maine. The year, however, was to be dominated not by new arrivals but by the heaviest losses of the war.

To date, all of Harrison ships' fatal encounters with the enemy had taken place in home waters or the Atlantic. In 1942 the dangers became global in scope. The first brush with the enemy occurred on the recently established Russian

convoy route. The *Harmatris* (2) was acting as the Commodore ship of PQ.8 and had led her charges safely to the entry of Kola Inlet when *U 454* launched a daring solo attack in the early evening of 17th January. One of his torpedoes struck the *Harmatris* on the starboard side abreast of number 1 hold. Although the hold filled rapidly, it became obvious that the ship was in no danger of sinking, and Captain Brundle kept his crew aboard while awaiting a tow. While waiting, a mysterious tremor shook the ship. At the time, it was thought that it might have been a drifting mine, as nobody had realized that the original assailant was a submarine. It was in fact a second torpedo from the persistent *U 454*, which failed to explode. *Harmatris* was lucky, but one of the escorts, the Tribal class destroyer HMS *Matabele* was not – before departing the scene *U 454* launched one last attack. The torpedoes missed their intended target, a tanker, but hit the destroyer, causing her magazines to explode – there were only two survivors. The *Harmatris* eventually made it into Murmansk on 20th January with the assistance of Russian tugs and an escort of British minelayers.

The first loss of 1942 occurred far away in the Indian Ocean at the hands of a new enemy, the Japanese. The rapid Japanese conquest of South East Asia, combined by a sortie into the Indian Ocean by the enemy's main carrier strike force, precipitated a rapid evacuation of merchant shipping from the Bay of Bengal. The Japanese Navy, however, had anticipated just such a move, and had sent a supporting cruiser task force, bolstered by the light carrier *Ryujo*, into the northern Bay of Bengal to attack shipping. The *Harpasa* sailed from Calcutta for Mombasa on 1st April and joined up with a group of seven other ships at the mouth of the Hooghly on the morning of the 4th. Shortly afterwards, however, the *Harpasa* fell astern, being unable to maintain the speed of her consorts, but all remained well until 14.35 on the 5th when two Japanese aircraft were sighted. The aircraft, were identified as Zero fighters, but were actually bomb-carrying Kates from the *Ryujo*. They made two separate attacks. In the first pass the Master saw some six to eight small bombs explode about 100

A remarkable photograph taken from a Japanese aircraft of the *Harpasa* being bombed in the Bay of Bengal on 4th April 1942. [Author's collection]

yards off the starboard quarter. The second proved fatal, with five bombs exploding simultaneously in number 5 hold. Within minutes, the gunnies and oil stowed in the 'tween decks were burning fiercely and the fire had engulfed the poop. Captain Atkinson and his crew fought the fire to no avail for an hour before its progress forwards and the fact that the ship had settled to a point where the decks were only 12 feet above water made abandoning ship imperative. By 16.00 all the crew were clear of the ship, and an hour later the explosives aboard blew up, destroying the after part of the ship. The Acting Commodore ship *Taksang* (3,471/1935) turned back on hearing the explosion

After *Harpagon* (1) was torpedoed on 9th April 1942 members of her crew spent 34 days in boats until they were rescued. *[J. and M. Clarkson]*

and picked up the men from the lifeboats. Captain Atkinson tried to persuade the Master of the rescue ship to tow the blazing forepart of his command 30 miles to the coast, but the latter quite sensibly refused.

The rescue ship was to prove only a temporary haven. Early the next morning, warships were sighted which soon proved to be Japanese. The *Taksang* was shelled at point blank range by the task force flagship, the heavy cruiser *Chokai*, and sunk in less than 10 minutes. Captain Atkinson did not have time to find a boat and was forced to dive overboard. He eventually found a cluster of boats and rafts which had made it away from the disengaged side of the ship. A roll call revealed that five men from the *Harpasa* and 12 from the *Taksang* had died. The Japanese fleet sailed away in chase of other fleeing vessels and the survivors rowed ashore, landing safely on the morning of 7th April.

Before the month was out, the company would lose two further ships, the first being a victim of the increasingly fierce German assault on the Arctic convoys. When the *Harpalion* (3) sailed from the Kola Inlet on 10th April 1942 with convoy QP.10, she was on the homeward leg of her second round trip. The convoy came under sustained attack by aircraft and U-boats for three days between the Inlet and Bear Island, losing four ships and having a fifth turn back with serious damage. The *Harpalion* was subject to four separate bombing attacks by Ju 88s on the morning of the 13th. The first three attacks all resulted in bombs exploding within 50 yards of the ship. The fourth, a solo low level attack from astern dropped four bombs right under the counter, only 10 to 20 feet from the stern. The explosions shattered the rudder and rendered the vessel unmanageable. The escorting destroyer HMS *Fury* was asked for a tow, but answered that this was impossible due to rough weather and continuing air attack. Captain Williams then tried to organize the rigging of a jury rudder, but the ship was continually attacked by other aircraft, which machine-gunned the crew working at the stern. Eventually the *Harpalion* ran out of ammunition and could not even defend herself. Eventually HMS *Fury* returned and ordered Williams to abandon ship. He did so grudgingly only after confirming with the Chief Officer and Chief Engineer that even if they did manage to rig a jury rudder, their chances of making port unescorted were slim. An attempt to scuttle the vessel by opening the sea cocks failed, and after the crew were rescued by the destroyer, the latter sank the *Harpalion* with gunfire.

Thousands of miles away, the *Harpagon* (1) sailed from New York for a solo passage to Table Bay on 17th April. In addition to general cargo, the ship was carrying over 2,500 tons of explosives. U-boats had been very active off the east coast of the USA in the early months of 1942, taking advantage of the failure of the USA to introduce a coastal convoy system, and the *Harpagon* was clearly sailing into dangerous waters. At 23.15 on 19th April, roughly 150 miles north north west of Bermuda, she was hit on the starboard side by two torpedoes from *U 109*, the first hitting number 1 hold, and the second number 3 hold about 20 seconds later. Chief Officer R.D. Creser rushed on deck to discover that the vessel was already on fire, with minor explosions going off regularly in her munitions cargo, and sinking so quickly that he only had to step over the side of the bulwark to enter the sea. He had to swim hard up and away from the ship to prevent being sucked down with her, and by the time he made it back to the surface all he could see was the stern disappearing in a blaze of flame. After a terrible night in which individual groups of survivors found their way to rafts and one damaged lifeboat, dawn found the survivors clustered in four rafts and the lifeboat. There were only nine of them – the Master and 39 other officers and crew were missing. Luckily, the survivors included the Chief and Second Officers and the Chief and Fifth Engineers, there were adequate stocks of food and water, and they knew that they were only 150 miles away from Bermuda and had fair hopes of an early rescue. They cast away one damaged raft, placed all the food and water in two others and tied all three rafts to the lifeboat.

Hopes of early rescue proved misplaced, and although a plane was heard above the clouds on 22nd April and flares were lighted, no sighting was made. On the following day the weather worsened appreciably, with heavy rain and a northerly gale of about Force 7 – conditions which prevailed for six days. One raft was lost during the first night, but luckily it contained no stores. On 24th April the Third Wireless Officer started showing symptoms of pneumonia, and by the 26th, the Chief Officer had to reduce food and water rations. Although the weather cleared up there was still no sign of rescue, and the rations had to be reduced again on 3rd May. The Wireless Officer died on 14th May, and with spirits already low, Creser had to reduce rations yet again the next day. One of the crew objected violently and seized an axe, but was quickly subdued by the two officers, one of whom got him in a throttle grip and the other 'knocked him for six'. By this time all the survivors were suffering from sunburn and salt water boils, and supplementing their diet with seaweed. Finally, at 05.00 on 24th May a ship was sighted and after frantic use of the remaining flares, contact was achieved by flashing an SOS with a torch. The ship, which proved to be the Argentine *Rio Diamante* (5,159/1918), took them aboard after a sojourn of just over 34 days adrift. None of the men were able to walk when they reached the deck, but they had been coaxed back to full health by the time they docked at Buenos Aires on 21st June despite the fact that *Rio Diamante* did not have a doctor aboard.

The company experienced another rash of losses in quick succession in July. Two took place in the course of the destruction of convoy PQ.17 in the cold waters of the Arctic Sea. Both the company's own *Hartlebury* and the managed *Empire Byron* sailed with the convoy. The former carried the Vice Commodore and the latter was under the command of the redoubtable Captain Wharton, who had recently been awarded a well-deserved MBE for his saving his crew on a long ocean voyage after the *Harpathian* (2) had been torpedoed in April 1941. Both ships survived the initial enemy attacks, but both fell victim to U-boats after the convoy was dispersed in the mistaken belief that it was being menaced by German capital ships.

The *Empire Byron* was one of the first of the scattered ships to fall prey to a submarine. Following the order to scatter at 20.20 hours on 4th July, Captain Wharton altered course from 045 to 065 degrees and increased speed to 10 knots. All went well until 06.20 on the 5th, when the ship was struck by a single torpedo on the port side in number 4 hold just forward of the main mast. Many of the U-boats unleashed on PQ.17 were new to the war and commanded by very inexperienced captains. *U 703* had actually missed the *Empire Byron* with two separate two torpedo spreads. It was a fifth, fired from the stern tube which finally hit the ship. The explosion was particularly violent, and the ship started to sink rapidly. The Master rang the engine room telegraph to stop, but the engineers could not stop the machinery due to damage and the vessel had to be abandoned while underway. The main starboard boat capsized, but its three occupants swam safely to the port boat. By this time the ship was underwater up to the rafts in the main rigging, and there were still nine men aboard including Captain Wharton. The ship was going under quickly, and he only just managed to set loose a raft and swim towards it before she went under. He and others on rafts had been picked up by the smaller lifeboats when the U-boat surfaced and began to interrogate the survivors. When Wharton saw the submarine turning toward his boat he quickly took off his uniform coat and put it in the locker; when hailed from the U-boat he said that he had last seen the Master on the bridge, and the Germans only took prisoner an unfortunate army officer on his way to Russia as an instructor for the new Churchill tanks being delivered to the USSR.

When the U-boat moved away, Wharton called his three boats together and began what would have been a 300-mile journey southwards to land. Luckily, the boat was sighted on 10th July by the corvette HMS *Dianella* which had returned from Archangel to sweep the sea for survivors. The survivors were picked up at about 13.20 having been in their boats for 5½ days and covering roughly 250 days of their journey to land. It speaks volumes for Wharton's already well-established competence that none of his men suffered anything worse than swollen feet during the boat journey.

Only nine men were lost in the sinking, one of whom died of his injuries in a life-boat and was buried at sea. Compared to what was happening to the *Hartlebury*, the ordeal faced by the survivors of the *Empire Byron* had proved rather mild.

When the convoy was ordered to disperse, Captain Stephenson took the *Hartlebury* north east up to the edge of the ice barrier and then steamed at full speed, taking advantage of banks of fog to hide his ship, until 16.30 on 6th July when he reached Admiralty Inlet, Novaya Zemlya. At this point he turned south south west to head for Archangel, but within ten minutes the ship was struck on the starboard side under the bridge by a torpedo fired by *U 355*. The Master was knocked briefly unconscious by falling debris, but just as he came round there was a second explosion as another torpedo hit the ship in the engine room, blowing away the starboard boat which was just being lowered. Another minute later there was a third explosion further aft on the side on number 5 hold. This was far more violent than the other two, almost certainly because the ammunition stowed in the hold exploded. The *Hartlebury* broke into three pieces, across the forward part of the stokehold and the after part of the long bridge deck in front of number 5 hold. The crew managed to launch three rafts from the port side, as well as the port lifeboat, which had to be cut free from the falls and ended up in the sea in a waterlogged condition. By the time Stephenson gave the order to abandon ship at 16.45, there was only one other man left aboard, and both jumped into the sea just before the remains of the ship went under.

Given the devastating impact of the torpedo attack, it was surprising how many men survived to reach the boat and rafts. The Master managed to get himself and 16 others into the lifeboat, and he saw seven men on one raft and 14 on another before losing sight of them in the fog. Everybody aboard was suffering the after effects of immersion, not only in the nearly frozen sea, but also in the waterlogged lifeboat itself. Stephenson did everything possible to clear the boat of water, but four men died in the first five hours. The weather moderated and the fog cleared on the evening of the following day, and with the help of a bucket and the boat's pump the water was reduced down to the level of the boat's tanks. By this time, however, there were only four men left alive, the rest having all succumbed to exposure. On the following morning a sail was rigged and a course steered south east towards land which the Master estimated to be some 16 miles distant. At 10 in the morning nine men were picked up from one of the rafts, and 12 hours later the 13 survivors came ashore on an uninhabited island in Pomorski Bay. The men were able to dry themselves and keep warm and fed for two days until a ship was sighted stopped in the bay. The boat was launched and the ship was discovered to be the US *Winston-Salem* (6,223/1920), a refugee from the same convoy. She already had on board seven more survivors from the *Hartlebury*, but was herself now stranded on some rocks. A variety of rescue ships now descended on the bay, one of which took the 20 *Hartlebury* survivors to Archangel, while others pulled the *Winston-Salem* to safety. The latter finally arrived at Archangel on 28th July, the last ship of PQ 17 to make port.

While the *Hartlebury* and *Empire Byron* were meeting their fates in the cold waters of the Arctic Sea, another Harrison vessel was becoming the company's second loss at the hands of the Imperial Japanese Navy. The *Hartismere* (1) was proceeding through the Mozambique

Channel on the last leg of a long voyage from Philadelphia round Africa with military stores for the war in the desert when she fell victim to a rare exercise in the concentrated use of submarines against mercantile targets by the Japanese. Four large submarines sank no fewer than 22 merchant ships in and around the Mozambique Channel between 5th June and 9th July. The *Hartismere* was the penultimate victim, struck by a single torpedo from the submarine *I-10* on the port side in the way of number 1 hold just a few minutes past midnight on 7/8th July. The *Hartismere* began to settle quickly by the head and Captain Long decided to abandon ship within minutes. Both boats got away safely with the entire ship's complement aboard, and as the Master's boat, which had a motor, made its way round the stern to the disengaged side, the ship's propeller was already clear of the water. As he reached the Chief Officer's boat, he noticed shell flashes to starboard of the ship's bow. The shelling was brief but violent, with the first shell starting a fire amidships and several others following in quick succession. The Master decided that the boats were too close to the ship for safety and towed the second boat further off. By this time the shelling had stopped, but the *Hartismere* was burning furiously. The boat's occupants watched at a distance until the flames suddenly disappeared at 00.20 – the ship having sunk within just over a quarter of an hour of the first assault. Although the Portuguese coast was 136 miles away, the presence of the motor boat made all the difference and the crew landed safely on the coast in well under two days, the Master later calculating that he had made 136 miles towing the second boat at an average speed of 4½ knots, and still had one gallon of petrol left when he reached his destination. It was a considerable achievement, due in no small measure to the fact that the Master and Chief Officer had been together when their previous ship had been torpedoed.

After improved anti-submarine measures limited the chances of success off the east coast of America, a large number of U-boats were redeployed into the Caribbean and Gulf of Mexico, where most shipping still sailed independently. The *Harborough* (1) was nearing the end of a passage from Rio de Janeiro to Trinidad when at 02.00 on 14th September Captain Hibbert received a warning that a submarine was operating about three miles off his track. As the message was six hours old and he was only 60 miles from his destination, he decided to press on at full speed. He nearly made it, but at 08.30, the track of a torpedo was seen by the lookouts and the ship was shortly afterwards hit between the engine room and number 4 hold on the port side. The damage was severe, with both the engine room and number 4 hold flooding, and the deck cracking across the port side. The ship was clearly doomed and, although the port lifeboat had been destroyed in the explosion, the Master got all the survivors away in the starboard boat, a small jolly boat and several rafts. The attacker, *U 515*, surfaced soon after and fired several shells into number 5 hold to hasten the sinking. The ship did not last long, sinking vertically, stern first at 08.50, 20 minutes after the torpedo had struck. Only five men had been

lost in the attack and, apart from the injured Donkeyman, all the survivors were in good shape and near land. A northerly current diverted the craft from Trinidad, but everybody was safely ashore on the neighbouring island of Tobago by mid-morning on 16th September.

The irony of the heavy losses suffered by the company in 1942 was that only the last one took place on the North Atlantic convoy routes. The *Hartington* (2) sailed from Halifax on 27th October in SC.107. At this stage of the war, U-boats were operating far further to the west than had been the case in 1941, and the convoy first came under attack on the evening of 1st November. By midnight, three ships had been torpedoed, and at 01.00 on 2nd November, the *Hartington* became the fourth when a torpedo from *U 522* struck her between numbers 1 and 2 holds on the starboard side. Within five minutes of the attack, the ship was listing 10 to 15 degrees to starboard and the order was given to abandon ship. This was done quickly and efficiently, and within another five minutes both boats were away. The *Hartington* herself did not last much longer, rolling over and sinking at 01.20. When the Chief Engineer closed the boats together to divide the survivors evenly, it was discovered that two men were missing. Both had been seen on deck, and there was no indication as to why they had not made it into the boats.

Several ships from the convoy hailed the boats as they passed, but none returned to their rescue, and the survivors were subjected to an unexpected ordeal. After one day of good weather, the boats were buffeted by a six-day gale. The boats were well provisioned and the men were equipped with protective clothing, so spirits and health generally remained high. Nonetheless, the Carpenter, an elderly man, died on the fourth day, probably from simple exhaustion as he had not been injured. The Master, Captain Young, had been ill on the voyage due to an operation carried out before sailing, and the Second Officer eventually collapsed from exhaustion and exposure after many days sailing the Engineer's boat. The 23 survivors in the Chief Engineer's boat were eventually picked up by the destroyer HMS *Winchelsea* on 12th November, but no trace was ever found of the Chief Officer's boat, bringing the final death toll from the sinking to 24.

While historical analysis has subsequently shown that the Allies were winning the Battle of the Atlantic by the closing months of 1942, this was by no means obvious at the time. The first five months of 1943 were to see some of

After *Harborough* (1) was sunk on 14th September 1942, the survivors soon reached Tobago. *[J. and M. Clarkson]*

the largest convoy battles of the war, and to take a heavy toll of shipping. The now heavily depleted Harrison fleet was involved in some of these. It would lose three ships in the climactic Atlantic convoy battles and one in the summer in the South Atlantic. Ships under its management would also suffer considerable loss, one in the North Atlantic, and the rest supporting Allied offensives in the Mediterranean.

The only new arrival in the Harrison fleet itself was the *Harlesden* (3), the last of its four new motor ships. The company did, however, take on the management of a significant number of new standard ships for the MOWT: four more Canadian-built vessels – the *Fort Athabasca*, *Fort Frontenac*, *Fort Lennox* and *Fort Pic*; and two British-built ones – the *Empire Florizel* and the *Empire Crown*.

The first casualty of the year was the *Harmala*, which had left Halifax in convoy SC.118 on 27th January with a cargo of iron ore. Several ships straggled from the convoy and were subsequently lost to U-boats on 6th February, but the convoy itself did not come under attack until the night of 6/7th February. Three ships had already been sunk when at 01.25 on the 7th, the *Harmala* was hit by one torpedo from *U 614* on the port side in number 2 hold, just forward of the bridge. The ship took a list to port and began to settle rapidly by the head. She had already lost her starboard lifeboat in heavy weather, so the Master, Captain Anholm, went to the boat deck to get the port lifeboat away. This was managed successfully, but almost as soon as it became waterborne, the ship lurched heavily to port, and Anholm was able to step straight aboard to join the 12 men already there. The ship then gave another violent lurch to port and sank immediately, the backwash almost swamping the boat. The total time elapsed between the torpedo hitting and the ship sinking was less than two minutes, and there was no time to send a distress signal, launch flares or even give a formal order to abandon ship. The Master could not see anybody in the water or in several empty rafts, but he could hear men shouting. The Free French corvette *Lobelia* appeared after about an hour in response to signals flashed by torch, and took the 13 men in the lifeboat aboard. There was still shouting from the water, and a number of red survival lights could be seen from the corvette's bridge, but she was ordered off to engage a U-boat and could only leave a Carley float behind in the hope that some of those in the water could climb aboard. When she returned after about two hours, all the red lights had disappeared, and although she remained behind to search after daybreak, no other survivors were found – a total of 40 men had lost their lives.

There were to be no survivors' reports from the next loss – the managed *Radhurst*. Built back in 1916, and only capable of nine knots when completed, she was too small and too slow to keep up with convoy ONS.165S when it hit stormy weather. Nothing was ever heard or seen again of the ship or her crew of 40, and it was only confirmed after the war that she had actually been found and sunk by *U 525*.

The final two Harrison casualties of the Battle of the Atlantic were sunk on the same night in the same convoy. The *Harbury* (4) and *Harperley* (3) both sailed from Milford Haven on 20th April in convoy ONS.5. By this time of the war westbound convoys were fully escorted, and ships more often carried cargo (in both ships' cases, coal) than sailing in ballast. The vessels were on opposite sides of the convoy, *Harperley* being the third ship in the port wing column, and *Harbury* ending up as the leading ship in column 8 on the starboard side after the two vessels ahead of her had straggled. There was one submarine attack on the morning of 30th April, which resulted in the loss of a single vessel, but the convoy then proceeded without incident until the convoy was attacked simultaneously by several submarines from different directions starting at 22.50 on 4th May. The *Harbury* was the first ship hit; the *Harperley* on the other side of the convoy was hit less than ten minutes later.

The *Harbury* was struck by one torpedo from *U 628* on the starboard side in number 5 hold. The after peak bulkhead collapsed and the tunnel door fractured, flooding

Harbury (4) (above) and *Harperley* (3) (below) were both sunk by U-boats on the same night in convoy ONS.5. The *Harbury* was photographed in the Mersey and the *Harperley* in Buenos Aires during May 1935. [Basil Feilden/J. and M. Clarkson; Raul Maya/Nigel Farrell collection]

the engine room, and the ship began to settle rapidly by the stern. With the after well deck already under water, abandon ship was ordered. The two main lifeboats were successfully lowered, but the small starboard quarter boat had been damaged by the explosion and its port equivalent capsized after launch. Part of the crew had to jump overboard as they were cut off by the rapid flooding of the well deck. Captain Cook and two volunteers stayed on board to ensure that everybody had left the ship, searching the midships section thoroughly. At about midnight, grinding and wrenching noises from aft persuaded the three men to take to a raft and lay off the vessel until daylight. At 02.30 the trawler HMS *Northern Spray* found all the survivors from the raft and the two boats and took them aboard. Seven men were found to be missing, presumed drowned after having to jump into the sea from the stern section. The *Harbury* was found to be still afloat at daybreak, and the Master, Chief Officer and the First Lieutenant of the trawler re-boarded her to see if salvage was possible. The inspection quickly revealed that the vessel was doomed. There was eight feet of water in the engine room and stokehold, and sea was pouring into number 4 hold from the 'tween decks. The party returned to the trawler and the *Harbury* was left to founder. An air search on the following day found no trace of her.

The *Harperley* (3) was hit at 22.56 by two torpedoes from *U 264* on the port side, one under the foremast and one in the engine room. The ship listed very heavily to port and Captain Turgoose ordered a very prompt abandon ship, sending out a distress signal and firing rockets. Those in the engine room had little chance of survival, and the Second, Third and Fourth Engineers were all either killed by the blast or drowned. One boat had been lost in the explosion, but the other three were all successfully launched. After only about quarter of an hour in the boats, the Master saw the *Harperley* sink by the head. Two men were heard moaning in the water, but only one could be found. The Master then pulled over to the Second Officer's lifeboat – the only large capacity craft to survive the explosion – and the two rebalanced the survivors as best they could. He then pulled over to the other small boat and found it capsized with two men clinging to its bottom. He found it impossible to go alongside, not least because his own boat was already damaged, and so told the men to hang on until daybreak and kept his boat nearby. The trawler HMS *Northern Spray*, which would later pick up the survivors of the *Harbury* (4), appeared after the men had been in the boats for about 3½ hours. All the occupants of the two upright craft were rescued, but although the naval vessel saw the lights of the two men left on the upturned boat and made towards them, neither the men nor the boat was ever found. Thus the casualty total for the *Harperley* reached 11.

The 20th and last vessel lost by J. and C. Harrison during the war was the *Harmonic* (3). Although U-boats were being withdrawn from the North Atlantic after very heavy losses in the spring and early summer, long-range boats were still a considerable menace to unescorted ships in the South Atlantic and Indian Ocean. The *Harmonic* was in the early stages of a passage from Rosario and Buenos Aires for Freetown when she had the misfortune to be sighted by one of the most proficient of the long-range U-boat commanders, Kapitänleutant Carl Emmermann of *U 172*. Emmermann was on his fifth war patrol and had already accounted for 24 Allied merchant ships. The submarine war in distant waters could be less brutal than that waged further north, and having brought

Harmonic to a stop with one torpedo, Emmermann waited until her crew had abandoned ship before sinking her. As a result, Harrison's last war loss was one of the least costly in terms of lives lost; 46 of the crew of 47 surviving to be picked up by the Portuguese *Inhambane* (6,051/1912) on 22nd July.

The other casualties suffered during the year were all vessels managed for the Ministry of War Transport. All took place in the Mediterranean, where, despite a massive deployment of land, sea and air resources, progress was slowed down by dogged enemy resistance. No fewer than four Harrison-managed vessels were lost, three of them through air attack. The first, the 32-year-old *Hampton Lodge*, was the only one actually sunk at sea. On 20th January she was on her way from Algiers to Oran in convoy KMS.6 as the lead ship in the port wing column. During the same evening the heavily escorted merchant ships came under sustained attack when less than 50 miles clear of Algiers. The attacking Ju 88s came in across the bows of the convoy, diving as low as 200 feet to release their bombs. At 19.59 *Hampton Lodge* was near-missed twice on her starboard bow; a minute later she was struck with three bombs from one well-aimed stick. The first struck forward of the bridge, the second abaft the same structure, and the third went through the engine room skylight, penetrated the tank tops and lodged there without exploding. The first and second bombs did explode, causing massive damage – all the hatches were blown off and by the time Captain Stott picked himself up off the deck, the ship was already listing 35 degrees to port and was clearly sinking. Crew discipline was excellent and everybody was safely off the ship and clear of the ship by 20.05. They were all picked up by the rescue tug *St. Day* within half an hour, and later, when the *Hampton Lodge* showed no signs of foundering she was re-boarded and inspected. This revealed that numbers 2 and 3 holds, the stokehold and the engine room were all flooded to sea level, and that the midships bulkheads had collapsed. It was clear that the ship could not be saved, and Stott was almost certainly correct in his assumption that she was only floating on air pockets. The vessel was left to her fate and was last seen at 23.30 with her decks almost awash. She foundered at 07.00 on the following morning.

The next two losses did not occur until the summer. On 21st July a combined force of German and Italian bombers launched an air raid on Allied shipping concentrated in the recently captured harbour at Augusta, Sicily. Anti-aircraft defences were poorly prepared and a number of ships were sunk including the almost brand new *Empire Florizel*. The vessel had entered the harbour with a cargo of 4,000 tons of mixed military stores at 09.00 on 19th July during a bombing attack. There were two further attacks on the same day, followed up by a third at dawn on the 20th when an ammunition ship was hit and blown up. At 03.00 in the morning of 21st July a major dive-bombing attack developed. After 20 minutes the *Empire Florizell* received at least two direct hits in number 1 hold. There were about 200 tons of petrol in number 1 hold and ammunition in number 2 hold. A fire broke out immediately and the ship was then wracked by a series of violent explosions, some of which blew blazing petrol cans right over the bridge onto the after deck. The vessel settled rapidly in about 12 fathoms and within five minutes the fore-deck was underwater, and the transport vehicles which made up the bulk of the cargo were well ablaze. With the stern out of the water, Captain Mastermann could do nothing but tell his crew to jump into the harbour.

Ultimately 54 survivors were rescued, and the ship, ablaze as far aft as number 4 hold, was shelled and sunk by a warship. Seven D.E.M.S. gunners (almost certainly killed by the initial bomb strikes) and two of the crew were missing, and six men were in hospital. Given the apocalyptic nature of the sinking, it was a low casualty rate.

The accidental loss of the *Fort La Montee* a few weeks later produced much higher casualties. The vessel was lying alongside the wharf in Algiers harbour on 4th August 1943 discharging cargo. Only about 100 tons of explosives (mostly detonators) and 6,000 shells were left aboard; the explosives in four special magazines (three in number 1 hold and one in

Fort La Montee in June 1943. *[National Maritime Museum P22695]*

number 2 'tween decks) and the shells in number 2 lower hold. At about 11.00 smoke was seen issuing from number 1 magazine. Although hoses were played on the magazine from the ship itself, a fully loaded US ship lying alongside and a squad of Army fire-fighters, the entire ship was enveloped in thick yellow smoke from burning phosphorous shells within half an hour and, although some of the crew fled ashore, the remainder donned gas masks and kept at their task. Two tugs arrived to tow the ship clear of the harbour, and had her clear of the breakwater by noon. Two fleet barges and the destroyer HMS *Arrow* secured alongside, and at one stage around 15.15 it looked as if the battle had been won. The fire, however, quickly flared up again, and about 15.40 the *Fort La Montee* suddenly blew up. The ship broke in two, the after part sinking very quickly. The forward part remained afloat but the bow was twisted and bent back over the bridge. The *Arrow* also lost her bow in the blast. Of the 35 men who were still on board at the time of the blast, 19 were lost in the explosion, including the Third Officer, Chief and Third Engineers, the Chief Steward and the First and Third Wireless Operators. All of the 16 survivors were injured and six of them, including the Master, the Chief Officer and the Second and Fourth Engineers, subsequently died. What was left of the ship was subsequently sunk by naval gunfire.

The worst loss of all, however, was the last. On 2nd December, German bombers launched an attack on the Italian port of Bari. At the time of the attack roughly 40 cargo vessels and warships were at anchor in the harbour. One of these was the US Liberty *John Harvey* (7,177/1943), whose cargo included several hundred tons of mustard gas shells. She was hit and blew up, triggering a series of other explosions in munitions-laden ships elsewhere in the harbour. In all a total of 17 ships were totally lost, one of them the Harrison-managed *Fort Athabasca* which was unfortunate enough to be carrying two captured German glider bombs destined for analysis at home. These exploded, destroying the ship and leaving only ten of her crew of 56 alive.

The *Fort Athabasca* was the company's last war loss. 1944 saw the heavy loss of managed tonnage offset by the arrival of by two Liberty ships, the *Samaustral* and *Samderry*, both on bare-boat charter to the Ministry of War Transport from the US Maritime Commission. The most striking event of the year, however, was the sale of all four of the 1942-43 built Doxford motorships – the *Hardingham* (2),

Harpalyce (5), *Harpagus* (5) and *Harlesden* (3) – to the Hain Steamship Co. Ltd., a large tramp operator which had been part of the P&O Group since the middle of the First World War. It seems incredible that a company whose pre-war fleet had been reduced to a fifth of its original size would sell four almost new replacements, even for an attractive price. With shipping under total government control there was no commercial logic to the decision unless J. and C. Harrison Ltd. was considering leaving ship owning altogether. There is no reason to suspect this, and even if they had been intent on such a course then surely they would have sold their five surviving pre-war ships, all of which were only half way through their normal economic lives. It cannot even be that the company was unhappy with the design or with what had been their first venture away from steam, because it placed an order with Doxford in late 1944 for a vessel which was an almost exact replica of the ships sold. Hain might have offered a price that seemed too good to decline, but the company was condemning itself to a more difficult post-war re-construction challenge than need have been the case.

Thus when the war ended in 1945, J. and C. Harrison Ltd. owned a fleet of only five ships – the *Harberton* (2) and *Harmattan* (3) of 1930, the *Harmatris* (2) and *Hartlepool* of 1932, and the *Harpalycus* (1) of 1935. One other vessel was still afloat under the British flag, the *Empire Stour* (ex-*Harpenden*), but she was now owned by the Ministry of War Transport and would be sold to Indian owners in 1947. Hundreds of brave men had lost their lives on the ships lost. Some others had been lucky enough to survive several sinkings. The fleet was ravaged, and the British economy worn out by a long hard struggle. Post-war shipping competition was likely to be tough, with the massive US shipbuilding effort providing the means for both established firms and new entrants to fight for business which was likely to take years to return to normal peacetime levels. In addition, the war had accelerated nationalist sentiment in the colonies of the European powers, and the British merchant marine was likely to prove particularly vulnerable to new state-sponsored ventures in Southeast Asia, the Indian sub-continent and Africa. J. and C. Harrison Ltd. would need all of its years of experience and deep capital reserves to rebuild its fleet and maintain a profitable business.

The entire Harrison-owned fleet at the end of the war comprised: *Harberton* (2) (left) and *Harmattan* (3) of 1930 (middle), the *Harmatris* (2) (entering Vancouver on 6th June 1935) (bottom), *Hartlepool* of 1932 (opposite page, top) and the *Harpalycus* (1) of 1935 (opposite page middle). *[J. and M. Clarkson; Ships in Focus; J. and M. Clarkson; Kevin O'Donoghue; J. and M. Clarkson]*

The slow road back

As already mentioned, five ships of the pre-war fleet survived to resume normal trading as government control of shipping was gradually relaxed. In addition, the company had one new ship under construction. The *Hartington* (3), almost a carbon copy of the ships sold in 1944, had been launched in March 1945, but the amount of work pending at Doxford's Pallion yard meant that she was not actually completed until late October. Beyond her, there was little prospect of gaining immediate access to new tonnage with yards fully occupied with clearing wartime Government orders, the Ministry of War Transport itself still utilizing a large proportion of available ships to move men, stores and equipment from war theatres to destinations all over the world, and a significant part of the war-built fleet due to be returned to the USA under the terms of the lend-lease agreement.

In 1946 J. and C. Harrison Ltd., still under the firm control of John and Frank Harrison, both now in their mid-sixties, embarked on a cautious fleet rebuilding programme which was to feature a mixture of new tonnage and war standard ships purchased second-hand. The fleet planned was only about half the size of its predecessor. Building costs were now much higher, and market conditions likely to be more competitive, so the directors, who it must be remembered were running a family firm for the benefit of family trust members, could well have been concentrating on profitability rather than growth. While the replacement tonnage programme was being rolled out, the firm chartered some of the vessels they were still managing for the Government to supplement its cargo carrying capacity, and sustain its revenue streams.

The post-war fleet would never approach the size of its pre-war predecessor. Two points have to be kept in mind in coming to any judgement on this fact. The first is that the conditions which allowed for the construction of 26 ships in six years were the product of two extraordinary events – the amassing of a huge pool of capital due to the highly inflated freight rates and insurance pay-outs of the First World War; and the low cost of new construction during the years following the Great Depression. The second is that J. and C. Harrison Ltd. was run as a private family owned venture from beginning to end, and there is no evidence whatsoever that its principals were ever considering changing its status. With no significant sums for new investment available from inside the family, there was simply no additional capital to counterbalance the steep increase in shipbuilding costs after the Second World War. In addition, the obligation to maintain dividend payments at relatively high levels meant that inflation was actually eroding the capital base.

After the arrival of the *Hartington* (3) in late 1945, the company ordered two further new motor ships, one each from Doxford and from the Burntisland Shipbuilding Co. Ltd. The two ships dispensed with the shelter deck, and the vessels were fairly close to being hull sisters, although the Doxford ship was slightly larger. Oddly enough, however, although Doxford supplied the engines for both ships, the slightly earlier Burntisland-built ship received a three-cylinder engine, whereas the Doxford ship received a larger four-cylinder engine, giving her a very slight speed advantage. The most likely cause of the variation is simply that Doxford, which had been mass producing marine engines during the war, simply used one from stock for the earlier of the two ships.

The Burntisland-built *Harpalion* (4) joined the fleet in early May 1947. Before Doxford delivered the *Hartismere* (2) at the end of June, the company purchased three war standard ships – two Liberties and one Ocean. The two Liberty ships were the same vessels which the company had been managing since 1944. *Samaustral* was renamed *Harpathian* (3), and *Samderry* became the *Harpagon* (2). The third purchase was the *Empire Prowess*, an 11½ knot, 7,060-ton, shelter-decked steamer built by William Gray in 1943. She was renamed *Harperley* (4). Her arrival completed the post-war reconstruction programme. J. and C. Harrison Ltd. now owned a fleet of 11 ships – five 1930s steamers, three war-built steam-driven standard ships and three new motorships. While some of the pre-war ships were getting a bit long in the tooth, all were still perfectly capable of earning a profit, and the average age of the fleet was only eight years.

The Willis Steamship Co. Ltd. had been wound up in 1944 and its remaining ships transferred to the parent company, and after the arrival of the last new acquisitions in

June 1947 the remainder of the fleet was split between J. and C. Harrison Ltd. and its two remaining subsidiaries as follows:

J. and C. Harrison Ltd.
Harberton (2) (1930)
Harmattan (3) (1930)
Harmatris (2) (1932)
Hartlepool (1932)
Harpagon (2) (1944/1947)
Harpathian (3) (1944/1947)
National Steamship Co. Ltd.
Hartington (3) (1945)
Harpalion (4) (1947)
Harperley (4) (1943/1947)
Hartismere (2) (1947)
Gowland Steamship Co. Ltd.
Harpalycus (1) (1935)

In contrast to the aftermath of the First World War, the end of the Second did not trigger even a short-lived boom for British ship owners. The war itself had done far greater damage to the UK economy, both financial and physical, and national policy had to be driven by austerity imperatives. The war had also torn apart the British Empire, quite literally so in the Far East. It had also done much to undermine the strength of Britain's political position in India. The latter was the single most important component of the old imperial economy, and Indian independence (and the subsequent partition of the former colony into separate Indian and Pakistani states), had immediate consequences for British-flagged shipping, which soon found itself in direct competition with state-subsidised local firms, most of them operating second-hand British-built tonnage of roughly equal age and quality.

In addition to the fleets of new nations, even more formidable competition built up from two very different sources. While the USSR had been a relatively minor participant in the pre-war shipping world, the post-war Soviet Bloc was an entirely different proposition. The USSR itself, and its major maritime satellite nations, quickly built up large fleets of cargo vessels, not only to serve their own policy and trade needs, but also to earn foreign currency. The entire enterprise was more than just subsidized; it was state-owned, and could operate on a financial basis which no private sector western company could expect to match. If this source of competition was based on the ultimate form of

The six vessels joining the fleet in immediate post-war years: the newbuildings *Hartington* (3) of 1945 and *Harpalion* (4) of 1947 (top and upper middle); the Liberties bought in 1947 *Harpathian* (3) and *Harpagon* (2), the latter at Otago on 13th June 1954 (lower middle and bottom); the British war-built *Harperley* (4) also bought in 1947, and the newly-built *Hartismere* (2) of 1947 in charterer's colours (opposite page top and bottom). *[National Museum of Wales 1972/2044 and 1846/1925; J. and M. Clarkson; World Ship Society New Zealand Branch; Roy Fenton collection; World Ship Society Ltd.]*

year ending on 31st March 1949. They exist both for the parent company and for the consolidated group, including the Gowland Steamship Co. Ltd. Although the National Steamship Co. Ltd. was under complete Harrison control, the majority of the shares were owned by the various family trusts, and J. and C. Harrison Ltd. therefore showed its 31% share on its balance sheet as a trade investment, and took a share of its profits through dividends paid to it. The remaining trade investment was a significant minority stake in Harrisons (London) Ltd., the coaster company originally set up by John Harrison in the 1880s. This was treated the same way on both the balance sheet and the income statement.

It is instructive to look at these accounts in some detail, as they give a clear picture not just of the financial strength of the business, but also of its structure and the extent to which it was deriving profits from operating its fairly modest fleet, and earning interest on its financial assets.

There were only three directors, John Harrison, Frank

public ownership, the other came from the opposite extreme. Greek ship owners were quick to build new fleets around their established business networks. They were active buyers of war-standard tonnage, particularly Liberty ships, and they leveraged their own capital with extensive use of bank lending. They led the way in using flags of convenience, and in taking advantage of other market opportunities, such as the Canadian Government's desire to use its war-built tonnage to build up a national merchant marine. A large number of Fort and Park standard ships did indeed hoist the Canadian flag, but the ultimate owners of most of the vessels involved were almost invariably members of large Greek family shipping dynasties.

This then was the harsh environment in which J. and C. Harrison Ltd. operated its re-built fleet. The main business continued to revolve around worldwide tramping, but the company did re-start its Baltic to South America service when economic and political conditions permitted. When considering the company's post-war performance, it is again necessary to underline the internal dynamics of the business itself. It was still a private family-owned company, whose only outside shareholders were long-standing employees. It was being run increasingly as a source of income for the various family trusts set up in the 1930s and, although profits were kept within the business to allow the company to keep its fleet modern and efficient, there was no longer the expansionary motive which had driven the creation of the pre-war fleet. If the company was to grow, it would have needed to change its business model to allow an injection of public capital and/or the utilization of bank lending. This was not the road it chose to go down. Indeed there is no indication that the option was ever considered.

The first surviving set of annual company reports and accounts for J. and C. Harrison Ltd. cover the financial

Harrison and A.W.H. Turketine (son of the original company accountant Thomas). John Harrison was Chairman, and he and Frank were joint Managing Directors. The Company Secretary was still the long serving Eric Penfold, and just about the only thing that had changed was that the company had moved a few doors along the street from its original offices at 66 Mark Lane and was now based at Marlon House, 71/74 Mark Lane. The directors' report was as terse as was often the case with private family-owned companies – it did nothing more than announce the year's profit and declare the dividend.

A simplified version of the consolidated balance sheet, re-formulated along the lines of current day financial statements, is reproduced below. The salient points are so striking that they need little by way of interpretation. The total book value of the seven of the company's fleet of 11 vessels included in the accounts (the four modern vessels owned by National were excluded) was only just under £300,000. The bulk of this figure must have been contributed by the two recently acquired Liberty ships, and it is clear that the company had made extremely large allowances for depreciation on the rest. The older ships in the fleet must effectively have been on the books for less than their scrap value. Most of the company's total assets of just under £2,560,000 were held as investments, including the significant stakes in the two other family companies. The only surprising feature of this portfolio was the relatively large proportion which was in cash as opposed to long-term investments. The picture of strength was mirrored on the other half of the balance sheet; the company have issued share capital of just over £1 million and a similar amount held as reserves. Finally, the company had an extremely healthy liquidity position, current assets being just under three times current liabilities.

Assets

Fleet at cost less depreciation			£296,553
Office equipment etc			£600
		=	£297,153
Trade investments			£604,709
Quoted securities			£447,900
		=	£1,052,609
Current assets			
-	Debtors		£56,628
-	Unexpired insurance premiums		£10,319
-	Averages		£93,854
-	Voyages in progress		£11,456
-	Cash at bankers and in hand		£806,365
-	Tax reserve certificates		£200,000
-	Other current assets		£1,599
-		=	£1,210,221
TOTAL ASSETS		=	£2,559,983

Liabilities

Preference shares			£60,504
Ordinary shares			£1,000.000
		=	£1,060,504
Excess of net assets of subsidiaryover cost			
		=	£27,348
General reserve			£643,848
Profit and loss account			£398,078
		=	£1,041,926
Current liabilities			
-	Trade creditors		£160,009
-	Taxation provision		£131,868
-	Repairs and reconditioning provision		£83,129
-	Proposed dividend		£55,000
-	Other current liabilities		£199
-		=	£430,205
TOTAL LIABILITIES		=	£2,559,983

One other striking aspect of the group's organisation was that all three of the modern post-war motor ships were owned by the National Steamship Co. Ltd. This company had suffered the highest losses of the four group companies – ten in all – and thus must have ended the war sitting on the largest cash pile from insurance payments. It would also have benefited from the capital gain realised on two of the four 1942-built motor ships sold to Hain in 1944. It was thus almost certainly in the best position to fund new construction, and was therefore used as the vehicle for the first stage of re-building.

Fleet renewal for the rest of the group was always going to become necessary in the early 1950s, and the company paved the way with a series of disposals. The four oldest pre-war veterans were sold in 1951-52. The 1930 sister ships *Harberton* (2) and *Harmattan* (3) went to Japanese and German owners respectively. The 1932 pair, *Harmatris* (2) and *Hartlepool*, were sold to a Hong Kong firm and then on to a Japanese owner. The Director's Report for the year ending 31st March 1953 made it clear just how far these vessels had been written down in the accounts. The surplus over the combined book value of the four ships was no less than £969,801 – more than four times the book value of the whole fleet of seven Harrison and Gowland-owned vessels in 1951.

Selling well-maintained 20-year old steamers was one thing (several were to have fairly long subsequent careers, and the three Japanese acquisitions were all converted to motor ships), but building new tonnage was to prove a far more difficult proposition. British shipbuilding capacity was greatly reduced from the time of the fleet's great 1930s expansion programme, and building costs had escalated steeply. Indeed the same Director's Report spelled the problem out quite clearly. It was intended that two new ships be built for the National Steamship Co. Ltd., to be funded directly from its own resources. In addition, two more were planned for J. and C. Harrison Ltd., and one for the Gowland Steamship Co. Ltd. Delivery of two new vessels for the parent company could not be secured until the summer of 1957, and the combined purchase price of the pair was estimated at £1,237,000 – a figure which was likely to increase due to steadily rising building costs. The Directors therefore allocated the entire profit on the sale of the old vessels, together with a contribution of £100,000 from what had been an exceptionally good year's trading, to a Fleet Replacement Account, which had already stood at £200,000 at the end of the previous year. A berth was booked at the Blyth Dry Docks and Shipbuilding Co. Ltd. for the first National vessel, and two at William Doxford and Sons Ltd. for the pair intended for the parent company. Two further berths were booked later, one at Lithgows on the Clyde for the vessel intended for Gowland, and another one at Blyth for the second National ship.

As the table below shows, the year ending in March 1952 had indeed been exceptional. Trading profits for that single year were more or less equivalent to the combined total of the previous four. As might be expected given that the fleet had shrunk from eleven vessels to seven, the subsequent year's results were significantly lower, but the fact that they were lower still a year later, indicates that the company was affected at least as much by poor market conditions as by the reduced size of its fleet. By the middle years of the decade they had recovered to more normal levels.

In 1955 the company began a round of disposals to help fund the full delivery cost of its three new vessels. In July of that year, the British war standard *Harperley* (4) was sold to another British tramp owner. This was followed up by the sale of the last of the pre-war fleet, the 21-year old *Harpalycus* (1) to Greek owners in February 1956, the two sales together adding close to £183,500 to the Fleet Replacement Account.

Fleet trading profits (year ending 31st March)
Includes only the results for vessels owned by J and C Harrison Ltd and the Gowland Steamship Co. Ltd.

1947/48	£424,425
1948/49	£296,558
1949/50	£122,968
1950/51	£269,489
1951/52	£944,744
1952/53	£94,259
1953/54	£20,947
1954/55	£105,044
1955/56	£280,865

In November, the Liberty *Harpathian* (3) was sold to Italian owners bringing the account up to £2,000,000. To assist in the building of the vessel intended for the Gowland Steamship Co. Ltd., it was arranged that the latter would issue for cash to its parent the 169,898 shares of £1 which had to date not been issued from its authorized capital. The last of the company's post-war second-hand purchases, the other Liberty, *Harpagon* (2), was eventually sold in May 1958, but by that time, the

company was finally taking delivery of its new ships. In addition, the passing of the second generation of company directors would open what were to prove the final chapters in the J. and C. Harrison story.

New ships and new men

The company finally took delivery of its first new vessel when the 6,670-ton, 14-knot Blyth-built motor ship *Harborough* (2) was registered at London in early December 1956 in the name of the National Steamship Co. Ltd. The two ships building at Doxford's Pallion yard were both launched in 1957, the *Harpagus* (6) in September and the *Harpalyce* (6) in early November. The Director's Report for that year noted glumly that the present estimated building cost would indeed be well in excess of the original basic cost. The Report was destined to be the last issued under the names of John Harrison and Francis Joseph Harrison as Managing Directors.

Frank Harrison died in Reading on 11th December 1957 aged 76. His cousin John followed him just over a month later, dying at home in West Sussex on 20th January 1958. The two men had run J. and C. Harrison Ltd. together for four decades. There can never be any doubt that the firm owed its success first and foremost to the their uncle Charles, but John and Frank had supported him strongly while he built up the company's large fleet in the 1930s, a feat which might have proved beyond even him considering that he embarked on the venture when already in his 70s. They had then managed the fleet through a war

Deliveries from 1956 to 1957 were the *Harborough* (2) from Blyth Dry Docks and Shipbuilding Co. Ltd. (top), the *Harpagus* (6) (middle, in August 1970 after lengthening) and the *Harpalyce* (6) (bottom, again after her 1967 lengthening) from William Doxford and Sons Ltd., Sunderland. *[Nigel Farrell collection; Les Ring/World Ship Society Ltd. 67526; Roy Fenton collection]*

which had seen the company lose no fewer than 24 of its own ships, and had taken on the management of a total of 20 vessels for the British Government. The high standard of bravery and sacrifice among Harrison crews, and the awards they won in the many seas in which the enemy prowled, was a testament to the quality of the men and their commitment to the company which the cousins helped sustain. After the war they had assembled a small but competitive fleet from a judicious mixture of new building and second-hand acquisition and, most importantly, they had built up funds to finance what steeply rising costs always meant would be an extremely expensive fleet modernization programme. Oddly enough, the Director's Report for 1958 made no mention of the passing of either man – perhaps it was simply not deemed necessary considering that the company itself was very much a family affair.

The company had been strengthening its board for several years to prepare for departure of John and Frank. The first addition, in 1953, had been Derek Harrison-Sleap, a grandson of the founder, James Touchet Harrison via his daughter Caroline. In 1956 it had been further reinforced by elevation of the long-serving Eric Penfold to the Board and the appointment of one of the few remaining eligible family males, Reginald F.L. Harrison, a grandson of Frederick Angier Harrison. Following the deaths of Frank and John, the office of Managing Director was temporarily allowed to lapse, and A.W.H. Turketine served as Chairman for two years. Family membership of the board was reinforced by the appointment of Mrs J.A. Wightman-Harrison, granddaughter of Charles Willis Harrison.

The *Harpagus* (6) and *Harpalyce* (6) were delivered in January and March 1958 at a combined cost of £1,888,203. They were 6,800-ton sisters, each capable of 13½ knots. Any joy felt at the realistion of a project which had been planned for so many years, must have been tempered, if not completely wiped away,by a collapse of company profits. After earning just over £270,000 in 1956-57, the fleet only just managed to break even in the following year. The commentary in the Director's Report was a very gloomy one.

During the year under review, freights slumped to a lower level than has been known since 1946. The results do not wholly reflect this fall, as favourable earnings were made in the first four months of the year's trading. The depressed condition of the freight market has persisted and worsened in the current year. In consequence even if it is possible to keep the Companies' vessels fully employed, present trading is not likely to provide adequate depreciation, and, with greatly reduced prices obtainable from the sale of ships due for replacement, the schemed redevelopment of the fleet will inevitably be restricted.

As stated before, the second Liberty, the *Harpagon* (2), was sold in September 1958, the last two ships of the 1950s replacement programme were launched in the same year, the *Harmattan* (4) by Lithgows in April, and the *Harpalycus* (2) by Blyth in November. They would join their respective subsidiary companies in February and April 1959 respectively. Both vessels followed the same basic design specification as the previous three, but the *Harmattan* (4) was given a shelter deck, raising her gross tonnage from the normal 6,800 tons to 9,230 tons. Their arrivals left the group fleet at eight ships, all, for the first time since 1947, built to the company's own specifications.

J. and C. Harrison Ltd.
Harpagus (6) (1958)
Harpalyce (6) (1958)
National Steamship Co. Ltd.
Hartington (3) (1945)
Harpalion (4) (1947)
Hartismere (2) (1947)
Harborough (2) (1956)
Harpalycus (2) (1959)
Gowland Steamship Co. Ltd.
Harmattan (4) (1959)

The consolidated balance sheet of J. and C. Harrison Ltd. for the year ended 31st March 1959 makes an interesting comparison with that for a decade before. Actual comparison of the numbers is of little use as the latter set show the effects

Harmattan (4) (upper, on trials) and Harpalycus (2) (lower, Port Chalmers, 27th January 1966) were the last conventional tramps delivered to Harrisons. [W. Ralston/Peter Harrison-Sleap; D. Wright]

of a decade of inflation. What is telling is several differences in the respective make-ups of the statements. The fleet accounted for less than 15% of total assets in 1949, while in 1959 the figure was just under 60%. In contrast, the figure for cash and investments had fallen from roughly 75% to about 20%. Finally, the firm had enjoyed an excellent short-term trade position in 1949, but by 1959 current assets were only just above current liabilities.

	31/3/1949	31/3/1959
Fleet and other fixed assets	£297,153	£2,952,740
Investments	£1,052,609	£1,756,053
Current assets	£1,210,221	£550,667
Total assets	£2,599,983	£5,259,460
Share capital	£1,060,504	£1,060,504
Reserves	£1,069,274	£3,823,600
Current liabilities	£430,205	£375,356
Total liabilities	£2,559,983	£5,259,460

After all the planning and effort that had gone into building the new fleet, the company actually lost the first of the new vessels less than a month after the delivery of the last. On 18th April 1959, the *Harborough* (2) sank in the Weser Estuary after running over the wreck of the Russian steamer *Kholomogory*. The vessel had been on the company's now firmly re-established service from the Baltic to South America and was on passage from Gdynia to Buenos Aires at the time of her loss. It is interesting that the company made no move to replace her. Only three years old, she is likely to have been insured at close to her building cost, but with continued inflation, and the National Steamship Co. Ltd.'s capital reserves depleted by the final payments on the *Harpalycus* (2), management probably took the view that replacement was not justified by either market conditions or the state of their own balance sheet.

The company Chairman Alan Turketine died in 1960 prompting another change in the senior management structure. No fewer than three Joint Managing Directors were appointed, Derek Harrison-Sleap, Reginald Harrison, and the first non-family member to hold such a post, L.S. Morgan FCA, the company finance director. As had been indicated in the 1958 report, business conditions remained difficult, and although things improved slightly after the near-loss of 1957/58, the profits were hardly sufficient to support the capital costs of the new vessels and the dividend.

Fleet trading profits (year ending 31st March)
Includes only the results for vessels owned by J. and C. Harrison Ltd. and the Gowland Steamship Co. Ltd.

1955/56	£280,865
1956/57	£271,668
1957/58	£4,975
1958/59	£27,334
1959/60	£110,857
1960/61	£81,453
1961/62	£132,158

In 1959 the long-standing dividend of 5% for Ordinary Shares was cut to 4%. As the new next decade began, the Board, far from considering fleet expansion, was thinking more in terms of disposing of its older motor ships. 1962 and 1963 were the critical years. In their report for the year ending 31st March 1962, the directors reported that a sum of £295,168 had been written off reserves to reduce the book value of the *Harpagus* (6) and *Harpalyce* (6) 'towards meeting the capital loss sustained having regard to present market values'. They

also reported that a £289,482 write-down had been taken to reduce the book value of Gowland's *Harmattan* (4) to £700,000. In the following year, when the company registered a trading loss of £33,177 before depreciation, they were forced to cut the dividend from 4% to 1½%.

By this time the company had disposed of its three 1945-1947 vintage motor ships. All of these vessels were owned by the National Steamship Co. Ltd., so there was no impact on the consolidated balance sheet of J. and C. Harrison Ltd. (nor, more strangely, were the sales mentioned in the Director's Report). The *Hartington* (3) was sold to Hong Kong interests, and the *Hartismere* (2) on to the Bermuda register in February 1962. The third of the trio, the *Harpalion* (4), went to Greek owners in June. The *Hartington* (3) became a marine casualty a few years after her disposal, but the other two vessels had subsequent careers of over a decade. They had not been sold because they were obsolete, and it is unlikely that their maintenance and repair costs were that onerous. The simple fact was that foreign owners could afford to operate them profitably while Harrison, like many other British companies in the tramping business, could not.

J. and C. Harrison Ltd. was now operating a fleet of only four ships, the *Harpagus* (6) and *Harpalyce* (6) under their direct ownership; the *Harmattan* (4) owned by their direct subsidiary the Gowland Steamship Co. Ltd.; and the *Harpalycus* (2) owned by the associated National Steamship Co. Ltd. All were modern vessels, well fitted for the requirements of a trade which had not yet seen any significant change in ship design or size. The first problem was that foreign ship owners, either those operating under a flag of convenience or those receiving some form of state subsidy, could operate their vessels far more cheaply and thus hold charter rates down at levels where the Harrison ships were not economical. The second problem was that the ships had been built at expensive British shipyards, and, even with extraordinary write-downs, represented a capital cost which it would be difficult to support from a narrow earnings base.

Fleet trading profits (year ending 31st March)
Includes only the results for vessels owned by J. and C. Harrison Ltd. and the Gowland Steamship Co. Ltd.

1961/62	£132,158
1962/63	- £33,177
1963/64	£38,481
1964/65	£70,304
1965/66	£182,152
1966/67	£7,405
1967/68	£143,052
1968/69	£110,924
1969/70	£82,123

As can be seen trading results through the 1960s were generally low, with the occasional reasonable year balanced by a very bad one. Having cut the dividend on the ordinary shares to 1½% in 1963, the Directors were forced to pass it altogether in 1964. After this, the company seems to have adopted a policy of distributing as much income as possible, drawing down on retained earnings from previous years. In 1965 the dividend was restored to a full 5% and in 1966 even pushed up to 7½%. A 5% dividend was paid despite a very poor trading year in 1967 largely because the company was able to sell its substantial residual holding in Harrisons (London) Ltd. – the coaster company originally founded by John Harrison the Elder in the 1880s – at a book profit of £258,698.

The picture of what was now a small company drawing down on its balance sheet to pay out more in dividends than its ships were actually earning would normally indicate that its directors were intent on winding the business slowly down. At the time a large number of British tramp owners were indeed deciding that it was no longer possible to operate under such conditions and were seeking to sell off their fleets or diversify into other business activities. J. and C. Harrison, however, was not quite finished yet. Indeed it was about to launch one last new programme in an attempt to enhance fleet competitiveness and profitability.

The last hurrah
J. and C. Harrison had not enjoyed a happy decade since the completion of its fleet modernization programme. One of its new vessels had been lost within a few years of completion. It had sold its three post-war motor ships rather earlier than it might have done had trading conditions been better, and it had been forced to take significant write-downs on its fleet, and follow a decidedly erratic dividend policy. In 1967-68, however, the company began a concerted effort to revive its fortunes. The first step taken was innovative. Rather than build new tonnage, which it would have only been able to afford by taking on significant amounts of debt, it decided to lengthen its existing ships to improve their earning capacity.

The company approached the Dutch shipbuilder, the Netherlands Dock and Shipbuilding Co. Ltd. of Amsterdam,

to quote for lengthening each of the four vessels in the fleet by inserting a new 50 foot section in the hull between the existing numbers 2 and 3 holds, just forward of the mid-ships deckhouse, and terms were quickly agreed. Engineers from the Dutch yard flew out to the Far East to take exact hull measurements of the *Harpalyce* (6), the first vessel to be 'jumboised', and then the yard started to prefabricate the new hull section before the vessel's arrival at the ship yard. The ship actually arrived at the yard on 1st October 1967. With the new section already available for fitting, the entire process of cutting the ship in two, inserting the new section and re-uniting the three parts – together with some general overhaul work on the ship's machinery – was completed within a month, and *Harpalyce* (6) was re-surveyed and re-registered at London on 2nd November. The three other ships in the fleet followed in succession. The *Harpagus* (6) was ready in May 1968, the *Harmattan* (4) in July and the *Harpalycus* (2) in September. The overall result of the work was an addition of roughly 3,000 more tons of carrying capacity to each vessel without any reduction in speed. Functionally, the company had increased its earning ability by roughly the same proportion as it would have through building two medium or one large-sized new freighters, but had done so at a fraction of the cost and the time.

Although it was probably no more than a coincidence, it was in some way fitting that this bold innovation should occur at a time when the Managing Director's responsibilities passed

Harmattan (4) being lengthened at Amsterdam. *[Kevin O'Donoghue collection]*

back entirely into family hands. Eric Penfold retired early in 1968 and L.S. Morris moved down to the board as a consultant, leaving Derek Harrison-Sleap and Reginald Harrison as Joint Managing Directors. The latter would step down in the early 1970s, leaving Derek Harrison-Sleap as the sole, and as it turned out, last, Managing Director of the family business. As we have already seen, the improvement in the carrying capacity of the fleet did produce some improvement in trading profits in the late 1960s, but the vessels were still not really doing much more than breaking even. In addition, the company had to cope with some wild variations in market conditions. The effects of these can be understood by looking at the financial year ending at 31st March 1970, the first year in which all of the vessels operated at their increased capacity for a full 12 months. As can be seen, the vessels did not earn enough themselves to cover depreciation, and the company's generous dividends were actually funded from a combination of investment income and retained earnings carried forward from earlier years.

J. and C. Harrison Ltd.,
consolidated profit and loss account, 1969/70

Trading profit	£82,113
Trade investments	£25,921
Quoted investments	£83,984
Loans	£100,367
Gross profit	£292,385
Depreciation	£163,058
Other expenses	£24,491
Tax	£53,000
Net profit	£51,836
Balance from previous years	£97,763
Distributable earnings	£149,599
Dividend – 10% preference shares	£6,050
Dividend – 11% on ordinary shares	£110,000
Balance carried forward	£33,549

The fleet would do better in 1970/71, earning a trading profit of £146,842, which was at least sufficient to cover depreciation, but the Directors had already decided that a major new investment was needed to drive the business forward. This investment programme, which was destined to be the last the company undertook, was revolutionary in a number of ways. To date, all of the company's vessels had been designed for general tramping, with each successive wave of ships being built to the general size, speed, efficiency and carrying capacity standards prevalent at the time. In 1970 the company moved away from a ship type which was rapidly becoming obsolescent, and decided to order two larger vessels designed specifically to carry bulk cargoes. The step up in size was significant from the stretched conventional tramps the company was now operating, but so too was the design. The ships, built with their engines aft, would measure 16,715 gross tons, with a deadweight lifting capacity of just over 26,000 tons at a speed of 15 knots.

The ships themselves marked a huge step forward in size and design, but they also took the company into an entirely new world in terms of ship finance. Each ship would cost £3,000,000. To put this into context, the total consolidated assets of J. and C. Harrison Ltd. on 31st March 1970 were only £4,833,689. Even if the company sold off all its other assets – and it clearly had no intention to do so – it was going to have to take on a significant amount of loan finance for the first time in its history.

The orders were placed with the recently created Upper Clyde Shipbuilders, a government sponsored consolidation of a number of yards undertaken in an attempt to support an industry which was no longer able to compete with foreign rivals. The ships were to be built at Upper Clyde's Scotstoun yard (formerly that of Charles Connell) and were due for delivery in 1972. In retrospect, the company would have been better advised to go to a foreign yard, but government incentives were available for building with Upper Clyde, and it was not clear in 1970 just how disastrously wrong the whole Upper Clyde experiment would go.

Before it became obvious that there would be problems with the new ships, the company had to face a series of setbacks with its existing business. The business year ending 31st March 1972 was quite simply a nightmare. The trading result moved from a profit of £146,842 to a loss of £112,708. Worse yet, the company lost one of its ships. The *Harmattan* (4) was an accidental casualty of the brief war between India and Pakistan in late 1971. She was in Karachi when war broke out, and had not been able to leave the port, which had already been subject to Indian air attack, when the Indian Navy launched a missile attack on the port on 18th

Damage to the *Harmattan* (4), including (right) the port side sheer strake where the missile stuck. *[Peter Harrison-Sleap]*

December. Anchored two miles off the port, she was struck by a Styx missile amidships and caught fire. Seven men were killed and another six injured in the initial explosion, with almost all of the casualties occurring in the engine room and galley. The Master, Captain Hubert Houston, was also slightly injured, but managed to get all the survivors safely away in the ship's boats. The *Harmattan* suffered severe structural damage and was also partially gutted by fire. She was abandoned to the underwriters as a constructive total loss and broken up at Karachi in the following spring.

By the time that the *Harmattan* went to the breakers, the new shipbuilding programme had been derailed by the effective collapse of Upper Clyde Shipbuilders. Work was delayed as the company lurched into insolvency, and with the ships being built with reduced staff under the management of receivers, it became obvious that delivery would be delayed. In the meantime, the two existing ships owned directly by J. and C. Harrison Ltd. were sold to help raise funds to pay for the new bulkers. The *Harpalyce* (6) went to the Panamanian flag in February 1972. The Director's Report does not indicate the actual sale price, but the accounts show a book profit of £98,619. The *Harpagus* (6) was sold to Greek owners in October 1973. In this case, the Director's report does give the full figures. The sale price was £675,000 and the book value £240,000, producing an accounting profit of £435,000. It is not immediately obvious why there should have been such a discrepancy in the profits – the most likely cause is that, by the time of the second sale, the company had already partially written down the ship's book value.

The first of the new bulkers was launched as *Harfleet* in March 1973 and registered with the Gowland Steamship Co. Ltd. in June. Her sister, *Harfleur* (2), was launched in September and registered with J. and C. Harrison Ltd. in December. The Harrison shipping group had now effectively become three single ship companies: the parent company and Gowland each with one of the new bulkers, and the associated National Steamship Co. Ltd. with the *Harpalycus*

(2). The investment in the two bulkers had transformed the Group's balance sheet. Happily, the accounts for the 1970s are far more detailed than those for the earlier period, and it is possible to paint a clear picture of where the Group stood on 31st March 1974, with both bulkers in service.

J and C Harrison Ltd., consolidated balance sheet, 1973/74

Fleet	£6,118,000
Other fixed assets	£2,472
Trade investments	£517,819
Quoted investments	£2,827,534
Current assets	£2,182,616
(Less current liabilities)	£284,574)
TOTAL	£11,364,237
Share capital	£1,060,504
Income on consolidation	£27,347
General reserve	£3,899,165
Profit and loss account	£580,256
Investment grant reserve	£1,156,967
Bank shipbuilding loans	£4,650,000
TOTAL	£11,364,237

The biggest difference from any Harrison balance sheet before was, of course, the presence of a significant bank loan. The loan itself was repayable over eight years from 1973 with an annual interest rate of 5½%. There was nothing dangerous about the level of gearing itself. A debt-to-total-assets ratio just in excess of 40% was at the lower end of what was normal in the shipping industry at the time. What was unusual was simply that J. and C. Harrison Ltd. now had a significant debt obligation. In practical terms this meant that its two bulkers had to earn enough each year to cover both depreciation and interest costs before breaking even, and that they together with the Group's other investments had also to generate sufficient capital to repay each annual loan instalment. The biggest risk, apart from the volatility of bulk

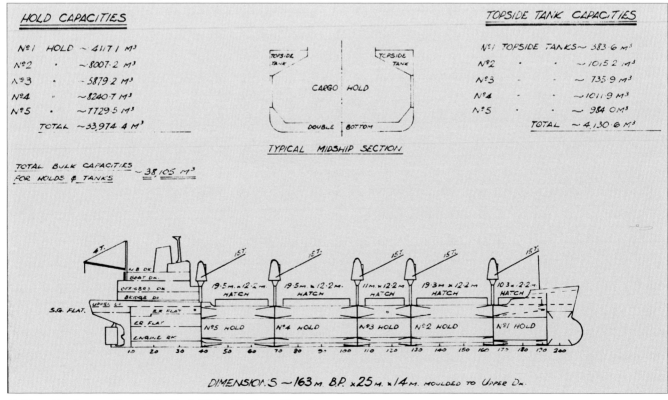

Hold and tank capacities of *Harfleet*. [Peter Harrison-Sleap]

shipping rates, was that the group quite literally had most of its eggs in only two baskets – there was nothing to take up the slack if either of the ships required lengthy maintenance or repairs.

The *Harfleet* and *Harfleur* (2) did not begin their careers as the only ships flying Harrison colours. The National Shipping Co. Ltd. continued to operate the *Harpalycus* (2) until August 1975, when she was sold to Greek owners. While her contribution was small in terms of the overall Group venture, she did make positive returns. The National Steamship Co. Ltd. contributed £41,664 to Group earnings in the year ending March 1973, £64,900 in 1974, and £77,439 in 1975. These results (which represented only 38% of National's total earnings) suggest that the *Harpagus* (6) and *Harpalyce* (6) could have made a positive contribution for another two or three years each if the need to raise funds to build the bulkers had not dictated their sale.

In the year ended 31st March 1974, the company registered a trading profit of £138,373 from its fleet, but the combined impact of depreciation and interest charges was such as to transform this to an operating loss of £231,426. Investment income in turn made this into a taxable profit of just under £100,000, and the full result was boosted by the £435,000 gain on the sale of the *Harpagon*. As the *Harfleet* did not enter service until June 1973 and the *Harfleur* not until December, the figures did not really indicate what the full earning power of the vessels would be. However, they did show how challenging it would be to meet depreciation and interest costs. The two bulkers were not actually the last ships bought by the company. This distinction fell to the 14-year old 530 tons motor vessel *Timber Queen,* purchased for £70,750 in February 1975 and renamed *Harcourt.*

J. and C. Harrison had not been involved in the coastal trade since selling their collier fleet to Cory in 1896. With their fleet about to be reduced to just two bulkers, both employed on long-term charters in the Pacific, it seems likely that the firm decided to utilize the surplus management capacity in its London office in order to re-enter the European coaster business. The *Harcourt* was the only vessel the company bought, but in the mid to late-1970s it took over the management of six similar vessels for four different British owners.

The two last deep-sea ships: *Harfleet* (above) and *Harfleur* (2) (below) both in Macmillan Bloudel funnel colours. *[World Ship Society Ltd.: 67504 and 67513]*

Harrison's last owned ship: *Harcourt* at Plymouth on 3rd April 1976. *[World Ship Society Ltd. 29874]*

47

The managed coaster *Borelly* sailing from Aberdeen on 1st July 1976. *[J. and M, Clarkson]*

The bulkers, which were largely deployed on the northern trans-Pacific trade, earned respectable freights from the start. They appear to have been sturdy, reliable vessels well suited to operating in what were often demanding sea conditions. The only problem of note occurred when the *Harfleet* suffered a structural failure in her forepeak while heading eastwards into rough seas. Luckily, the problem occurred near the end of her voyage and she was got safely into a Japanese port for repairs. Whatever their merits as ships, however, it was soon obvious, that they had no chance of operating profitably under the British flag and with a British cost-base. A very small trading profit was registered in 1974-75, and a more respectable one in 1975-76, but in both years the combined impact of depreciation and interest charges produced a loss before financial income of over £400,000. Financial income produced a small profit in the first year and a modest loss in the second, but that really only proved one point. The company could make a far better return on capital through financial investments than it could through ship ownership.

This point was driven brutally home in the next two trading years (see table below). While the ships maintained a steady level of turnover, they produced significant trading losses, just over £280,000 in 1976-77 and double that in 1977-78. Although interest costs were falling as the bank loan was paid off, not even investment income could stop the company from registering large losses at the net profit line, the loss figure falling just short of half a million in 1977-78. Throughout the whole period, the Board had, quite rightly,

paid no dividend, but the time had clearly arrived for it to decide whether it was meeting the best interests of its shareholders – the three family charitable trusts – by remaining in the shipping business.

The results for 1978-79 merely confirmed that it was time to sell. The vessels registered a record trading loss of £740,035. By the financial year end, the company was already disposing of its fleet. The *Harfleur* (2) was sold on 14th February 1979, the *Harfleet* on 19th April and the little *Harcourt* on 18th July. As far as ship owning was concerned, it was the end of the road for J. and C. Harrison Ltd. However, the company maintained the tradition established by its founders of realizing significant gains on the ship disposals. The contract selling price for each of the two bulkers was £3,100,000 less three percent commission to the broker who arranged the sale to a Taiwanese company. The profit on the sale of the *Harfleur* (2) alone was still £890,272. As the contract for her sale had already been signed, the company re-valued *Harfleet* at £2,800,000 in the 1978-79 financial year, thereby bringing forward the profit of £561,851 on her sale into the same accounts.

The Directors' Report issued on 12th December 1980 contained the following statement, which serves as a terse obituary on 90 years of ship ownership.

The principal activities of the group were those of ship operating, but since the sale of the group's ships, income is at present derived from investments and loans.

Derek Harrison-Sleap had resigned as Managing Director on 31st March 1980 (although he remained on the board itself), and the accounts for the financial year ending on that day demonstrate that he had left the helm of a healthy and profitable company. The consolidated balance sheet of J. and C. Harrison Ltd. showed total net assets of £6,727,340, all of which were effectively investments and loans. This figure was slightly in excess of the equivalent figure two years before, when the company still owned its three ships. Inflation means that the numbers cannot be compared on a like-for-like basis, but basically, Derek, the sole representative of the third and last generation of family ship owners, had engineered its exit from the business while preserving most, if not all of its financial capital. His great uncle, Charles Willis Harrison, would have approved.

Financial results during the mid-1970s				
	1974-75	**1975-76**	**1976-77**	**1977-78**
Turnover	£1,027,370	£1,124,693	£1,261,279	£1,348,152
Trading profit (loss)	£17,140	£84,383	(£252,361)	(£446,895)
Depreciation	(£249,385)	(£261,453)	(£261,495)	(£249,069)
Interest	(£238,655)	(£206,046)	(£172,776)	(£139,745)
Other costs	(£24,843)	(£27,719)	(£27,812)	(£29,463)
Net operating loss	(£495,743)	(£410,835)	(£714,444)	(£865,172)
Trade investments	£76,417	£96,668	£104,772	£112,832
Quoted investments	£164,196	£207,146	£225,209	£211,950
Loan interest	£250,849	£238,393	£102,102	£43,149
Net profit (loss) before tax	(£4,281)	£131,372	(£282,361)	(£497,241)
Tax	(£32,563)	(£1,919)	(£2,432)	(£2,179)
Net profit (loss) after tax	(£36,844)	£129,453	(£284,793)	(£499,420)

Harrison men

A quiet hero: Captain John Wharton, MBE, DSC, LM

In many ways, Captain John Wharton was typical of the men who served J. and C. Harrison, and indeed the British Merchant Marine as a whole, during the Second World War. A seaman for his entire working life, he was already used to shouldering the almost endless responsibilities of a tramp ship skipper, and took on all the strain and danger of the war at sea without complaint. He sailed alone in distant waters and in convoy in some of the most dangerous theatres of conflict. He was not unique in having more than one ship sunk under him. What placed him in a smaller and select group was a special and quiet courage, which helped save the lives of those under his command, and won him honours on three separate occasions.

Captain John Wharton. *[Pauline Cowen]*

John Wharton was born in Barrow-on-Furness on 20th January 1905. He went to sea in 1922 aged 17, ranked as a Boy on the *Jervis Bay*, which at the time served as a training ship while maintaining her commercial service between the UK and Australia. He served aboard until 1927, being promoted first to Ordinary Seaman and then to AB. After a brief stint on another vessel, he received his ticket as the Third Mate of the Watts, Watts tramp *Finchley*. By 1930, he was Second Mate of another Watts,Watts vessel, the *Ascot*. During the depths of the Great Depression, he managed to secure one year's employment as Second Mate of Souter's *Sheaf Crown*, before joining J. and C. Harrison as Second Mate of the *Harbledown* in May 1933. He was to serve the company for his remaining 34 years at sea.

When the war began, Wharton was serving as First Mate of the *Hartlebury*. He moved to the *Harpagus* (4) in 1940 before taking his first command as captain of

the *Harpathian* (2) on 27th February 1941. It was to prove a brief and violent introduction to the rank of Master Mariner. Wharton took his ship from Middlesbrough north around Scotland to the Clyde and then south towards Freetown in convoy OG.57. The convoy dispersed as it passed Gibraltar and Wharton sailed on alone. A day after dispersal in the early evening of 8th April, Wharton was on the bridge with the Third Officer when the *Harpathian* was hit forward on the port side by a torpedo from *U 107*. The explosion must have opened both forward holds to the sea, as the ship started sinking rapidly by the head. Whatever his relative inexperience, Wharton obviously had a cool head and had drilled his crew well. Both after lifeboats were launched before the ship sank, some four minutes after the torpedo strike. Wharton was the last man to leave the ship, shepherding four others before him into the starboard boat. By the time he stepped aboard the ship was already submerged up to her funnel, and the boat was so close that it was blown yards sideways when the boilers exploded. One man in the water was quickly rescued, and the men re-distributed between the two boats. The Canary Islands were some 350 miles away, and although the boats set off together, they lost touch during the night. Wharton's boat made the Canaries on 18th April, having lost just one elderly fireman to the rigours of the journey. His cool conduct during the attack and his admirable seamanship across an empty ocean earned him a well deserved MBE in February 1942.

Wharton was back on the bridge again within two months of his landing in the Canaries, this time in command

Harpathian (2) loading timber in Vancouver. *[Ships in Focus]*

of the elderly Ministry of War Transport-owned *Hampton Lodge*. He stayed with her until the end of 1941, when he took over the new *Empire Byron* from her Sunderland builders. While the ship was completing, Wharton found time to marry Sadie Harvey, a local lass. By the time his MBE citation was announced he had gone to sea, and his mother greeted the newspaper reporter who brought the news with the words 'Oh, that will be for what happened in April'. If the man from the Mail was hoping for tales of high adventure, he left disappointed. Mrs Wharton told him her son was very quiet at home, and that she had never even seen him in uniform.

The *Empire Byron* was to spend all of her brief career on Arctic convoy duty. Wharton took her to Russia in convoy PQ.12 in March without incident, and back again safely in QP.9 at the end of the same month. Unfortunately, his next outward convoy was PQ.17, and the *Empire Byron* was found quickly by *U 703* after the infamous order to scatter was given. The enemy submarine's captain was not as accomplished as the man who had sunk the *Harpathian*, but he finally hit the *Empire Byron* with his fifth torpedo. Eight men were killed in the explosion but, once again, Captain Wharton got all of the surviving crew into the boats safely. *U 703* surfaced and would have taken Wharton prisoner had he not already had the foresight to hide his uniform coat in the boat's locker. The enemy settled for an unfortunate army officer and departed. The Arctic in July was a far worse proposition than the mid-Atlantic in April, but Wharton kept

his boats together and his men alive until the boats were found by the corvette HMS *Dianella* after covering 250 miles in five and a half days. His courage won him a well-deserved DSC.

After some well deserved leave, Wharton assumed command of the *Harmattan* (3) in November 1942, sailing her from Greenock to Algiers. There, the enemy found him again. On 12th December, a force of Italian two-men human topedoes attacked shipping in Algiers Bay, successfully sinking two ships, and damaging another two, one of them *Harmattan*, with limpet mines. The damaged ships were beached, and *Harmattan*, the least damaged, was eventually able to sail to the UK for final repair in April 1943. Wharton's prompt action in getting his damaged vessel beached won him his third award, a Lloyd's Gold Medal for Gallantry.

Captain Wharton served as Master of four different ships between June 1943 and the end of the war in Europe, by which time he was back with the *Harmattan*. For more than three years he then captained the Canadian-built *Fort Pic*, before returning to company-owned vessels in 1949. He served on with J. and C. Harrison until retiring at the age of 60 in April 1967, his last command being the motor ship *Harpalycus* (2). By his own calculation, he had sailed a total of 1,724,950 miles during his career at sea. He enjoyed a long and quiet retirement in Sunderland, dying on 23rd January 1981, three days after his 76th birthday.

The Third Mate's story: Captain David Davies

After a period in a liner company as fourth mate, with only a second mate's ticket and on effective sea time only, I left them and ended up on the officer's pool in the Minories, London. Within minutes of entering the building I was on my way to 74 Mark Lane to an interview at J. and C. Harrison who insisted that their third mates be certificated. At Mark Lane I was shown a glass-cased model of the *Hartington* (3) and told that I would be joining her in Rotterdam in a few days. What I was not told was that I would be taking the crew as well. On arrival at Liverpool Street Station I was grabbed by the man from the Shipping Federation who seemed relieved to hand over to me and hastily left after getting me to sign for the motley crew that surrounded me demanding their subsistence money of 2/6d. My long craved for sense of responsibility (and power?) had arrived.

Captain David Davies *[David Davies]*

After a thankfully incident-free journey via Harwich and the Hook, we arrived in Rotterdam where I hired a launch to take us out to *Hartington* lying in the Maashaven. After a few minutes some of the hung-over crowd pointed out a large, illuminated Harrison funnel and told the launch driver to take us to that ship, which he did. On arrival alongside we all boarded to be welcomed by the night watchman who informed us we had boarded the *Harperley* (3)! My career with J. and C.'s had not got off to a good start.

Captain Phelps, master of the *Hartington*, was not impressed, and didn't think it was at all unusual for two ships of a very small company to be in the same port at the same time.

He was elderly and approaching retirement, a Welsh tramp-ship master of the old school. Only occasionally wearing uniform, he mostly wore a civilian suit and his master's cap. I was disappointed it was not a bowler hat. I had signed on a B agreement which meant I should be paid overtime for any work in excess of laid down hours but not if the work was classified as 'safety of ship'. After coming off watch I spent many hours overhauling the equipment of the four lifeboats and recharging fire extinguishers, all safety of ship according to Captain Phelps who made me responsible for cleaning the wheel house windows, with the remark that all good third mates cleaned the brass whilst on watch. I was not a good third mate... I finally entered his good books in thick fog off Newfoundland. I was the only officer competent at radar plotting. I plotted all the traffic, telling him what other ships were doing and what action to take. He was so impressed that I spent not only my watch but the 12 to 4 as well, and part of 4 to 8 on the radar, and of course no overtime – 'safety of ship'. He did make one concession to me: I was permitted to smoke in his presence whilst plotting.

We made several voyages to Wabana, Newfoundland returning to Glasgow with iron ore. Whilst in Glasgow, Captain Phelps was relieved by Captain Champion, a tall, swarthy West Countryman with a dominating bearing and black penetrating eyes. He came from a naval background, which had an immediate effect on *Hartington*. By example he raised the standard of dress amongst the officers, with full uniform on Sundays and a social gathering in the smoke room before lunch, and after morning rounds, which he took very seriously. No longer was I expected to clean the brass, and I had a cadet to assist me with the lifeboats. Above all he was a very competent radar observer, culminating with our last voyage to Wabana when he took *Hartington* into Wabana in thick fog without the pilot, who we couldn't find. Arriving off the berth with all hands at stations we came out of the fog and into the berth, as we moored up Captain Champion picked up the megaphone, pointed it at the wharf and began to sing the well known song 'Has any body here seen Kelly, K-E-double L-Y' – the pilot's name was Kelly.

That was our final trip to Wabana. Our next voyage was to Lulea in Sweden, again iron ore for Glasgow and then on to Torrevieja, Spain to load bulk salt for Japan. At last we would leave the cold, drab, dull and dirty industrial ports behind and head for warmer climes with the Hombre bars, vino, women and corruption. On arrival on a Saturday the crew all drew large subs, got dressed up and headed for the fleshpots of sailor town. Come Monday morning many were missing, all banged up in the 'calabozo' to supplement the wages of the local Guardia Civil. The Chief Steward had to cook breakfast, and the Bosun and a lot of the deck crowd, along with the Second Engineer, were missing. After breakfast Captain Champion, dressed in a smart tropical linen suit and Panama hat, set off ashore. About mid day he returned with all the miscreants in tow. How he achieved it no one knew, not even the liberated. A rising Levanter dictated a hasty departure from Torrevieja only to find that we had sailed with two Spanish policemen sleeping it off in the hospital. This necessitated a deviation of course to Gibraltar where we landed them at the Detached Mole.

Our passage to Tokyo was pleasant and uneventful, with my mate the Radio Officer regaling with me accounts of the wonderful nightlife to be enjoyed by lonely sailors in Japanese ports. On our arrival he and myself dressed in our best sports jackets and flannels and with a £20 sub were about to go ashore when the Chief Steward gave me the Captain's complements and would I step up to his cabin. On entering I found the two first trip cadets also dressed to go ashore. Captain Champion thanked me for coming up and asked (ordered) me to take the cadets ashore and to look after them, making sure they were back by midnight. This, of course, really dampened my ardour and I was promptly dumped by the Radio Officer. In the course of the evening we did enter a more respectable-looking bar where the young cadets were overwhelmed by the resident bar girls calling them their 'cherry boys' and offering them a good time free. We returned to the *Hartington* well before midnight and the cadets were still 'cherry boys'. I'd done my bit but I don't know if the cadets were cherry boys when we sailed for Vancouver.

A composite great circle course was set across the North Pacific with courses being steered to half a degree through the course recorder. The *Hartington* was not parish rigged as many tramps of that period were. In fact, we were better equipped than many liner company cargo ships – we had radar, gyro compass with repeaters and a course recorder along with a gyro pilot. On passage we prepared the ship for bulk grain, erecting shifting boards, bins and feeders, and arrived in Vancouver with the ship passing the grain survey and ready to load. The grain cargo was a free gift from the UK and other western governments to the people of Poland. During our passage from Vancouver to Panama the Chief Engineer challenged Captain Champion's authority. The result was that the Chief Engineer was sacked and sent home DBS, and the company flew a new Chief out to join *Hartington*. I never knew, and neither did anyone else, the true facts of the matter, only that the Chief liked the bottle.

The fact that our destination was Poland created a serious problem for the Second Mate. He was Polish

Hartington (3) at Vancouver, 21st June 1958. *[F.W. Hawks]*

and had served as an officer throughout the war with some distinction in destroyers of the Polish Navy. In light of the Katyn revelations that thousands of Polish officers had been massacred by the Russians, it would have been unwise for him to return to his homeland whilst it was under communist rule. We anchored off Kiel to enable Mr. Loscashinski to be paid off and a new Second mate to join. Whilst at anchor two gentlemen, one from Royal Naval Intelligence and another from the Foreign Office (MI6), came on board to brief an officer to gather intelligence in Gyndia. This was common practice with any British merchant ship going behind the Iron Curtain, with the job going to the Third or Second Mate. In our case it was the Third Mate – me – and on completion of my briefing, which took some time, I asked them why we were making a gift of food to a potential enemy. The MI6 man put it this way: 'the only way the Soviet Union could be brought down would be by the internal subversion of a discontented population, with the most likely country to start the ball rolling being Poland'. In the Soviet Bloc, people were always short of food while we in the west had food to give away. How right he was even in 1956. Throughout our stay in Gyndia, we were made to feel very welcome and even spent a pleasant evening in the Interclub drinking with some friendly Russians. While in Poland we received our orders to sail for New Orleans to load grain so we said goodbye to our 'enemies' and went to meet our allies: what a contrast awaited us.

The USA was in the grip of McCarthyism at the time and the crew of any foreign ship entering a US port from a Soviet Bloc port was considered to be crewed by communists or communist sympathisers. When *Hartington* picked up the American pilot we were also invaded by a horde of tin-hatted, gun-toting US Coast Guards. As Third Mate, I was on the bridge working the telegraph and keeping the movement book. Throughout I was shadowed by a man with a carbine and pistol as was Captain Champion and the man on the wheel, much to the embarrassment of the pilot who apologised for their behaviour.

When we were alongside, further US officials boarded and set up in the saloon and smoke room, showing a complete contempt for our accommodation by not using the ash trays but treading their stubs out on the carpeted decks. On deck posters depicting a Russian soldier with the caption 'Ivan is Watching You' were posted. The whole crew were then questioned, or should I say interrogated. The arrogant and aggressive attitude of the 'interrogators' and John Wayne gun slingers swaggering around our decks eventually got a response from the crew and a policy of 'goon-baiting' began.

In response to the question 'have you got venereal disease' the stock answer was 'no, I've not been ashore yet'. Another ploy was to enquire within hearing of the officials of another shipmate whether he had finished reading the ship's copy of 'Das Capital', which immediately instigated a frenzied search for subversive literature. The mildest girlie magazines were condemned as pornographic and destroyed (they were very modest compared to the ones on open sale ashore). Some of us got shore passes and some did not. Armed tin-hatted guards were placed ashore at the bow and stern and of course on the gangway. The top of the pops with the crew became 'The International' and the final incident was when the shore guard at the stern was struck by a potato. If it had been a hand grenade the response could not have been more dramatic, with Coast Guards swarming all over the ship. Captain Champion somehow resolved the situation, the Americans realised that their over reaction was counter productive and the crowd agreed to back off. We were not sorry to leave New Orleans and could understand the US fear of communism when we saw the third world conditions that prevailed in certain areas of New Orleans.

On arrival in Rotterdam I paid off to take my first mate's ticket, and said goodbye to Captain Champion, who thanked me and for the first time called me by my Christian name as did Mr. Steele the Mate.

Hartington (3). *[Ships in Focus]*

Fleet lists

Notes on the ships' histories.

The number '1' to '6' in brackets after a ship's name indicates that she is the first, second, etc. ship of that name in the fleet where the name has been used more than once. The dates following the name are those of entering and leaving Harrisons' ownership or management. Hulls are made of steel unless otherwise stated.

On the next line is given the ship's Official Number in the British registry. This is followed by her tonnages, gross (g) and net (n), at the time of acquisition. Dimensions given on the following line are the overall length x breadth x draft expressed in decimal feet. Tonnages and dimensions following any rebuild are quoted on subsequent lines.

On the next line is a description of the engine at the time of acquisition with the following abbreviations: 2-cyl. two-cylinder simple, C.2-cyl. for compound two-cylinder,

T.3-cyl. triple-expansion, Q.4-cyl. quadruple expansion, 4SC four-stroke cycle, 2SC two-stroke cycle, SA single-acting and DA double-acting. Then follows the name and location of the engine builder, dimensions of the cylinders, horse powers and speed as recorded in registration documents. If the vessel was re-engined at some point in its career, the new engine details are given on the next line.

Subsequent lines give the completion date, name and location of the builder and yard number followed by details of the ship's full career, including wherever possible dates of UK registration and port numbers. The place named after the title of the owner is the owner's domicile, and not necessarily the port of registry. Unless otherwise stated, the vessel flies the national flag of the owner's domicile.

The ships' histories have been corrected according to information published in February 2012.

J. and C. Harrison

1. JAMES SOUTHERN/HARLOW (1) 1887-1895 Iron
O.N. 52755 693g 539n
198.2 x 28.3 x 15.9 feet
1872: 801g 513n
218.2 x 28.3 x 15.8 feet
2-cyl. by R. and W. Hawthorn, Newcastle-upon-Tyne (2 x 38 x 30 inches); 90 NHP, 9 knots.
1890: C.2-cyl. by the Wallsend Slipway Co. Ltd., Wallsend-on-Tyne (27/50 x 30 inches); 107 NHP, 450 IHP, 9 knots.
5.1865: Launched by T. and W. Smith, North Shields (Yard No.25) for Frederick W. Harris, London.
8.8.1865: Registered at London (243/1865) in the ownership of Frederick W. Harris, London (24/64), Thomas E. Smith, Newcastle-upon-Tyne (12/64), Thomas Day, North Shields (6/64), John K. Welsh, London (4/64), Thomas D. Hopper, London (4/64), James Southern, London (3/64) and four others as JAMES SOUTHERN.
2.5.1872: Re-registered at London (100/1872) in the ownership of James Dixon (15/64), Frederick W. Harris (10/64), James L Wylie (8/64) and others (31/84), London.
1875: Owners became Henry Harris and James Dixon, trading as Harris and Dixon, London.
9.12.1887: Sold (8/64) by Henry Harris to James T., Charles W. and Frederick A. Harrison, London; 7/64 further shares sold by Harris and other holders between 10 and 16.12.1887.
12.1.1888: Management of vessel transferred to J. and C. Harrison.
3 and 26.11.1888: Further shares sold by H. Harris (7/64) and J. Dixon (8/64) to James T., Charles W. and Frederick A. Harrison.
4.3.1889: Further shares sold by H.A. Harris (2/64) to James T., Charles W. and Frederick A. Harrison.
9.1.1890: Harrison brothers' shareholdings divided between James (11/64), Charles (11/64) and Frederick (10/64).
22.5.1890: Renamed HARLOW.
24.10.1890: On the death of James T.

Harrison his shares pass to his trustee William G. Harrison.
2.3.1891: William G. Harrison sells the shares held in trust to Charles W. Harrison.
13.7.1895: Charles W. (22/64) and Frederick A. (11/64) Harrisons' shares sold to Mrs Elizabeth Jobling, Snaresbrook, Essex trading as the Harlow Steamship Co. (John H. Pearson, manager), London.
15-20.7.1895: Remaining 31/64 shares sold by minority holders to Mrs Elizabeth Jobling.
2.12.1905: Sank following a collision with the Belgian steamer PHILIPPEVILLE (4,091/1899) off Dungeness whilst on a voyage from Guernsey to London with a cargo of stone.
26.1.1906: Register closed.

2. CANNEL/CLAPTON 1887-1889 Iron
O.N.56892 758g 449n
201.3 x 28.1 x 17.4 feet
2-cyl .by Palmers' Shipbuilding and Iron Co. Ltd., Jarrow; 98 NHP.
1871: C.4-cyl. by Palmers' Shipbuilding and Iron Co. Ltd., Jarrow; 98 NHP.
3.8.1867: Launched by Palmers' Shipbuilding and Iron Co. Ltd., Jarrow (Yard No.214) for the General Iron Screw Collier Co. Ltd., London as J.E. McCONNELL.
3.12.1867: Registered at London (329/1867).
6.4.1880: Sold to James Dixon junior, trading as Harris and Dixon, London.
4.8.1880: Renamed CANNEL.
23.12.1887: Acquired (16/64) by James T., Charles W. and Frederick A. Harrison, London.
12.1.1888: Management of vessel transferred to J. and C. Harrison.
17.11.1888: Renamed CLAPTON.
31.5.1889: Remaining (48/64) shares acquired by James T., Charles W. and Frederick A. Harrison, London.
5.7.1889: Sold to John Thomas Harrison, trading as John T. Harrison and Co., London.
4.8.1900: Sold to the Antwerp Steamship Co. Ltd. (John Defty, manager), London.
16.8.1910: Owners renamed the Clapton Steamship Co. Ltd., London.

21.5.1913: Sold to Joseph Constant, London.
14.8.1913: Register closed on sale to S. Atychides and Th. B. Vahratoglou, Constantinople, Turkey; registered at Bandar Abbas, Persia and renamed SHIRAZ.
1914: Owners renamed Compagnie Perso-Ottomane de Navigation a Vapeur (S. Atychides. and Th. B. Vahratoglou, managers), Constantinople, Turkey.
11.1914: Abandoned on fire.

3. BENAMAIN 1888-1889 Iron
O.N.77446 381g 247n
150.2 x 23.2 x 13.0 feet
C.2-cyl. by Hall, Russell and Co., Aberdeen (19/30¾ x 22 inches), 43 NHP.
15.5.1878: Launched by Hall, Russell and Co., Aberdeen (Yard No.210) for James and Alexander Davidson, Aberdeen.
1.6.1878: Registered at Aberdeen as BENAMAIN.
17.11.1888: Sold to James T. Harrison, London.
28.11.1888: Registered at London (381/1888).
5.7.1889: Sold to John T. Harrison, London.
29.3.1890: Struck rocks off Lundy Island while on a voyage from Swansea to Treport with general cargo; refloated and got into Oxwich Bay, Glamorgan before foundering in position 51.34 north, 03.08 west. The entire crew of 12 was saved.
17.6.1890: Register closed.

4. GODREVY/HARBURY (1) 1889-1894 Iron
O.N.89620 1,570g 996n
255.7 x 36.0 x 18.4 feet
C.2-cyl. by J. W. and F. Wilson and Co., Monkwearmouth (33/62 x 42 inches); 160 NHP.
1892: T.3-cyl. by Wallsend Slipway Co. Ltd., Wallsend-on-Tyne (21/33/58 x 42 inches); 160 NHP, 1,000 IHP, 10 knots.
26.4.1884: Launched by Joseph Priestman and Co., Sunderland (Yard 10) as GODREVY for J. T. Matthews, London.
19.9.1884: Registered at London (146/1884).
29.11.1888: Sold to Thomas Briggs, Manchester.

16.10.1889: Sold to James T. Harrison, London, trading as J. and C. Harrison.
18.12.1889: 24/64 shares sold to Charles W. Harrison and 16/64 shares sold to Frederick A. Harrison.
24.10.1890: Death of James T. Harrison; his shares pass to his trustee William G. Harrison.
2.3.1891: William G. Harrison sells the shares held in trust to Charles W. Harrison.
27.1.1892: Renamed HARBURY.
11.3.1894: Wrecked on Mitahen Rocks, Elketaine Point, Algiers while on a voyage from Odessa to the United Kingdom with a cargo of maize.
28.4.1894: Register closed.

5. HARLYN (1) 1891-1895

O.N.99021 1,453g 929n
245.0 x 34.0 x 16.2 feet
T.3-cyl. by North Eastern Marine Engineering Co. Ltd., Wallsend-on-Tyne (18½/30/49 x 33 inches); 130 NHP, 9 knots.
11.1891: Launched by Edward's Shipbuilding Co. Ltd., Newcastle-upon-Tyne (Yard No.58) for J. and C. Harrison, London.
30.11.1891: Registered at London (185/1891) in the ownership of Charles W. and Frederick A. Harrison as HARLYN.
8.12.1891: 54/64 shares sold back to the shipbuilder.
19.12.1892: 10/64 shares resold to Charles W. and Frederick A. Harrison.
18.12.1893: 11/64 shares resold to Charles W. and Frederick A. Harrison.
28.11.1894: 33/64 shares resold to Charles W. and Frederick A. Harrison.
20.2.1895: 16/64 shares sold to Thomas W. Mann (Julius E. Guthe, manager), West Hartlepool.
3.7.1895: 48/64 shares sold to Thomas W. Mann (Julius E. Guthe, manager), West Hartlepool.
28.3.1899: Sold to the West Hartlepool Steam Navigation Co. Ltd. (J.E. Guthe, manager), West Hartlepool.
15.4.1899: Registered at West Hartlepool (6/1899).
8.7.1906: Wrecked at Cape Negro, near Cape Sable, Nova Scotia while on a voyage from Trapani to Gloucester, Massachusetts, USA with a cargo of salt.
31.8.1906: Register closed.

Harlyn (1), now owned by the West Hartlepool Steam Navigation Co. Ltd., wrecked near Cape Sable in 1906. [Kevin O'Donoghue collection]

Harberton (1) of 1894 in the colours of William Cory and Son Ltd. after 1896. The location is probably Penarth, where the photographer worked. [Wehrley/Kevin O'Donoghue collection]

6. HARBOURNE 1893-1894

O.N.101965 1,158g 714n
225.0 x 33.4 x 14.4 feet
T.3-cyl. by North Eastern Marine Engineering Co. Ltd., Wallsend-on-Tyne (18½/30/49 x 33 inches); 130 NHP, 9 knots.
17.12.1892: Launched by S.P. Austin and Son Ltd., Sunderland (Yard No.178) for J. and C. Harrison, London.
24.1.1893: Registered at London (7/1893) in the ownership of Charles W. and Frederick A. Harrison as HARBOURNE.
29.3.1894: Foundered off Flamborough Head after a collision with the British steamship EPPLETON (947/1882) while on a voyage from Blyth to London with a cargo of coal.
28.4.1894: Register closed.

7. HARBERTON (1) 1894-1896

O.N.102892 1,443g 893n
247.0 x 35.3 x 15.6 feet
T.3-cyl. by North Eastern Marine Engineering Co. Ltd., Wallsend-on-Tyne (19/31/51 x 33 inches); 130 NHP, 690 IHP, 9½ knots.
16.6.1894: Launched by S. P. Austin and Son Ltd., Sunderland (Yard No.185) for J. and C. Harrison, London.
16.7.1894: Registered at London (75/1894) in the ownership of Charles W. and Frederick A. Harrison as HARBERTON.
7.11.1896: Sold to William Cory and Son Ltd., London.
6.4.1916: Transferred to Cory Colliers Ltd., London.
29.3.1917: Missing after leaving Blyth for London with a cargo of coal; presumed to have sunk on 30.3.1917 in the North Sea after striking a mine laid by the German submarine UC 31. Her entire crew of 15 was lost.
2.11.1917: Register closed.

8. GLENFINLAS 1894-1895

O.N.68109 2,154g 1,409n
330.0 x 35.3 x 24.8 feet
C.2-cyl. by the builder (44/79 x 45 inches); 320 NHP.
17.12.1872: Launched by London and Glasgow Engineering and Iron Shipbuilding Co. Ltd., Govan, Glasgow (Yard No.174) for Alan C. Gow and Co., Glasgow.
4.6.1874: Registered at Glasgow (67/1874) in the ownership of Leonard Gow, Glasgow (32) and James McGregor, London (32) as GLENFINLAS.
1880: Managing company re-styled McGregor, Gow and Co.
12.1890: Sold to William J. Jobling, Newcastle-upon-Tyne.
15.9.1892: Ownership transferred to the Glenfinlas Steamship Co. Ltd. (William J. Jobling, manager), Newcastle-upon-Tyne.
7.1894: Sold to Charles W. Harrison and Frederick A. Harrison, London.
31.7.1894: Registered at London (85/1894).
4.1895: Sold to K.O.F. Dalman, Gothenburg, Sweden and renamed ELFSBORG.
26.4.1895: Register closed.
8.12.1895: Foundered in the North Sea while on a voyage from Iggesund to London with a cargo of wood and iron ore.

9. HARDEN 1894-1897

O.N.104775 1,958g 1,262n
279.0 x 36.9 x 16.8 feet
T.3-cyl. by North Eastern Marine Engineering Co. Ltd., Wallsend-on-Tyne (21/35/57 x 39 inches); 185 NHP, 1,000 IHP, 9¼ knots.
8.1894: Launched by Edward's Shipbuilding Co. Ltd., Newcastle-upon-Tyne (Yard No.70) for J. and C. Harrison, London.
11.8.1894: 54/64 shares sold back to the builder.
13.8.1894: Registered at London (91/1894) in the ownership of Charles W. and Frederick A. Harrison as HARDEN.
19.8.1896: 54/64 shares resold to Charles W. and Frederick A. Harrison.

11.1.1897: Wrecked at Cape Passero, Sicily while on a voyage from Novorossisk to Rotterdam with a cargo of grain and wood.
24.2.1897: Register closed.

10. HARLINGTON 1895-1896
O.N.104864 1,032g 628n
220.0 x 31.5 x 13.6 feet
T.3-cyl. by William Allan and Co., Sunderland (17½/29/47 x 33 inches); 110 NHP, 580 IHP, 9½ knots.
5.4.1895: Launched by S.P. Austin and Son Ltd., Sunderland (Yard No.188) for J. and C. Harrison, London.
30.4.1895: Registered at London (43/1895) in the ownership of Charles W. and Frederick A. Harrison as HARLINGTON.
17.1.1896: Sold to the Peninsular and Oriental Steam Navigation Co., London for £14,272.
2.12.1914: Wrecked on Middle Sunk Sand in the Thames Estuary while on a voyage from the Tees to London with a cargo of iron and general.
8.1.1915: Register closed.

11. HARPALUS 1895-1896
O.N.104888 1,445g 907n
247.0 x 35.3 x 16.0 feet
T.3-cyl. by George Clark Ltd., Sunderland (19/31/51 x 33 inches); 130 NHP, 700 IHP, 9 knots.
4.5.1895: Launched by J.L. Thompson and Sons Ltd., Sunderland (Yard No.329) for J. and C. Harrison, London.
5.6.1895: Registered at London (68/1895) in the ownership of Sir Christopher Furness and Charles W. Harrison, London as HARPALUS.
2.11.1896: Sold (64/64) to Charles W. Harrison, London.
10.11.1896: Sold to William Cory and Son Ltd., London.
6.4.1916: Transferred to Cory Colliers Ltd., London.
3.5.1916: Sold to the Federated Coal and Shipping Co. Ltd., Cardiff.
2.12.1916: Captured and sunk with bombs by the German submarine UB 23 in the Atlantic 34 miles south south west of Galley Head in position 50.56 north, 08.58 west while on a voyage from Penarth to Nantes with a cargo of coal. Her entire crew was saved.
20.12.1916: Register closed.

12. HARCALO (1) 1895-1899
O.N.104894 2,401g 1,538n
295.0 x 42.3 x 17.2 feet
T.3-cyl. by George Clark Ltd., Sunderland (22/36/59 x 39 inches); 200 NHP, 900 IHP, 9 knots.
9.5.1895: Launched by William Pickersgill and Sons, Sunderland (Yard No.107) for J. and C. Harrison, London.
8.6.1895: Registered at London (73/1895) in the ownership of Charles W. and Frederick A. Harrison as HARCALO.
5.7.1898: Sold (64/64) to Charles W. Harrison, London.
9.8.1898: Sold (64/64) to J. and C. Harrison Ltd, London.
4.1899: Sold to Compania Bilbaina de Nav. (Aznar y Compania, managers), Bilbao, Spain and renamed GANECOGORTA.
12.4.1899: Register closed.
1903: Managers renamed E. Aznar y Tutor.
1907: Sold to Compania Maritima del Navervion (Urquijo y Aldecoa, managers), Bilbao, Spain and renamed MAR ADRIATICO.
14.2.1917: Captured and sunk with bombs by the German submarine UC 21 in the Bay of Biscay in position 45.43 north, 01.24 east while on a voyage from New York and Lisbon to Bordeaux with general cargo.

13. HARBURY (2) 1896
O.N.105858 1,838g 1,147n
268.0 x 37.7 x 17.0 feet
T.3-cyl. by George Clark Ltd., Sunderland (20½/33/54 x 39 inches); 160 NHP, 900 IHP, 9½ knots.

Above: The *Harlington* of 1895 during her P&O career. *[Nautical Photo Agency/ World Ship Society Ltd.]*

Harpalus (1) of 1895 was another Harrison collier transferred to Cory in 1896. *[M. Barnard/J. and M. Clarkson]*

Harbury (2) of 1896 in the colours of William Cory and Son Ltd. Despite the owner's coal business, she is delivering timber. *[Nigel Farrell collection]*

15.4.1896: Launched by S.P. Austin and Son Ltd., Sunderland (Yard No.191) for J. and C. Harrison, London.
17.8.1896: Registered at London (110/1896) in the ownership of Charles W. and Frederick A. Harrison as HARBURY.
10.11.1896: Sold to William Cory and Son Ltd., London.
3.1912: Sold to Kjøbenhavn Bunkerkul Depot (J. Hansen and A. Erlandson, managers), Copenhagen, Denmark and renamed SMUT.
18.3.1912: Register closed.
1925: Management transferred to Knut Hansen.
1926: Sold to A/B Trävarutransport (Kristian Hansen, manager), Helsingfors, Finland.
1926: Owner renamed A/B Trætramp.
1939: Sold to Alfred Kalm, Tallinn, Estonia and renamed AARNE.
6.1940: Seized by Soviet naval forces in the Baltic.
10.1940: Formally expropriated and placed in the ownership of Estonskoye Gosudarstvyennoye Morskoye Parokhodstvo, Tallinn, Estonia.
5.7.1941: Captured in damaged condition by the German army at Windau.
10.1941: Entered German service as HEINRICH VON PLAUEN under the ownership of Deutsches Reich - Adm der KMD (Helmsing and Grimm, managers), Hamburg, Germany.
6.6.1943: Torpedoed and sunk by Soviet aircraft in the Baltic off Domesnes, Ösel in position 57.47 north, 22.26 east while on a voyage from Danzig to Riga with a cargo of coal.

14. HARBORNE 1896
O.N. 105880 1,278g 785n
235.1 x 34.1 x 33 feet
T.3-cyl. by John Dickinson and Sons Ltd., Sunderland (18½/30/49 x 33 inches); 120 NHP, 680 IHP, 9½ knots.
27.8.1896: Launched by S.P. Austin and Son Ltd., Sunderland (Yard No.192) for J. and C. Harrison, London.
1.10.1896: Registered at London (138/1896) in the ownership of Charles W. and Frederick A. Harrison as HARBORNE.
7.11.1896: Sold to William Cory and Son Ltd., London.

6.4.1916: Transferred to Cory Colliers Ltd., London.
31.3.1920: Transferred to the Rea Shipping Co. Ltd. (R.J. Speller, managers), London.
30.12.1920: Renamed CORBURN.
10.1921: Sold to Compania Anonima Navieros del Norte, San Sebastian, Spain and renamed EA.
31.10.1921: Register closed.
1923: Sold to Compania Maritima Elanchove, San Sebastian.
1942: Sold to Carbones de Tenerife, San Sebastian.
1943: Sold to Compania Anonima Navieros del Norte, San Sebastian.
1952: Sold to Santiago Rivero Morán, Gijón, Spain and renamed SOMIÓ.
1962: Sold to Sociedad Anonima Letasa, Bilbao, Spain.

1968: Sold to Recuperaciones Submarinas S.A., Santander, Spain for breaking up.
16.2.1968: Work began.

15. HARPENDEN (1) 1896-1899
O.N.108155 3,071g 1,941n
312.0 x 43.2 x 24.3 feet
T.3-cyl. by George Clark Ltd., Sunderland (23/38/62 x 42 inches); 220 NHP, 1,100 IHP, 9½ knots.
5.11.1896: Launched by S.P. Austin and Son Ltd., Sunderland (Yard No.184) for J. and C. Harrison, London.
2.12.1896: Registered at London (167/1896) in the ownership of Charles W. and Frederick A. Harrison as HARPENDEN.
5.7.1898: Sold (64/64) to Charles W. Harrison, London.
9.8.1898: Sold (64/64) to J. and C. Harrison Ltd, London.
17.2.1899: Sold to James A. Salton and Assheton N. Curzon, London.
18.10.1899: Sold to the Anglo-Algerian Steamship Co. (1896) Ltd. (F.C. Strick, manager), Swansea.
23.10.1899: Registered at Swansea (6/1899).
2.10.1900: Renamed SERBISTAN.
19.9.1906: Transferred to La Commerciale Steam Navigation Co. Ltd., London (F.C. Strick, Swansea, manager).
28.10.1912: Returned to the Anglo-Algerian Steamship Co. (1896) Ltd.
1.1.1913: Owner renamed Strick Line Ltd.
11.11.1916: Sailed from St. Nazaire for Cardiff with a cargo of munitions.
14.11.1916: Chased by a German submarine

The *Harborne* (1) in Cory colours at Boston, Lincolnshire (above), and in the Avon during her Spanish career as the monosyllabic *Ea* (below). *[Both: Roy Fenton collection]*

Strick's first *Serbistan* was originally *Harpenden* (1).*[Nigel Farrell collection]*

Photographed in King's Dock, Swansea, the coaster *Hardy* spent most of her career working for John T. Harrison. *[Roy Fenton collection]*

off Ushant and took refuge in Brest Roads.
16.11.1916: Sailed again and went missing with her crew of 24.
29.12.1916: Register closed.

16. MANDARIN/HARDY 1896-1897 Iron
O.N.84289 639g 366n
180.3 x 27.3 x 13.9 feet
C.2-cyl. by Hutson and Corbett, Glasgow (23/45 x 33 inches); 85 NHP.
10.12.1880: Launched by Hugh MacIntyre and Co., Paisley (Yard No.68) for Baird and Brown, Glasgow as MANDARIN.
8.2.1881: Registered at Glasgow (11/1881) in the ownership of James Brown, Glasgow.
15.11.1882: Sold to James and Alexander Wyllie, Troon.
30.11.1882: Mortgaged (32/64) to James Dickie, Glasgow.
23.12.1896: Sold (32/64) by James Dickie as mortgagee to Charles W. and Frederick A. Harrison, London.
24.12.1896: Sold (6/64) by Robert Wyllie and (28/64) minority shareholders and mortgagees to Charles W. and Frederick A. Harrison, London.
1.1.1897: Registered at London (1/1897) in the ownership of Charles W. and Frederick A. Harrison.
7.5.1897: Renamed HARDY.

9.8.1897: Sold to John Thomas Harrison, London.
30.6.1905: Transferred to John Harrison Ltd. (John Defty, manager), London
18.2.1907: Transferred to Services Maritimes du Tréport Ltd. (John Defty, manager), London.
11.12.1911: Sunk by explosion off Ault while on a voyage from Tréport to London with general cargo.
19.12.1911: Register closed.

17. HARLECH (1) 1897-1898
O.N.108198 1,282g 785n
235.8 x 34.3 x 14.3 feet
T.3-cyl. by John Dickinson and Sons Ltd., Sunderland (19¾/31/51 x 33 inches); 130 NHP, 800 IHP, 9½ knots.
1.4.1897: Launched by S.P. Austin and Son Ltd., Sunderland (Yard No.194) for J. and C. Harrison, London.
26.4.1897: Registered at London (52/1897) in the ownership of Charles W. and Frederick A. Harrison as HARLECH.
5.1898: Sold to the United States Navy for use as a collier and renamed POMPEY.
25.5.1898: Register closed.
1911: Converted to a torpedo boat tender.
7.1922: Transferred to the United States Army Quartermaster Corps for use as a transport.

1923: Sold to the National Coal Company, Manila, Philippines.
1928: Transferred to the National Development Company, Manila, Philippines.
1931: Sold to Compania Maritima (Fernandez Hermanos Inc., managers), Manila and renamed SAMAL.
12.1941: Lost during the Japanese invasion of the Philippines.

18. HARMONIC (1) 1897-1899
O.N.108238 2,876g 1,798n
314.1 x 45.5 x 21.0 feet
T.3-cyl. by George Clark Ltd., Sunderland (22½/37/61 x 42 inches); 210 NHP, 1,050 IHP, 9¼ knots.
1.6.1897: Launched by S.P. Austin and Son Ltd., Sunderland (Yard No.193) for J. and C. Harrison, London.
15.7.1897: Registered at London (103/1897) in the ownership of Charles W. and Frederick A. Harrison as HARMONIC.
8.7.1898: Sold (64/64) to Charles W. Harrison, London.
9.8.1898: Sold (64/64) to J. and C. Harrison Ltd, London.
11.12.1899: Sold to the Anglo-Algerian Steamship Co. (1896) Ltd. (F.C. Strick, manager), Swansea.
15.12.1899: Registered at Swansea (7/1899).
4.5.1900: Renamed BALUCHISTAN.
1.1.1913: Owner renamed Strick Line Ltd.
4.1913: Sold to J. Christensen, Bergen, Norway and renamed RITA WALLEM.
1.5.1913: Register closed.
1914: Sold to Minamimanshu Tetsudo K.K., Dairen, Japan and renamed RYUSHO MARU.
1919: Sold to Dairen Kisen K. K., Dairen.
1923: Sold to Dairen Sato Kuni Kisen K.K., Dairen.
4.1934: Sold for breaking up in Japan.

19. HARMONY (1) 1897-1899
O.N.108242 1,118g 674n
224.5 x 33.5 x 13.9 feet
T.3-cyl. by George Clark Ltd., Sunderland (19/31/51 x 33 inches); 156 NHP, 730 IHP, 10 knots.
13.7.1897: Launched by S.P. Austin and Son Ltd., Sunderland (Yard No.195) for J. and C. Harrison, London.
3.8.1897: Registered at London (112/1897) in the ownership of Charles W. and Frederick A. Harrison as HARMONY.
8.7.1898: Sold (64/64) to Charles W. Harrison, London.
9.8.1898: Sold (64/64) to J. and C. Harrison Ltd, London.
3.1.1899: Sold to the Red Cross Iquitos Steamship Co. Ltd. (William Isaacs, manager), Liverpool.
9.1.1899: Registered at Liverpool (7/1899).
1.2.1899: Renamed NAPO.
30.9.1905: Owner renamed the Iquitos Steamship Co. Ltd.
23.5.1913: Transferred to the Booth Steamship Co. Ltd, Liverpool on its subsidiary company going into liquidation.
3.1914: Sold to the Reval Shipping Co.

Harmony (1) was sold to the Red Cross Iquitos Steamship Line as *Napo*. [Kevin O'Donoghue collection]

Ltd. (Joh. Pitka and Co., managers), Reval, Estonia and renamed KODUMAA.
1.4.1914: Register closed.
9.1915: Requisitioned by the Imperial Russian Navy as a Baltic Fleet transport.
6.1918: Taken over by Transbalt, Petrograd, and renamed TSIMMERVALD.
12.1918: Captured by Estonian forces in the Gulf of Finland.
1919: Sold to the Reval Shipping Co. Ltd., Reval, Estonia and renamed KODUMAA.
1930: Transferred to the Tallinn Shipping Co. Ltd., Tallinn, Estonia.
10.9.1940: Detained at Greenock following the Soviet occupation of Estonia.
15.10.1940: Requisitioned by the British Government.
21.12.1940: Registered at Glasgow (36/1940) in the ownership of the Ministry of Shipping, London (E.P. Atkinson and Sons, Goole, managers).
26.9.1942: Capsized and sank outside Goole locks in the River Ouse while on a voyage from Goole to Ispwich with a cargo of coal.
5.2.1946: Register closed.

20. SAINT HELEN 1897-1899
O.N. 102250 2,599g 1,658n
314.0 x 44.1 x 20.8 feet
T.3-cyl. by William Gray and Co. Ltd., West Hartlepool (23/36½/62 x 39 inches); 240 NHP, 1,100 IHP, 9 knots.
12.8.1897: Launched by William Gray and Co. Ltd., West Hartlepool (Yard No.544) for Smith and Scaramanga, London.
16.9.1897: Registered at London (122/1897) in the ownership of Basil A. Smith and John G. Scaramanga (Frederick A. Harrison, ship's husband) as SAINT HELEN.
16.9.1897: 55/64 shares sold back to William C. Gray, West Hartlepool; 9/64 shares sold to Charles W. Harrison and Frederick A. Harrison.
21.9.1898: 23/64 shares sold by William C. Gray to J. and C. Harrison Ltd.
9.3.1899: 32/64 shares sold by William C. Gray to J. and C. Harrison Ltd.
14.3.1899: 9/64 shares sold by Charles W. Harrison and Frederick A. Harrison to J. and C. Harrison Ltd.
11.12.1899: Sold to the Anglo-Algerian Steamship Co. (1896) Ltd. (F.C. Strick, manager), Swansea.
22.12.1899: Registered at Swansea (8/1899).

29.10.1900: Renamed BARDISTAN.
25.9.1905: Sold to Robert K. Kelley, Liverpool.
3.10.1905: Registered at Liverpool (74/1905).
17.10.1905: Renamed ARCOLA.
30.10.1905: Sold to the Steamship Arcola Co. Ltd. (Robert and Percy Thomson, managers), Rothesay, New Brunswick, Canada.
1.6.1907: Registered at St John, New Brunswick, Canada (18/1907).
9.7.1908: Wrecked in Hay Cove, St Paul's Island, Cape Breton, Nova Scotia, Canada while on a voyage from Preston to Miramichi in ballast.
22.7.1908: Register closed.

21. HARPERLEY (1) 1897-1899
O.N.108279 2,366g 1,498n
300.0 x 43.0 x 20.4 feet
T.3-cyl. by W. Allan and Co. Ltd., Sunderland (23/37½/61½ x 39 inches); 240 NHP, 1,150 IHP, 10 knots.
27.10.1897: Launched by R. Craggs and Sons Ltd., Middlesbrough (Yard No.138) for J. and C. Harrison, London.
23.12.1897: Registered at London (161/1897) in the ownership of Sir Christopher Furness and Charles W. Harrison, London as HARPERLEY.

5.7.1898: Sold (64/64) to Charles W. Harrison, London.
9.8.1898: Sold (64/64) to J. and C. Harrison Ltd., London.
13.3.1899: Sold to James A. Salton and Assheton N. Curzon, London.
24.7.1899: Sold to the Anglo-Algerian Steamship Co. (1896) Ltd. (F.C. Strick, manager), Swansea.
26.7.1899: Registered at Swansea (3/1899).
22.3.1900: Renamed NIGARISTAN.
19.9.1906: Transferred to La Commerciale Steam Navigation Co. Ltd., London.
1.1907: Sold to Wilhelm Kunstmann, Stettin, Germany and renamed BRITANNIA.
14.6.1920: Surrendered to Great Britain as a prize.
26.7.1920: Registered at London (415/1920) in the ownership of the Shipping Controller (J. Denholm Ltd., Greenock, managers).
10.1920: Transferred to the Greek Government.
21.10.1920: Register closed.
1921: Renamed ATHINÆ and placed in government ownership with the Service of Maritime Transport, Piraeus, Greece.
1923: Sold to Pnevmaticos, Rethymnis and Yannaghas, Syra, Greece and renamed AKTI.
11.2.1927: Stranded in the entrance channel to Alexandria while on a voyage from Constanza to Alexandria with a timber cargo.
2.3.1927: Refloated but subsequently declared a constructive total loss and sold for breaking up in Italy.

22. HARLINGEN (1) (1897)
O.N. 106106 3,084g 1,985n
325.0 x 47.1 x 22.4 feet
T. 3-cyl. by Central Marine Engine Works, West Hartlepool (25/40/62 x 42 inches); 260 NHP, 300 IHP, 9 knots
9.12.1897: Launched by William Gray and Co. Ltd., West Hartlepool (Yard No. 547) for J. and C. Harrison, London as HARLINGEN, having been ordered by

Harrowing's *Ethylbrytha* was ordered by Smith and Scaramanaga but launched as *Harlingen* (1) for J. and C. Harrison, only to be sold before completion. [M. Barnard/J. and M. Clarkson]

Smith and Scaramanga, London. She was sold before registration.

30.3.1898: Registered at Whitby (1/1898) in the ownership of John H. Harrowing, Whitby as ETHELBRYTHA.

2.6.1898: Sold (16/64) to Robert Harrowing, Whitby.

27.11.1898: Joint owners became David Beckwith, York; William Hodgson, Malton; Robert and John H. Harrowing, Whitby.

17.8.1908: Transferred to the Harrowing Steamship Co. Ltd. (John H. Harrowing and Co., managers), Whitby.

30.7.1916: Captured, shelled and sunk by the German submarine U 35, eleven miles west south west of Pantellaria whilst on a voyage from St. Louis du Rhône to Salonica with a cargo of hay.

8.8.1916: Register closed.

23. HARRINGTON 1898-1899
O.N.108354 1,730g 1,072n
268.0 x 37.8 x 17.0 feet
T.3-cyl. by George Clark Ltd., Sunderland (21½/35/57½ x 39 inches); 180 NHP, 950 IHP, 10 knots.

5.1898: Launched by S.P. Austin and Son Ltd., Sunderland (Yard No.199) for J. and C. Harrison, London.

24.5.1898: Registered at London (100/1898) in the ownership of Charles W. and Frederick A. Harrison as HARRINGTON.

5.7.1898: Sold (64/64) to Charles W. Harrison, London.

9.8.1898: Sold (64/64) to J. and C. Harrison Ltd., London.

11.12.1899: Sold to the Steamship Calgarth Co. Ltd. (W.R. Rea, manager), London.

11.1.1900: Renamed CALGARTH.

12.1.1900: Registered at Liverpool (7/1900).

3.6.1901: Transferred to the Rea Shipping Co. Ltd. (A.L. Rea, manager), London.

26.5.1911: Sold to Denaby and Cadeby Main Collieries Ltd. (H.J. Tremellem, manager), London.

5.7.1911: Registered at Hull (34/1911).

11.7.1911: Renamed SAMPAN.

19.2.1920: Owner renamed Denaby Shipping and Commercial Co. Ltd.

29.5.1923: Sold to the Abbey Line Ltd. (Frederick Jones, manager), Cardiff.

6.1923: Sold to W. Schuchmann, Geestemünde/ Bremerhaven, Germany and renamed SÜDSEE.

4.6.1923: Register closed.

1930: Sold to Bugsier Reederei-und Bergungs A.G., Bremerhaven, Germany.

1935: Sold back to W. Schuchmann, Bremerhaven, Germany.

5.1946: Allocated to the Netherlands and

9.1946: Towed to Rotterdam.

1947: Renamed BRESKENS under Dutch Government ownership (A. Veder N.V., manager), The Hague, Netherlands and entered service 2.1948.

1948: Sold to N.V. S.S. Hannah (F.W. Uittenbogaart, manager), Rotterdam, Holland.

17.9.1948: Capsized and sank about one mile west south west of Boistö Pilot Station while on a voyage from Kotka to Rotterdam with a cargo of timber.

24. HARPORT (1) 1898-1899
O N 108397 1,747g 1,077n
263.8 x 39.4 x 17.2 feet
T.3-cyl. by John Dickinson and Sons Ltd., Sunderland (21/38/57½ x 39 inches); 180 NHP, 1,055 IHP, 10 knots.

4.7.1898: Launched by S.P. Austin and Son Ltd., Sunderland (Yard No.200) for J. and C. Harrison, London.

8.8.1898: Registered at London (157/1898) in the ownership of J. and C. Harrison Ltd. as HARPORT.

6.9.1899: Sold to the Australasian Steam Navigation Co. Ltd., Brisbane, Australia.

15.1.1900: Registered at Brisbane (1/1900).

12.6.1900: Renamed MAREEBA.

31.7.1908: Wrecked on Stockton Beach, 10 miles north of Newcastle, New South Wales while on a voyage from Queensland ports to Sydney with general cargo.

18.8.1908: Register closed.

25. HARLECH (2) 1898-1899
O.N.209995 1,199g 725n
235.5 x 34.3 x 14.5 feet
T.3-cyl. by George Clark Ltd., Sunderland (19/31/51 x 33 inches); 130 NHP, 800 IHP, 10 knots.

15.9.1898: Launched by S.P. Austin and Son Ltd., Sunderland (Yard No.201) for J. and C. Harrison Ltd., London.

22.10.1898: Registered at London (207/1898) in the ownership of J. and C. Harrison Ltd. as HARLECH.

13.10.1899: Sold to the Red Cross Iquitos Steamship Co. Ltd. (William Isaacs, manager), Liverpool.

18.10.1899: Registered at Liverpool (119/1899).

20.10.1899: Renamed JAVARY.

30.9.1905: Owner renamed the Iquitos Steamship Co. Ltd.

23.5.1913: Transferred to the Booth Steamship Co. Ltd., Liverpool on its subsidiary company going into liquidation.

19.10.1914: D.H. Crompton, New York empowered to sell the vessel in the USA for not less than £8,000.

1914: Sold to L.C. Gillespie and Sons, New York, USA.

1916: Sold to the Darland Steam Ship Corporation, New York.

22.6.1916: Register closed.

1922: Sold to the Javary Steam Ship Corporation, New York.

1923: Sold to Donald Brothers Inc., New York and renamed JEANETTE.

1926: Renamed DONETTA.

1927: Sold to Charles Warner, Jacksonville, Florida, USA.

25.2.1927: Arrived at Baltimore for breaking up.

26. HARCALO (2) 1904-1907
O.N.118498 2,822g 1,826n
325.0 x 47.0 x 22.3 feet
T.3-cyl. by Richardsons, Westgarth and Co. Ltd., Hartlepool (23/40/65 x 42 inches); 305 NHP, 1,300 IHP, 9½ knots.

11.8.1904: Launched by Furness, Withy and Co. Ltd., West Hartlepool (Yard No.274) for J. and C. Harrison Ltd, London.

28.9.1904: Registered at London (156/1904) in the ownership of Charles W. and Frederick A. Harrison as HARCALO.

14.9.1906: Sold (64/64) back to the builder on the death of Frederick A. Harrison.

1.10.1906: Repurchased (64/64) by Charles W. Harrison.

9.7.1907: Sold to the Silver Wings Steamship Co. Ltd. (N.G. Hallett, manager), Cardiff.

10.7.1907: Renamed SILVER WINGS.

25.7.1913: Owner renamed the Wing Steamship Co. Ltd., London (N.G. Hallett, Cardiff, manager).

18.8.1915: Wrecked on Sable Island while on a voyage from New York with a cargo of steel rails and general.

2.10.1915: Register closed.

27. HARMONIC (2) 1905-1916
O.N.120491 2,827g 1,826n
325.0 x 47.0 x 22.3 feet
T.3-cyl. by Richardsons, Westgarth and Co. Ltd., Hartlepool (23/40/65 x 42 inches); 305 NHP, 1,300 IHP, 9½ knots.

Harcalo (2) owned by Norman Hallett as *Silver Wings* grounded on 10th February 1914 at Sully. She was quickly refloated and taken to Cardiff. *[Roy Fenton collection]*

After sale to Denmark the former *Harmonic* (2) returned to British registry in 1926 as *Eastbury* for Alexanders (Newcastle) Ltd. as seen here. *[Nigel Farrell collection]*

8.12.1904: Launched by Furness, Withy and Co. Ltd., West Hartlepool (Yard No.276) for J. and C. Harrison Ltd., London.
21.1.1905: Registered at London (10/1905) in the ownership of Charles W. and Frederick A. Harrison as HARMONIC.
14.9.1906: Resold (64/64) to the builder on the death of Frederick A. Harrison.
10.10.1906: Sold (64/64) to Charles W. Harrison, London and Stephen W. Furness, West Hartlepool.
7.5.1907: Repurchased (64/64) by Charles W. Harrison.
22.5.1916: Sold to R.W.J. Sutherland, Cardiff and immediately resold to Ivor H. Jones and Charles W. King, Cardiff.
26.7.1916: Transferred to the Tree Steamship Co. Ltd. (Ivor H. Jones, manager), Cardiff.
8.1916: Requisitioned by the Admiralty as a Q-Ship.
4.1918: Returned to her owners.
10.4.1919: Sold to the Maindy Shipping Co. Ltd. (Jenkins, Richards and Evans Ltd., managers), Cardiff.
13.2.1920: Renamed MAINDY HOUSE.

6.1921: Sold to Rederi A/S Triton (Torben Nielsen, manager), Copenhagen, Denmark and renamed OLAF L. KONGSTED.
30.6.1921: Register closed.
1923: Management transferred to Oscar Ovesen.
1924: Sold to D/S A/S Paris (O. Oveson, manager), Copenhagen, Denmark and renamed PARIS.
1.1926: Sold to Alexanders (Newcastle) Ltd. (E. Barnsfather, manager), Newcastle-upon-Tyne.
26.1.1926: Registered at Newcastle (3/1926) as EASTBURY.
16.9.1933: Sold to the Alexander Shipping Co. Ltd. (Capper, Alexander and Co., managers), London on liquidation of Alexanders (Newcastle) Ltd.
17.12.1937: Sold to Charles Strubin and Co. Ltd., London.
31.12.1937: Renamed LAKE GENEVA.
10.1.1938: Registered at London (6/1938).
2.1939: Sold to Usaldusühing Jakobson, ja Ko, Parnu, Estonia (C. Strubin and Co., managers, London).
23.2.1939: Register closed.

1940: Sold to Compagnie Belge d'Armement et de Gérance, Panama (L. and J. Lalement, Ghent, Belgium, managers) and renamed BOBBY.
23.4.1940: Sunk in collision with the Dutch steamship MIDSLAND (1,089/1915) about three miles south east of Dungeness whilst on a voyage from Safi to Ghent.

28. HARMONY (2) 1905-1912
O.N.120501 2,833g 1,830n
325.1 x 47.0 x 22.3 feet
T.3-cyl. by Richardsons, Westgarth and Co. Ltd., Hartlepool (23/40/65 x 42 inches); 305 NHP, 1,300 IHP, 9½ knots.
7.1.1905: Launched by Furness, Withy and Co. Ltd., West Hartlepool (Yard No.278) for J and C Harrison Ltd., London.
21.2.1905: Registered at London (19/1905) in the ownership of Charles W. and Frederick A. Harrison as HARMONY.
14.9.1906: Resold (64/64) to the builder on the death of Frederick A. Harrison.
16.10.1906: Repurchased (64/64) by Charles W. Harrison.
6.12.1911: Sold to Godfrey A. Simmonds acting as the Assistant Secretary of the Union Steamship Co. of New Zealand Ltd., Dunedin, New Zealand.
31.7.1912: Renamed KAURI and registered at Dunedin (1/1912) in the ownership of the Union Steamship Co. of New Zealand Ltd., Dunedin, New Zealand.
5.8.1927: Laid up at Lyttelton.
1928: Sold to N.E.A. Moller (Moller and Co., managers), Shanghai, China.
15.11.1928: Renamed MINNIE MOLLER and registered at Shanghai, China (British flag).
1935: Owners renamed Moller Line Ltd., Shanghai.
1936: Sold to the Hwah Sung Steamship Co. Ltd., Shanghai and renamed HWAH-FOO.
24.8.1937: Sunk as a blockship at Kiangyin in the Yangtse during the Sino-Japanese War.

Harmony (2) off Tilbury (above) and as *Kauri* of the Union Steamship Co. of New Zealand Ltd. (opposite page, top). *[National Maritime Museum G688; Ian J. Farquhar collection]*

29. HARLINGEN (2) 1905-1906

O.N.120606 3,471g 2,225n
342.0 x 49.5 x 22.7 feet
T.3-cyl. by Central Marine Engine Works,
West Hartlepool (25½/40½/67 x 45 inches);
335 NHP, 1500 IHP, 9 knots.
2.8.1905: Launched by William Gray and
Co. Ltd., West Hartlepool (Yard No.708)
for J. and C. Harrison Ltd., London.
16.9.1905: Registered at London
(136/1905) in the ownership of Frederick
A. Harrison as HARLINGEN.
20.9.1905: Resold (33/64) to the builder.
17.9.1906: Reacquired (31/64) to William
G. Harrison.
18.9.1906: Resold by William G. Harrison
(31/64) to Charles W. Harrison.
3.10.1906: Resold by the builder (17/64) to
Charles W. Harrison.
9.11.1906: Wrecked near Cabo Frio, Brazil
while on a voyage from Buenos Aires to
Port Eads in ballast.
20.12.1906: Register closed.

30. HARLEY (1) 1905-1906

O.N.120608 3,518g 2,279n
347.0 x 47.5 x 25.2 feet
T.3-cyl. by Richardsons, Westgarth and Co.
Ltd., Hartlepool (24/39/66 x 42 inches);
319 NHP, 1,300 IHP, 9 knots.
17.7.1905: Launched by Furness, Withy
and Co. Ltd., West Hartlepool (Yard
No.283) for J. and C. Harrison Ltd.,
London.
26.9.1905: Registered at London
(142/1905) in the ownership of Frederick
A. Harrison and Stephen Furness as
HARLEY.
30.5.1906: Sold (64/64) to William G.
Harrison.
6.1906: Sold to Compagnie Royale
Belgo-Argentine (Adolf Deppe, manager),
Antwerp, Belgium and renamed BARON
BAEYENS.
9.6.1906: Register closed.
1.1934: Broken up at Antwerp by Cyclops
Works S.A.

31. HARLECH (3) 1905-1914

O.N.120614 3,470g 2,224n
345.0 x 39.5 x 23.7 feet
T.3-cyl. by Central Marine Engine Works,
West Hartlepool (25½/40½/67 x 45

inches); 335 NHP, 1,500 IHP, 9 knots.
14.9.1905: Launched by William Gray and
Co. Ltd., West Hartlepool (Yard No.709)
for J. and C. Harrison Ltd., London.
12.10.1905: Registered at London
(150/1905) in the ownership of Frederick
A. Harrison as HARLECH.
13.10.1905: Resold (32/64) to the builder.
14.4.1906: Resold (15/64) to Frederick A.
Harrison.
18.9.1906: Sold by Frederick A. Harrison
(31/84) to William G. Harrison.
23.10.1906: Sold by Frederick A. Harrison
(16//64) to William G. Harrison.
5.10.1906: Resold (17/64) by the builder to
Charles W. Harrison.
4.1914: Sold to D.N. Calimeris, Syra,
Greece and renamed CALIMERIS.
16.4.1914: Register closed.
1916: Sold to M. Theodossion, Piraeus, Greece.
1917: Sold to Societa Nazionale di
Navigazione, Genoa, Italy.
1925: Sold to Epam L. Goulandris, Andros,
Greece and renamed ARISTIDES L.
GOULANDRIS.
1931: Owner renamed E.A. Goulandris and
Co., Andros.
1939: Sold to Werner Hackland, Pori,
Finland and renamed EDITH.
9.1943: Damaged by a mine in the Baltic;
stripped and laid up at Copenhagen.

21.9.1944: Seized by the German
authorities.
1945: Further damaged by air attack.
1945: Allocated to the United Kingdom and
returned to her Finnish owners.
1948: Sold to Petersen and Albeck A/S,
Copenhagen for breaking up.

32. HARPERLEY (2) 1906-1928

O.N.120666 3,990g 2,566n
360.3 x 50.1 x 25.8 feet
T.3-cyl. by Central Marine Engine Works,
West Hartlepool (26/42/70 x 45 inches); 350
NHP, 1,600 IHP, 9 knots.
25.1.1906: Launched by William Gray and
Co. Ltd., West Hartlepool (Yard No.717) for
J. and C. Harrison Ltd., London.
15.2.1906: Registered at London (25/1906)
in the ownership of Frederick A. Harrison as
HARPERLEY.
19.2.1906: Resold (40/64) to the builder.
29.8.1906: Resold (6/64) by the builder to
Charles W. Harrison.
18.9.1906: Shares (24/64) pass to William
G. Harrison as Trustee following the death
of Frederick A. Harrison; sold on the same
day to Charles W. Harrison.
27.2.1907: Resold (6/64) by the builder to
Charles W. Harrison.
7.7.1908: Sold (32/64) by Charles W.
Harrison to Basil A. Smith, London.
18.2.1909: Resold (28/64) by the builder to
Charles W. Harrison.
5.8.1915: Resold (32/64) by Basil A. Smith
to Charles W. Harrison.
22.3.1920: Transferred for £150,000 to
the Willis Steamship Co. Ltd. (J. and C.
Harrison Ltd., managers), London.
12.1928: Sold to Stamatios and Demetrios
Fafalios, Chios, Greece and renamed
STAMOS FAFALIOS.
14.12.1928: Register closed.
12.1933: Sold to Metal Industries Ltd.
About 25.12.1933: Arrived at Rosyth from
Liverpool for breaking up.
1.8.1934: Breaking up commenced.
About 9.1934: Hulk towed to Charlestown
for work to be completed.

Harperley (2). Note the position of the gangway. *[Kevin O'Donoghue collection]*

33. HARPENDEN (2) 1906-1914

O.N.123703 3,537g 2,241n
347.0 x 47.4 x 25.2 feet
T.3-cyl. by Richardsons, Westgarth and Co.
Ltd., Hartlepool (24/34/66 x 45 inches);
318 NHP, 1,300 IHP, 9 knots.
2.8.1906: Launched by Furness, Withy and
Co. Ltd., West Hartlepool (Yard No.295)
for J. and C. Harrison Ltd., London.
13.9.1906: Registered at London
(154/1906) in the ownership of Sir
Christopher Furness and Charles W.
Harrison, London as HARPENDEN.
16.3.1912: Sold (64/64) to Charles W.
Harrison.
4.1914: Sold to Société Les Affréteurs
Réunis (J. Stern, manager), Rouen, France
and renamed FLORE.
6.4.1914: Register closed.
26.7.1917: Struck a mine laid by the
German submarine U 71 and sank eight
miles east of Fetlar Island, Shetlands while
on a voyage from Archangel to Brest with
passengers and general cargo.

34. HARLYN (2) 1906-1914

O.N.123704 3,459g 2,224n
342.0 x 49.5 x 22.7 feet
T.3-cyl. by William Gray and Co. Ltd.,
West Hartlepool (25½/40½/67 x 45 inches);
335 NHP, 1,500 IHP, 9 knots.
21.8.1906: Launched by William Gray and
Co. Ltd., West Hartlepool (Yard No.731)
for J. and C. Harrison Ltd., London.
18.9.1906: Registered at London
(155/1906) in the ownership of Charles W.
Harrison as HARLYN.
20.9.1906: Re-sold (32/64) back to the
builder.
21.9.1906: Re-purchased (32/64) by
Charles W. Harrison.
10.11.1914: Sold to the Ioanna Shipping Co.
Ltd. (John A. Mango, manager), London.
11.11.1914: Renamed IOANNA.
9.3.1920: Sold to the Albany Steam
Navigation Co. Ltd. (H.R. Fletcher,
manager), Cardiff.
30.7.1920: Renamed ALBANY.
12.1931: Arrived at Briton Ferry to be
broken up by T.W. Ward Ltd.
1.9.1932: Register closed.

35. HARLEY (2) 1906-1913

O.N.123731 4,171g 2,707n
359.8 x 50.2 x 26.4 feet
T.3-cyl. by Richardsons, Westgarth and Co.
Ltd., Hartlepool (24/39/66 x 45 inches);
335 NHP, 1,400 IHP, 9 knots.
3.9.1906: Launched by Furness, Withy and
Co. Ltd., West Hartlepool (Yard No.296)
for J. and C. Harrison Ltd., London.
18.10.1906: Registered at London in the
ownership of Charles W. Harrison and
Stephen W. Furness as HARLEY.
23.10.1908: Sold (64/64) to Charles W.
Harrison.
29.1.1913: Sold to the Union Navigation
Co. Ltd., Montreal, Canada.
15.2.1913: Registered at Montreal
(2/1913).

Albany, formerly *Harlyn* (2), in Manchester, 24th August 1924. *[Nigel Farrell collection]*

18.12.1914: Henry Whiton and Clarence
A. Snider (President and Treasurer of the
Union Navigation Co. Ltd.) empowered to
sell the vessel at New York for not less than
$250,000.
23.12.1914: Sold to Walker, Armstrong and
Co., Savannah, Georgia, USA and renamed
SOUTHERNER.
8.2.1915: Register closed.
1916: Sold to the Garland Steamship
Corporation, New York, USA and renamed
CAROLINIAN.
10.1918: Requisitioned by the United
States Navy as No.1445 for the Naval
Overseas Transportation Service.
3.1919: Returned to commercial service.
1927: Sold to G.E. Kulukundis, Syra,
Greece and renamed PROTEUS.
1928: Transferred to Elias G. Culucundis
and S.C. Costomeni, Syra, Greece.
1929: Transferred to the Atlanticos
Steamship Co. Ltd., Syra, Greece.
1932: Sold to A.G. Lemos, Syra, Greece
and renamed STEFANIOS.
16.4.1934: Wrecked two miles west by
south west of East Point, Mayo Island,
Cape Verde Islands while on a voyage from
Bahia Blanca to Las Palmas with a cargo
of wheat.

36. HARTINGTON (1) 1907-1933

O.N.125598 4,043g 2,500n
360.0 x 50.0 x 25.7 feet
T.3-cyl. by William Gray and Co. Ltd.,
West Hartlepool (26/42/70 x 45 inches);
350 NHP, 1,600 IHP, 9 knots.
26.6.1907: Launched by William Gray and

Co. Ltd., West Hartlepool (Yard No.747)
for J. and C. Harrison Ltd., London.
23.7.1907: Registered at London
(122/1907) in the ownership of Charles W.
Harrison as HARTINGTON.
25.7.1907: Resold (36/64) to the builder.
30.7.1910: Reacquired (36/64) by Charles
W. Harrison.
22.3.1920: Transferred for £150,000 to
the Willis Steamship Co. Ltd. (J. and C.
Harrison Ltd., managers), London.
6.1933: Sold to Constantine D. Calafatis,
Syra, Greece and renamed FRED.
30.6.1933: Register closed.
1934: Passed to the Executors of the late
Constantine D. Calafatis.
1935: Management transferred to Petros M.
Nomikos, Piraeus, Greece.
1940: Management transferred to D.A.
Psychoyos.
1948: Management transferred to D. Calafatis.
1952: Sold to Van Heyghen Frères for
breaking up while laid up at Bruges.
1.12.1952: At the breakers awaiting
demolition.

37. HARLOW (2) 1907-1912

O.N.114647 4,212g 2,668n
370.2 x 48.8 x 28.8 feet
T.3-cyl. by John Dickinson and Sons Ltd.,
Sunderland (26/43/71 x 51 inches); 450
NHP, 2,250 IHP, 11 knots.
7.7.1902: Launched by Short Brothers
Ltd., Sunderland (Yard No.306) for the
New York and Oriental Steam Ship Co.
Ltd. (Barber and Co., managers), Liverpool
as SAGAMI; purchased while fitting out

Hartington (1). *[Nigel Farrell collection]*

Harlow (2) loading a coal cargo. *[Kevin O'Donoghue collection]*

Harport (2). *[Nigel Farrell collection]*

Incharran (above) was bought in 1908 and renamed *Harcroft* (below). *[Nigel Farrell collection; Kevin O'Donoghue collection]*

by the Hindustan Steam Shipping Co. Ltd. (J.W. Squance and Co., managers), Newcastle-upon-Tyne.
27.10.1902: Registered at Sunderland (10/1902).
25.10.1906: Management transferred to Common Brothers, Newcastle-upon-Tyne.
15.10.1907: Sold to Charles W. Harrison.
18.10.1907: Renamed HARLOW.
11.1912: Sold to Societa Anonima Lloyd del Pacifico, Savona, Italy and renamed AMISTA.
22.11.1912: Register closed.
c9.1932: Sold for breaking up while laid up at Savona.

38. HARPORT (2) 1907-1912
O.N.125644 3,986g 2,5203n
370.0 x 50.2 x 24.4 feet
T.3-cyl. by John Readhead and Sons Ltd., South Shields (26/42/70 x 45 inches); 300 NHP, 2,250 IHP, 10 knots.
8.10.1907: Launched by John Readhead and Sons Ltd., South Shields (Yard No.404) for J. and C. Harrison Ltd., London.
16.11.1907: Registered at London (179/1907) in the ownership of Charles W. Harrison as HARPORT.
15.11.1907: Re-sold (40/64) to the builder.
23.8.1911: Re-purchased (40/64) by Charles W. Harrison.
6.1912: Sold to Deutsch-Amerikanische Petroleum Gesellschaft, Hamburg, Germany and converted to a tanker (5,294g).
15.6.1912: Register closed.
8.1914: In port at Pisagua at the outbreak of the First World War; sold to the Standard Oil Company (New Jersey), Bayonne, New Jersey, USA and renamed DAYTON.
1923: Sold to J.M. Botts, New York, USA.
1925: Sold to the Olympic Steamship Co. Inc., Seattle, USA and renamed OLYMPIC.
1940: Sold to Compania International de Vapores S.A. and Compania General de Vapores S.A. (S.S. Niarchos, manager), Panama.
22.1.1942: Torpedoed and sunk by the German submarine U 130 in position 36.01 north, 75.30 west while on a voyage from Curacao to Baltimore with a cargo of crude oil. Her entire crew of 31 was lost.

39. HARCROFT 1908-1913
O.N.118096 4,034g 2,587n
375.0 x 47.5 x 25.8 feet
T.3-cyl. by George Clark Ltd., Sunderland (25/42/71 x 48 inches); 424 NHP, 2,000 IHP, 10½ knots.
20.3.1904: Launched by William Pickersgill and Sons, Sunderland (Yard No.143) for the Rover Shipping Co. Ltd. (Hamilton, Fraser and Co., managers), Liverpool as INCHARRAN.
16.5.1904: Registered at Liverpool (41/1904).
14.7.1908: Acquired by Charles W. Harrison.
21.7.1908: Sold (32/64) to John Holman and Sons Ltd., London.
29.7.1908: Renamed HARCROFT.

2.4.1912: Reacquired (32/64) by Charles W. Harrison.
21.1.1913: Sold to the Guarantee Insurance and Investment Co. Ltd. (C. Cartwright, manager), London.
24.3.1913: Renamed RIO PALLARESA.
23.5.1913: Transferred to the Taconic Steamship Co. Ltd. (C. Cartwright, London, manager) Toronto, Canada.
21.1.1915: Sold to the Kyle Transport Co. Ltd. (Bicket and Co., managers), Liverpool.
29.7.1918: Torpedoed and sunk by the German submarine UC 25 in the Mediterranean 62 miles east north east of Malta while on a voyage from Alexandria to Hull. Two members of her crew were lost.
29.8.1918: Register closed.

40. HARFLEUR (1) 1909-1912
O.N.125753 4,596g 2,847n
385.0 x 51.1 x 26.4 feet
T.3-cyl. by William Gray and Co. Ltd., West Hartlepool (26/42/70 x 48 inches); 391 NHP, 1,700 IHP, 9 knots.
9.11.1908: Launched by William Gray and Co. Ltd., West Hartlepool (Yard No.759) for J. and C. Harrison Ltd., London.
2.1.1909: Registered at London (3/1909) in the ownership of Charles W. Harrison as HARFLEUR.
4.1.1909: Re-sold (50/64) to the builder.
22.4.1912: Re-acquired (50/64) from the builder.
7.5.1912: Registered at Montreal (9/1912) in the ownership of Charles W. Harrison.
3.6.1912: Sold to the Union Navigation Co. Ltd., Toronto, Canada.
2.4.1913: Register papers re-issued to reflect change in ownership.
1.12.1914: Henry Whiton and Clarence A. Snider (President and Treasurer of the Union Navigation Co. Ltd.) empowered to sell the vessel at New York for not less than $270,000.
4.12.1914: Sold to Walker, Armstrong and Co., Savannah, Georgia, USA and renamed GEORGIANA.
8.2.1915: Register closed.
1916: Sold to the Garland Steamship Corporation, New York, USA and renamed NORLINA.
5.1918: Requisitioned by the United States Navy as No.1597 for the Naval Overseas Transportation Service.
5.1919: Returned to commercial service.
4.8.1926: Wrecked at Horseshoe Point, 45 miles north of San Francisco while on a voyage from San Francisco to Seattle with general cargo.

41. HARFORD 1909
O.N.125756 4,412g 2716n
375.0 x 51.5 x 25.7 feet
T.3-cyl. by John Readhead and Sons Ltd., South Shields (26½/43/71 x 48 inches); 430 NHP, 2,500 IHP, 12 knots.
7.11.1908: Launched by John Readhead and Sons Ltd., South Shields (Yard No.407) for J. and C. Harrison Ltd., London.

Harfleur (1) in Harrison funnel colours (above) and with a different funnel, possibly after her sale in 1912 (below). *[Nigel Farrell collection; Kevin O'Donoghue collection]*

1.1.1909: Re-sold (34/64) to the builder.
5.1.1909: Registered at London (5/1909) in the ownership of Charles W. Harrison as HARFORD.
6.11.1909: Badly damaged by fire in bunkers at Barracouta while on a voyage to Melbourne with a cargo of timber; abandoned to the underwriters as a constructive total loss.
26.8.1910: Register closed.
1911: Repaired and sold to Fujioka Koichiro, Kobe, Japan and renamed KOJU MARU.
1914: Sold to T. Mikami, Kobe.
9.1915: Sold to the Bellevue Steamship Co. Ltd. (Bell Brothers and Co., managers), Glasgow and renamed BELLEVUE.
21.9.1915: Registered at Glasgow (40/1915).
1.12.1915: Sold to the Town Line (London) Ltd. (Harrison, Sons and Co.,

managers), London and registered at London (330/1915).
7.9.1916: Renamed COURTOWN.
27.9.1924: Sunk in collision with the French steamer LA ROCHEFOUCAULD (2,275/1920) three miles north of Pendeen while on a voyage from Cardiff to Montevideo with a cargo of coal.
16.10.1924: Register closed.

42. HARLESDEN (1) 1909-1916
O.N.125768 4,334g 2,724n
365.0 x 50.5 x 26.9 feet
T.3-cyl. by North Eastern Marine Engineering Co. Ltd., Sunderland (26/42/72 x 48 inches); 396 NHP, 2,100 IHP, 10½ knots.
22.2.1909: Launched by John Readhead and Sons Ltd., Sunderland (Yard No.243) for J. and C. Harrison Ltd., London.
25.3.1909: Registered at London (26/1909) in the ownership of Charles W. Harrison and John B. Adam as HARLESDEN.

Harlesden (1). *[Nigel Farrell collection]*

Harpeake. [Nigel Farrell collection]

4.10.1911: Sold (64/64) to Charles W. Harrison.
17.4.1916: Sold to the Mondrich Steamship Co. Ltd. (F.V. Japp, manager), London.
29.6.1916: Renamed FENCHURCH.
20.3.1920: Management transferred to

Oliver Hatch, London.
5.1927: Sold to N. Pateras Sons, Syra, Greece and renamed KRYSANTHI PATERA.
1.6.1927: Register closed.
24.11.1930: Abandoned on fire and foundered

75 miles from Cristobal while on a voyage from Antofagasta to the Mediterranean with a cargo of nitrate.

43. HARPEAKE 1909-1913
O.N.129034 4,601g 2,840n
385.0 x 51.1 x 26.4 feet
T.3-cyl. by William Gray and Co. Ltd., West Hartlepool (26/42/70 x 48 inches); 391 NHP, 1,700 IHP, 9 knots.
5.7.1909: Launched by William Gray and Co. Ltd., West Hartlepool (Yard No.764) for J. and C. Harrison Ltd., London.
10.8.1909: Registered at London (108/1909) in the ownership of Charles W. Harrison as HARPEAKE.
11.8.1909: Re-sold (50/64) to the builder.
27.4.1912: Purchased back (50/64) from the builder.
19.7.1913: Sold to the Moss Steamship Co. Ltd., Liverpool.
24.7.1913: Registered at Liverpool (61/1913).
28.7.1913: Renamed SEBEK.
21.4.1917: Torpedoed and sunk by the German submarine U 70 in the North Atlantic 145 miles north west of Tory Island in position 56.12 north, 12.20 west while on a voyage from Alexandria to Liverpool with general cargo. One of her crew was lost.
23.5.1917: Register closed.

The *Harlingen* enigma

Always willing to seize a commercial opportunity, the Harrisons sold ships before they had been registered on several occasions. The 'Marine Engineer' noted that this ship had been laid down for J. and C. Harrison Ltd., London as *Harlingen*, but she was completed - over 18 months after launching - for Furness, Withy and Co. Ltd. If this was correct, she would have been the third of the name in the fleet. However, there must be serious doubts as to whether Harrisons did indeed order her. She was much smaller than the vessels the company were currently building, and from a yard they never otherwise dealt with. The long gap between launch and registration would also argue against Harrison ownership: such a dynamic organisation is unlikely to have had a ship lingering in a yard for that long. The author concludes that, despite the report in the 'Marine Engineer' and the coincidence of her name, this *Harlingen* had no connection with the Harrisons, but she is included for completeness.

HARLINGEN (1909)
O.N. 127452 938g 545n
210.0 x 33.2 x 14.1 feet
T. 3-cyl. by Richardsons, Westgarth and Co. Ltd., Sunderland (16/27/44 x 30 inches); 105 NHP, 600 IHP, 9¼ knots.
12.11.1909: Launched by Osbourne, Graham and Co., Hylton, Sunderland (Yard No. 150) as HARLINGEN.

19.6.1911: Registered at West Hartlepool (8/1911) in the ownership of Furness, Withy and Co. Ltd., West Hartlepool as HARLINGEN.
3.7.1911: Register closed on sale to Friedrich Schulz, Memel, Germany.
8.6.1912: Registered at Leith (6/1912) in the ownership of G.V. Turnbull and Co. Ltd., Leith as PETER PAN.
23.9.1916: Sold to Furness, Withy and Co. Ltd., Liverpool.
17.8.1922: Register closed on sale to Rederi A/B Sirius (E.R. Killmann, manager), Helsingborg, Sweden and renamed SIRIUS.
9.4.1923: Registered at Newport (1/1923) in the ownership of Ensign Shipping Co. Ltd. (George J. Dunn, manager), Newport, Monmouthshire as NEWBURN.

27.1.1927: Register closed on sale to D/S A/S Als (A.M. Vollmund and N. Winther, managers), Copenhagen, Denmark as FEDDY.
1931: Management transferred to Aage Vollmund.
9.4.1940: At Grangemouth.
9.5.1940: Requisitioned by the Ministry of Shipping, London.
13.5.1940: Registered at London (123/1940) in the ownership of Ministry of Shipping (later Ministry of War Transport) (William Cory and Son Ltd., managers), London.
5.4.1942: Sunk in collision with the British armed trawler HMS VISENDA off North Ronaldsay whilst on a voyage from Thorshavn to Methil in ballast.
6.6.1942: Register closed.

The collier *Harlingen* in Furness Withy colours at Bristol. *[Roy Fenton collection]*

44. HARPAGUS (1) 1910-1917
O.N.129100 5,866g 3,672n
428.0 x 53.5 x 29.1 feet
T.3-cyl. by William Gray and Co. Ltd., West
Hartlepool (28/45/75 x 51 inches); 574 NHP,
2,700 IHP, 10 knots.
25.4.1910: Launched by William Gray and
Co. Ltd., West Hartlepool (Yard No.771) for
J. and C. Harrison Ltd., London.
8.6.1910: Registered at London (50/1910)
in the ownership of Charles W. Harrison as
HARPAGUS.
10.6.1910: Re-sold (50/64) to the builder.
30.4.1912: Re-purchased (50/64) from the
builder.
9.5.1917: Torpedoed and sunk
by the German submarine U 34 in the
Mediterranean 62 miles south west of Planier
Island while on a voyage from New York to
Marseilles with general cargo. Three of her
crew were lost, and the the master and chief
engineer were taken prisoner.
16.5.1917: Register closed.

45. HARPALION (1) 1910-1915
O.N.129152 5,867g 3,669n
428.0 x 53.5 x 29.1 feet
T.3-cyl. by William Gray and Co. Ltd., West
Hartlepool (28/45/75 x 51 inches); 574 NHP,
2,700 IHP, 10 knots.
4.10.1910: Launched by William Gray and
Co. Ltd., West Hartlepool (Yard No.779) for
J. and C. Harrison Ltd., London.
4.11.1910: Registered at London (109/1910)
in the ownership of Charles W. Harrison as
HARPALION.
15.11.1910: Re-sold (50/64) to the builder.
19.6.1912: Purchased back (50/64) from the
builder.
24.2.1915: Torpedoed and damaged by
the German submarine U 8 in the English
Channel 6½ miles west of the Royal
Sovereign Light Vessel while on a voyage
from London to Newport News in ballast.
26.2.1915: Foundered as a result of torpedo
damage 40 miles off Cap d'Antifer. Three of
her crew were lost.
5.3.1915: Register closed.

46. HARMATTAN (1) 1911-1917
O.N.129162 4,791g 3,046n
390.0 x 50.6 x 27.8 feet
T.3-cyl. Swan, Hunter and Wigham
Richardson Ltd., Wallsend-on-Tyne
(26/42½/70 x 48 inches); 510 NHP, 2,050
IHP, 10¾ knots.
30.11.1910: Launched by Swan, Hunter and
Wigham Richardson Ltd., Wallsend-on-Tyne
(Yard No.838) for J. and C. Harrison Ltd.,
London.
3.1.1911: Registered at London (3/1911) in
the ownership of Charles W. Harrison and
Charles S. Swan as HARMATTAN.
8.7.1912: Sold (64/64) to Charles W.
Harrison.
5.5.1917: Sank after striking a mine laid
by the German submarine UC 37 in the
Mediterranean 30 miles off Cape Bon while
on a voyage from Avonmouth and Gibraltar
to an Eastern Mediterranean port with a part

Sisters from William Gray and Co. Ltd. in 1910 were *Harpagus* (1) (above) and *Harpalion* (1) (below). *[Both: Nigel Farrell collection]*

In contrast to the long bridge deck design of the Hartlepool sisters above was the *Harmattan* (1), built by Swan, Hunter and Wigham Richardson Ltd. at Wallsend. *[Nigel Farrell collection]*

cargo of government stores. 42 members of
her crew were lost.
9.5.1917: Register closed.

47. HARPALYCE (1) 1911-1915
O.N.132551 5,940g 3,691n
428.0 x 53.5 x 29.1 feet
T.3-cyl. by William Gray and Co. Ltd., West

Hartlepool (28/45/75 x 51 inches); 574 NHP,
2,700 IHP, 10 knots.
1.5.1911: Launched by William Gray and
Co. Ltd., West Hartlepool (Yard No.789) for
J. and C. Harrison Ltd., London.
16.6.1911: Registered at London (64/1911)
in the ownership of Charles W. Harrison as
HARPALYCE.

Although dimensionally similar to *Harpagus* (1) and *Harpalion* (1), *Harpalyce* (1) had a distinctly different profile, her four masts making her look like contemporary German steamers. The lower photograph was taken

on trials. For such a short-lived steamer, she was well photographed, and a further photograph, taken just before her loss, appears on page 15. *[Roy Fenton collection; Nigel Farrell collection]*

17.6.1911: Re-sold (50/64) to the builder.
1.7.1912: Purchased back (50/64) from the builder.
10.4.1915: Torpedoed and sunk by the German submarine UB 4 in the North Sea seven miles east by south from the North Hinder Lightvessel while on a voyage from Rotterdam to the Tyne in ballast. 15 members of her crew were lost.
21.4.1915: Register closed.

48. CALYX/HARFIELD 1912-1914
O.N. 118110 3,465g 2,245n
340.6 x 46.1 x 25.9 feet
T.3-cyl. by John G. Kincaid and Co.,
Greenock (25/41/67 x 48 inches); 343 NHP,
2,000 IHP, 9½ knots.
27.6.1904: Launched by Russell and Co.,
Port Glasgow (Yard No.522) for the Hill
Steamship Co. Ltd. (Hugh Evans and Co.,
managers), Liverpool as HILLGROVE.

26.7.1904: Registered at Liverpool
(61/1904).
4.5.1907: Sold to the Phoenix Steamship Co.
Ltd. (Hoyland and Co., managers), London.
10.5.1907: Registered at London (74/1907)
as CALYX.
6.6.1907: Mortgaged to Charles W. Harrison
and Francis A. Beane.
13.11.1911: Management transferred to J.
and C. Harrison Ltd.

3.1.1912: Acquired from the mortgagees by Charles W. Harrison.
6.5.1912: Renamed HARFIELD.
5.1914: Sold to Pelli and Co. (Fortunato Pelli, manager), Genoa, Italy and renamed PRIMO.
30.5.1914: Register closed.
17.12.1916: Wrecked at Hormigas while on a voyage from Philadelphia to Genoa with general cargo.

49. HARMATRIS (1) 1912-1916
O.N.135160 4,863g 3,109n
410.2 x 52.0 x 27.9 feet
T.3-cyl. by Earle's Shipbuilding and Engineering Co. Ltd., Hull (28/46½/78 x 54 inches); 602 NHP, 3,000 IHP, 11½ knots.
9.10.1912: Launched by the Northumberland Shipbuilding Co. Ltd., Sunderland (Yard No.200) for J. and C. Harrison Ltd., London.
5.12.1912: Registered at London (207/1912) in the ownership of Charles W. Harrison as HARMATRIS.
8.3.1916: Torpedoed and sunk by the German submarine UB 18 in the English Channel ¼ mile north east by east from the Boulogne breakwater while on a voyage from St. John, New Brunswick to Le Havre and Boulogne with a cargo of oats and hay. Four lives were lost.
4.4.1916: Register closed.

50. HARPATHIAN (1) 1913-1918
O.N.135190 4,588g 2,870n
380.0 x 53.0 x 26.1 feet
T.3-cyl. by North Eastern Marine Engineering Co. Ltd., Sunderland (26/42/70 x 48 inches); 443 NHP, 2,000 IHP, 10 knots.
23.12.1912: Launched by the Sunderland Shipbuilding Co. Ltd., Sunderland (Yard No.274) for J. and C. Harrison Ltd., London.
14.2.1913: Registered at London (18/1913) in the ownership of Charles W. Harrison as HARPATHIAN.
5.6.1918: Torpedoed and sunk by the German submarine U 151 in the North Atlantic 80 miles off Cape Henry, Virginia while on a voyage from Plymouth to Newport News in ballast. The entire crew was saved.
11.7.1918: Register closed.

51. HARLOW (3) 1913-1914
O.N.135222 6,550g 4,108n
470.0 x 58.0 x 28.5 feet
T.3-cyl. William Doxford and Sons Ltd., Pallion, Sunderland (29/49/80 x 60 inches); 724 NHP, 3,600 IHP, 12¼ knots.
12.2.1913: Launched by William Doxford and Sons Ltd., Pallion, Sunderland (Yard No.453) for J. and C. Harrison Ltd., London.
10.5.1913: Registered at London

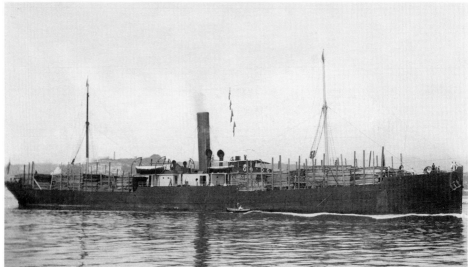

Hillgrove (upper) was renamed *Calyx* (middle) in 1907 and in 1912 acquired by Harrisons and renamed *Harfield*. *[Nigel Farrell collection; Kevin O'Donoghue collection]*

Harpathian (1). *[Nigel Farrell collection]*

(59/1913) in the ownership of Charles W. Harrison as HARLOW.
1.1914: Sold to Roland Linie A.G., Bremen, Germany and renamed GERNIS.
24.1.1914: Register closed.
8.1914: Laid up by owners at Sabang, Dutch East Indies for the duration of the war.
c12.1918: Transferred to the Netherlands as war reparations.
1919: Allocated to Nederlandsche-

Amerikaansche Stoomvaart Maatschappij, Rotterdam, Netherlands and renamed NOORDERDIJK.
1932: Sold to Fratelli Rizzuto, Genoa, Italy and renamed PROVVIDENZA.
22.9.1940: Torpedoed and sunk by the British submarine TRUANT in the Mediterranean 3½ miles south east of Punta Imperatore, Ischia while on a voyage from Naples to Cagliari.

Harlow (3) (above) and as the Dutch *Noorderdijk* (below). *[Nigel Farrell collection; World Ship Society Ltd.]*

Harflete. [Nigel Farrell collection]

52. HARFLETE 1913-1917

O.N.135224 4,814g 3,021n
390.0 x 50.5 x 28.1 feet
T.3-cyl. by John Dickinson and
Sons Ltd., Sunderland (26/43/71 x
48 inches); 401 NHP, 1,960 IHP, 11
knots.

8.3.1913: Launched by Bartram
and Sons Ltd., Sunderland (Yard
No.227) for J. and C. Harrison Ltd.,
London.

15.5.1913: Registered at London
(61/1913) in the ownership
of Charles W. Harrison as
HARFLETE.

26.4.1917: Torpedoed and sunk
by the German submarine U 70
200 miles north west by west of
the Fastnet Rock in position 51.54
north, 14.48 west while on a voyage
from Cienfuegos to Queenstown
with a cargo of sugar. One member
of the crew was lost.

4.6.1917: Register closed.

53. HARBURY (3) 1913-1917

O.N.135279 4,572g 2,778n
380.0 x 53.0 x 26.1 feet
T.3-cyl. by North Eastern Marine
Engineering Co. Ltd., Sunderland
(26/42/70 x 48 inches); 443 NHP,
2,000 IHP, 10 knots.

16.9.1913: Launched by the
Sunderland Shipbuilding Co. Ltd.,
Sunderland (Yard No.278) for J.
and C. Harrison Ltd., London.

17.10.1913: Registered at London
(137/1913) in the ownership of
Charles W. Harrison as HARBURY

9.6.1917: Torpedoed and sunk by the German submarine U 70 in the North Atlantic 170 miles west by half north of Ushant in position 47.47 north, 09.16 west while on a voyage from Buenos Aires to Cherbourg with a cargo of oats and maize. Twelve members of the crew were lost.
10.7.1917: Register closed.

54. HARLINGEN (3) (1914)
6,874g 4,262n
425.0 x 54.0 x 34.9 feet
T.3-cyl. by Blair and Co. Ltd. Stockton-on-Tees (28/46/75 x 51inches); 622 NHP, 10 knots.
12.2.1914: Launched by the Sunderland Shipbuilding Co. Ltd., Sunderland (Yard No.279) for Nederlandsche-Amerikaansche Stoomvaart Maatschappij (Holland-Amerika Lijn), Rotterdam, Netherlands as VEENDIJK.
She had been laid down for J. and C. Harrison Ltd., London as HARLINGEN.
4.1914: Completed.
3.1918: Requisitioned by the United States Government.
4.1918: Transferred to the United States Navy as Naval Overseas Transport Service No. 2515.
8.1919: Returned to owners.
1933: Broken up by Frank Rijsdijk's Industrie Onderneming at Hendrik-Ido-Ambacht during the second quarter.

55. AVONMEDE/HARPALION (2) 1925-1931
O.N.140284 4,240g 2,661n
390.0 x 53.3 x 23.5 feet
T.3-cyl. by John Dickinson and Sons Ltd., Sunderland (27/45/74 x 48 inches); 466 NHP, 2,270 IHP, 9¾ knots.

Harbury (3). [Nigel Farrell collection]

Above: the Dutch *Veendijk*, laid down for Harrisons and intended to be *Harlingen*. [Martin Lindenborn]
Below: *Avonmede* of D. and T.G. Adams was bought in 1925 and renamed *Harpalion* (2). [Nigel Farrell collection]

70

29.9.1916: Launched by William Pickersgill and Sons Ltd., Sunderland (Yard No.191) for Evan Thomas, Radcliffe and Co. Ltd., London. She had been laid down for the Newcastle Steamship Co. Ltd. (J. and C. Forster, managers), Newcastle-upon-Tyne.

14.1.1917: Registered at London (17/1917) in the ownership of the Swindon Steamship Co. Ltd., (Evan Thomas, Radcliffe and Co. Ltd., managers), Cardiff as SWINDON.

16.5.1917: Sold to the Johnston Line Ltd., Liverpool.

2.7.1917: Renamed COTTESMORE and registered at Liverpool (37/1917).

25.6.1920: Sold to the Mede Line Ltd. (D. and T. G. Adams, managers), Newcastle-upon-Tyne and subsequently renamed AVONMEDE.

19.12.1924: J. and C. Harrison Ltd appointed managers by the mortgagee, the Midland Bank Ltd.

2.4.1925: Acquired from the mortgagee by the Willis Steamship Co. Ltd. (J. and C. Harrison Ltd., managers), London.

9.4.1925: Registered at London (62/1925) as HARPALION.

10.1931: Sold to Livanos Brothers (N.G. Livanos, manager), Chios, Greece and renamed THEOFANO.

9.10.1931: Register closed.

1935: Transferred to Theofano Maritime Co. Ltd. (N.G. Livanos, manager), Piraeus, Greece.

1937: Sold to Vassilios J. Pateras, Chios and renamed DIRPHYS.

8.6.1941: Torpedoed and sunk by the German submarine U 108 in the North Atlantic in position 47.44 north, 39.02 west after dispersing from a convoy while on a voyage from Swansea to Montreal with a cargo of 6,152 tons of anthracite. Six members were lost from a crew of 25.

In 1925 *Shannonmede* became *Harpalyce* (2) (above) and in 1932 *Leonidas Z. Cambanis* (below). *[Roy Fenton collection; J. and M. Clarkson collection]*

56. SHANNONMEDE/ HARPALYCE (2) 1925-1931

O.N.140294 4,274g 2,671n
290.0 x 53.3 x 23.5 feet
T.3-cyl. by Richardsons, Westgarth and Co. Ltd., Hartlepool (27/45/74 x 48 inches); 475 NHP, 2,150 IHP, 10¼ knots.

17.2.1917: Launched by William Pickersgill and Sons Ltd., Sunderland (Yard No.193) for Evan Thomas, Radcliffe and Co. Ltd., London. She had been laid down for the Newcastle Steamship Co. Ltd. (J. and C. Forster, managers), Newcastle-upon-Tyne.

2.5.1917: Registered at London (89/1917) in the ownership of the Llanover Steamship Co. Ltd. (Evan Thomas, Radcliffe and Co. Ltd., managers), Cardiff as LLANOVER.

5.6.1917: Sold to the Johnston Line Ltd, Liverpool.

3.7.1917: Renamed LINMORE and registered at Liverpool (38/1917).

9.8.1920: Sold to the Canute Steamship Co. Ltd. (D. and T.G. Adams, managers), Newcastle-upon-Tyne and renamed SHANNONMEDE.

19.12.1924: J. and C. Harrison Ltd. appointed managers by the mortgagee, the Midland Bank Ltd.

2.4.1925: Acquired from the mortgagee by the Willis Steamship Co. Ltd. (J. and C. Harrison Ltd., managers), London.

9.4.1925: Registered at London (63/1925).

27.7.1925: Renamed HARPALYCE.

30.1.1929: Sold to the Edward Nicholl Steamship Co. Ltd., London.

1.2.1929: Renamed LITTLETON.

4.1932: Sold to the heirs of the late L.Z. Cambanis, Andros, Greece and renamed LEONIDAS Z. CAMBANIS.

8.4.1932: Register closed.

3.4.1941: Torpedoed and sunk by the German submarine U 74 in the North Atlantic in position 58.12 north, 27.40 west while on a voyage from Halifax, Nova Scotia to Swansea in convoy SC 26 with a cargo of 6,500 tons of wheat. Two were lost from a crew of 20.

57. CLYDEMEDE/HARPAGUS (2) 1925-1928

O.N.140549 4,269g 2,670n
390.0 x 53.3 x 23.5 feet
T.3-cyl. by John Dickinson and Sons Ltd., Sunderland (27/45/74 x 48 inches); 466 NHP, 2,270 IHP, 10 knots.

5.6.1917: Launched by William Pickersgill and Sons Ltd., Sunderland (Yard No.194) for Johnston Line Ltd., Liverpool as OAKMORE. She had been laid down for the Newcastle Steamship Co. Ltd. (J. and C. Forster, managers), Newcastle-upon-Tyne; sold on the stocks to Evan Thomas, Radcliffe and Co. Ltd., Cardiff; and then re-sold prior to launch.

3.12.1917: Registered at Liverpool (78/1917).

11.8.1920: Sold to the Canute Steamship Co. Ltd. (D. and T.G. Adams, managers), Newcastle-upon-Tyne.

12.8.1920: Renamed CLYDEMEDE.

19.12.1924: J. and C. Harrison Ltd. appointed managers by the mortgagee, the Midland Bank Ltd.

2.4.1925: Acquired from the mortgagee by the Willis Steamship Co. Ltd. (J. and C. Harrison Ltd., managers), London.

9.4.1925: Registered at London (64/1925).

13.5.1925: Renamed HARPAGUS.

Clydemede was another of the ships of D. and T.G. Adams acquired by Harrison after initially being managed by the company on behalf of the mortgagees, who took over the ships in 1924. She was renamed *Harpagus* (2) by Harrisons, and is seen entering Vancouver on Sunday 1st August 1926. *[J. and M. Clarkson]*

12.1928: Sold to D.A. Pateras, Chios, Greece and renamed MAROUKA PATERAS.

6.12.1928: Register closed.

1938: Owners became Anastassios Pateras and Sons, Chios.

3.11.1941: Stranded in fog on Double Island, Strait of Belle Isle, in position 52.15 north, 53.33 west while on a voyage from Probolingo via Cape Town and Sydney, Nova Scotia to Loch Ewe with a cargo of sugar.

5.11.1941: Refloated and sank two miles south west of Double Island.

58. NILEMEDE/HARMATTAN (2) 1925-1928

O.N.142713 4,453g 2,697n

375.6 x 51.7 x 26.5 feet

T.3-cyl. by Rankin and Blackmore Ltd., Greenock (27/44/73 x 48 inches); 518 NHP, 3,000 IHP, 11½ knots.

9.1918: Launched by Robert Duncan and Co. Ltd., Port Glasgow (Yard No.404) for the Shipping Controller, London (Lang and Fulton, Greenock, managers).

15.11.1918: Registered at London (413/1918) as WAR FANTAIL.

15.10.1919: Sold to the Brand-Adams Steamship Co. Ltd. (D. and T. G. Adams, managers), Newcastle-upon-Tyne.

25.10.1919: Renamed NILEMEDE.

19.12.1924: J. and C. Harrison Ltd. appointed managers by the mortgagee, the Midland Bank Ltd.

3.4.1925: Acquired from the mortgagee by the Willis Steamship Co. Ltd. (J. and C. Harrison Ltd., managers), London.

7.4.1925: Registered at London (60/1925).

17.7.1925: Renamed HARMATTAN.

12.5.1928: Sold to the Brynymor Steamship

Middle: *Harmattan* (2), formerly *War Fantail* and *Nilemede*. *[J. and M. Clarkson]*
Bottom and opposite top: two views of the *Lamington*, that above at Avonmouth, the other laid up on the Dart in 1932. *[J. and M. Clarkson; Roy Fenton collection]*

Co. Ltd., Swansea (Ambrose, Davies and Matthews, London, managers).

16.5.1928: Renamed DANYBRYN.

2.1931: Sold to Jadran Brodarsko d.d. (K. Polic, manager), Bakar, Yugoslavia and renamed JADRAN.

17.2.1931: Register closed.

1933: Sold to Société Misr de Navigation Maritime, Alexandria, Egypt and renamed ARAFAT.

1936: Sold to Carras Brothers, Chios, Greece and renamed FOTINI CARRAS.

7.6.1939: Wrecked on South Bellona Reefs in position 21.25 south, 159.34 east while on a voyage from New Caledonia to Bowen, Queensland and Europe with a cargo of chrome ore.

59. LAMINGTON 1929-1931

O.N. 124210 3,539g 2,283n

350.4 x 48.0 x 24.3 feet

T.3-cyl. by A. Rodger and Co., Port Glasgow (24/40/65 x 42 inches); 294 NHP, 1,700 IHP, 10 knots.

25.7.1907: Launched by A. Rodger and Co.,

Port Glasgow (Yard No.396) for J. Stevenson and Co., Glasgow.

15.8.1907: Registered at Glasgow (65/1907) in the ownership of the Lanarkshire Steamship Co. Ltd. (J. Stevenson and Co., managers), Glasgow as LAMINGTON.

20.8.1907: Mortgaged to the Clydesdale Bank Ltd., Glasgow.

18.8.1914: Mortgage discharged.

27.10.1916: Sold to the National Steamship Co. Ltd. (Fisher, Alimonda and Co. Ltd., managers), London.

10.11.1916: Mortgaged for £130,000 to the London and South Western Bank Ltd., London.

23.5.1929: Mortgage transferred to J. and C. Harrison Ltd., London.

1.6.1929: Management transferred to J. and C. Harrison Ltd., London.

13.3.1931: Mortgage discharged.

11.1931: Sold to T.N. Epiphaniades, Syra, Greece and renamed KONISTRA.

3.12.1931: Register closed.

29.4.1941: Beached after being bombed in Suda Bay Crete while on a voyage from Piraeus to Alexandria. Later refloated and

repaired by German salvors; re-entered service under control of Mittelmeer Reederei G.m.b.H.

8.1944: Found scuttled at Marseilles.

7.1945: Declared a constructive total loss.

8.2.1946: Refloated and beached.

12.7.1946: Left Marseilles under tow to be broken up at Fos.

60. FOTINIA 1929-1932

O.N. 133314 4,584g 2,835n

383.0 x 51.7 x 26.6 feet

T.3-cyl. by George Clark Ltd., Sunderland (26/42/71 x 48 inches); 431 NHP, 2,200 IHP, 10½ knots.

5.6.1913: Launched by William Pickersgill and Sons Ltd., Sunderland (Yard No.179) for Joseph Robinson and Sons, South Shields.

10.7.1913: Registered at North Shields (13/1913) in the ownership of Stag Line Ltd. (Joseph Robinson and Sons, managers), North Shields as PHOTINIA.

5.4.1917: Sold to the National Steamship Co. Ltd. (Fisher, Alimonda and Co. Ltd., managers), London.

11.4.1917: Mortgaged for £227,500 to the London and South Western Bank Ltd., London.

12.7.1917: Renamed FOTINIA.

23.5.1929: Mortgage transferred to J. and C. Harrison Ltd., London.

29.5.1929: Management transferred to J. and C. Harrison Ltd., London.

13.3.1931: Mortgage discharged.

12.1932: Sold to S. Perivolaris, Chios, Greece and renamed MARGARITIS.

22.12.1932: Register closed.

1939: Sold to Mrs A. Perry (S. Perivolaris, manager), Panama.

1941: Sold to Kokoku Kisen K.K., Kobe, Japan and renamed EIZAN MARU.

18.1.1942: Torpedoed and sunk by the submarine USS PLUNGER west of Shionomisaki, Honshu in position 33.30 north, 135 east.

Fotinia was, like *Lamington*, one of the few ships that Harrisons never renamed. *[World Ship Society Ltd.]*

Harberton survived the Second World War only to be damaged by a mine in early 1947. *[Ships in Focus]*

61. HARBERTON 1930-1951
O.N. 161432 4,585g 2,728n
400.0 x 54.5 x 24.6 feet
T.3-cyl. by George Clark Ltd., Sunderland (25/41/68 x 45 inches); 417 NHP, 2,200 IHP; 10¾ knots.
1957: Oil engine 8-cyl. 2SCSA by Mitsubishi Nippon Heavy Industries, Yokosuka, Japan (350mm x 520mm).
28.4.1930: Launched by Short Brothers Ltd., Sunderland (Yard No.442) for J. and C. Harrison Ltd., London.
2.6.1930: Registered at London (112/1930) in the ownership of the National Steamship Co. Ltd. (J. and C. Harrison Ltd., managers), London as HARBERTON.
25.5.1942: Transferred to J. and C. Harrison Ltd.

2.1.1947: Damaged by a mine in the Mediterranean in position 40.20 north, 24.05 east while on a voyage from Alexandria to Stratoni in ballast. Towed to Kavalia with ten feet of water in numbers 1, 2 and 3 holds. Temporary repairs were carried out at Piraeus and Messina before dry docking at Genoa.
1951: Sold to Meiji Kaiun K.K., Kobe, Japan and renamed MEISEI MARU.
19.6.1951: Register closed.
1952: Sold to Nichiro Gyogyo K.K., Tokyo, Japan.
1957: Converted to a motor vessel.
1960: Sold to Hokuyo Suisan K.K., Tokyo and renamed SHINYO MARU.
14.11.1965: Stranded and sank in heavy weather at Estori on the east coast of Sakhalin Island.

62. HARPATHIAN (2) 1930-1941
O.N. 161434 4,671g 2,775n
400.9 x 54.5 x 24.7
T.3-cyl. by North Eastern Marine Engineering Co. Ltd., Sunderland (25/41/68 x 45 inches); 408 NHP, 2,200 IHP, 10¾ knots.
29.4.1930: Launched by Bartram and Sons Ltd., Sunderland (Yard No.269) for J. and C. Harrison Ltd., London.
5.6.1930: Registered at London (120/1930) in the ownership of the National Steamship Co. Ltd. (J. and C. Harrison Ltd., managers), London as HARPATHIAN.
8.4.1941: Torpedoed and sunk by the German submarine U 107 in position 32.22 north, 22.53 west while on a voyage from the Tees and Clyde to West Africa with a cargo of RAF stores. Four were lost from a crew of 43.
13.9.1941: Register closed.

Harpathian (2) docks at Avonmouth. *[J. and M. Clarkson]*

63. HARMATTAN (3) 1930-1952

O.N. 161438 4,558g 2,709n
395.5 x 54.6 x 24.6 feet
T.3-cyl. by North Eastern Marine
Engineering Co. Ltd., Sunderland
(25/41/68 x 45 inches); 408 NHP, 2,200
IHP, 10¾ knots.
14.5.1930: Launched by Robert Thompson
and Sons Ltd., Sunderland (Yard No.338)
for J. and C. Harrison Ltd., London.
16.6.1930: Registered at London
(120/1930) in the ownership of the
National Steamship Co. Ltd. (J. and C.
Harrison Ltd., managers), London as
HARMATTAN.
20.10.1942: Transferred to J. and C.
Harrison Ltd.
12.12.1942: Severely damaged in Algiers
Harbour by underwater charges set by
frogmen from two-man maiale carried
by the Italian submarine AMBRA and
beached.
4.1943: Following temporary repairs at
Algiers, sailed for a permanent overhaul in
the United Kingdom.
2.1952: Sold to Willy H. Schlieker and
Co. Zweigniederlassung Hamburg (Robert
M. Sloman, junior, managers), Hamburg,
Germany and renamed MARGA.
13.3.1952: Register closed.
1957: Owner re-styled Reederei Willy H.
Schlieker and Co.
27.5.1960: Sold to Compania de
Navegacion Puerto Nueva, S.A., Panama
(Sebastiano Tuillier, Lugano, Switzerland).
1.11.1971: Arrived at Split to be broken up
by Brodospas.
15.1.1972: Demolition began.

64. HARPAGUS (3) 1930-1937

O.N. 161451 4,689g 2,857n
395.0 x 54.2 x 24.8 feet
T.3-cyl. by John Readhead and Sons Ltd.,
South Shields (25/41/68 x 45 inches); 435
NHP, 2,180 IHP; 10½ knots.
15.5.1930: Launched by John Readhead

Harmattan (3) (above) and as *Marga* (below), the letter T on the funnel indicating owner-ship by Sebastiano Tuillier. *[National Museum of Wales D1005702; Ships in Focus]*

Harpagus (3) (below). *[National Museum of Wales D1005706]*

and Sons Ltd., South Shields (Yard
No.502) for J. and C. Harrison Ltd.,
London.
1.7.1930: Registered at London
(133/1930) in the ownership of the
National Steamship Co. Ltd. (J. and C.
Harrison Ltd., managers), London as

HARPAGUS.
11.1937: Sold to Robert M. Sloman
Junior, Hamburg, Germany and renamed
SIZILIEN.
18.11.1937: Register closed.
4.5.1943: Bombed and sunk by RAF
aircraft off Terschelling.

Harperley (3) at Vancouver. *[Ships in Focus]*

65. HARPERLEY (3) 1930-1943
O.N. 161459 4,586g 2,744n
400.2 x 54.6 x 24.5 feet
T.3-cyl. by Central Marine Engine Works
(William Gray and Co. Ltd.), West
Hartlepool (25/41/68 x 45 inches); 425 NHP,
2,060 IHP; 10½ knots.
12.6.1930: Launched by William Gray and
Co. Ltd., West Hartlepool (Yard No.1041)
for J. and C. Harrison Ltd., London.
14.7.1930: Registered at London (141/1930)
in the ownership of the National Steamship
Co. Ltd. (J. and C. Harrison Ltd., managers),
London as HARPERLEY.
5.5.1943: Torpedoed and sunk by the
German submarine U 264 in the North
Atlantic in position 55.03 north, 42.58
west while on a voyage from Newport and
Milford Haven to Buenos Aires with a cargo
of 6,005 tons of coal and 200 bags of mail
in convoy ONS 5. Eleven members of her

crew were lost from a total of 49.
16.6.1943: Register closed.

66. HARMONIC (3) 1930-1943
O.N. 161490 4,558g 2,709n
395.5 x 54.6 x 24.6 feet
T.3-cyl. by North Eastern Marine
Engineering Co. Ltd., Sunderland (25/41/68
x 45 inches); 408 NHP, 2,200 IHP, 10¾
knots.
29.7.1930: Launched by Robert Thompson
and Sons Ltd., Sunderland (Yard No.339) for
J. and C. Harrison Ltd., London.
20.8.1930: Registered at London (173/1930)
in the ownership of the National Steamship
Co. Ltd. (J. and C. Harrison Ltd., managers),
London as HARMONIC.
15.7.1943: Torpedoed and sunk by the
German submarine U 172 in the South
Atlantic while on a voyage from Rosario and
Buenos Aires to Freetown and the UK with

a cargo of 7,368 tons of linseed oil. One
member of her crew of 47 was lost.
7.12.1943: Register closed.

67. HARPENDEN (3) 1930-1940
O.N. 162474 4,678g 2,774n
400.9 x 54.5 x 24.7 feet
T.3-cyl. by North Eastern Marine
Engineering Co. Ltd., Sunderland (25/41/68
x 45 inches); 408 NHP, 2,200 IHP, 10¾ knots.
1941: T.3-cyl. by John Brown and Co. Ltd.,
Clydebank (28½/37½/68 x 48 inches), 439
NHP, 11 knots.
29.7.1930: Launched by Bartram and Sons
Ltd., Sunderland (Yard No.270) for J. and C.
Harrison Ltd., London.
30.8.1930: Registered at London (177/1930)
in the ownership of the National Steamship
Co. Ltd. (J. and C. Harrison Ltd., managers),
London as HARPENDEN.
11.9.1940: Damaged by a torpedo from

Harmonic (3) arriving at Vancouver. *[J. and M. Clarkson]*

Harpenden (3). *[Ships in Focus]*

the German submarine U 28 in the North
Atlantic in position 55.34 north, 45.46
west while on a voyage from Hull to the
St. Lawrence River in ballast in convoy
OA.210. One member of the crew was
killed.
16.9.1940: Arrived in the Clyde under tow
and beached in Kilchattan Bay.
2.11.1940: Register closed. Moored in the
Gareloch until 19.11.1940; engines removed
and used for a new vessel.
20.8.1941: Hulk moved to Rothesay Bay
where it remained until it was moved to
Glasgow to be rebuilt. Stern rebuilt and
vessel re-engined by John Brown and Co.
Ltd., Clydebank.
15.12.1941: Re-registered under the
ownership of the Ministry of War Transport
(J. and C. Harrison Ltd., managers), London
as EMPIRE STOUR.
1946: Sold to Bharat Line Ltd., Bombay,

India and renamed BHARATJAL.
1.7.1948: British register closed following
Indian independence.
1957: Sold to Linea Adriatico Golfo Persa
Ltda., Monrovia, Liberia (C.A. Petroutsis,
Trieste, Italy) and renamed AL RIYADH.
1958: Renamed SPETSAI PATRIOT.
29.6.1963: Arrived at Split to be broken up
by Brodospas.

68. HARPALYCE (3) 1930-1937
O.N. 162484 4,708g 2,824n
395.0 x 54.3 x 24.6 feet
T.3-cyl. by John Readhead and Sons Ltd.,
South Shields (25/41/68 x 45 inches); 435
NHP, 2,180 IHP; 10½ knots.
12.8.1930: Launched by John Readhead and
Sons Ltd., South Shields (Yard No.503) for
J. and C. Harrison Ltd., London.
15.9.1930: Registered at London (188/1930)
in the ownership of the National Steamship

Co. Ltd. (J. and C. Harrison Ltd., managers),
London as HARPALYCE.
10.1937: Sold to N.V. Stoomvaart
Maatschappij 'Oostzee' (Vinke and Co,
managers), Amsterdam, Netherlands and
renamed LOPPERSUM.
26.10.1937: Register closed.
5.1940: Seized by the Germans at
Rotterdam, served as the transport/
accommodation ship Ro.1 and VB.3.
8.1945: Recovered at the end of the war.
11.1945: Returned to service.
1956: Sold to F. Italo Croce S.p.A., Genoa,
Italy and renamed LUISITA CROCE.
28.1.1960: Struck submerged object and
stranded about five miles west of Cape
Palmas in position 04.25 north, 07.49 west
while on a voyage from Naples to Takoradi,
with general cargo and cement.
30.1.1960: Wreck submerged and breaking
up.

Harpalyce (3) *[Ships in Focus]*

The newly-built *Harpalion* (3) on the Thames, 2nd September 1932. Judging by the poor survival of images of her, she was the least frequently photographed of the Harrison ships of the 1930s. *[R. Snook/F.W. Hawks]*

69. HARPALION (3) 1932-1942
O.N. 162707 5,486g 3,220n
427.7 x 56.3 x 26.1 feet
T.3-cyl. by North Eastern Marine
Engineering Co. Ltd., Wallsend-on-Tyne
(23.5/40/68 x 48 inches); 408 NHP, 2,200
IHP, 10½ knots.
6.4.1932: Launched by R. and W. Hawthorn
Leslie Co. Ltd., Hebburn-on-Tyne (Yard
No.585) for J. and C. Harrison Ltd., London.
10.5.1932: Registered at London (47/1932)
as HARPALION.
13.4.1942: Sunk by gunfire from a naval
escort after being bombed and badly
damaged by German Ju-88 aircraft in the
Arctic Sea in position 73.33 north, 29.19
east while on a voyage from Murmansk
to Reykjavik with a cargo of 600 tons of
manganese ore in convoy QP.10. The entire
crew of 52 and 18 Distressed British Seamen
were saved.
11.6.1942: Register closed.

70. HARMATRIS (2) 1932-1951
O.N. 162711 5,395g 3,195n
428.0 x 56.3 x 26.0 feet
T.3-cyl. by David Rowan and Co. Ltd.,
Glasgow (25/43/72 x 48 inches); 502 NHP,
2,200 IHP, 11 knots.
1960: Oil engine 6-cyl. 2SCSA by Kobe
Hatsudoki Seizosho, Kobe, Japan (520 x
1050 mm).
20.4.1932: Launched by Lithgows Ltd.,
Port Glasgow (Yard No.853) for the Willis
Steamship Co. Ltd. (J. and C. Harrison Ltd.,
managers), London.
12.5.1932: Registered at London (51/1932)
as HARMATRIS.
17.1.1942: Torpedoed by the German
submarine U 454 in the Arctic Sea in
position 16.00 north, 38.08 east while on
a voyage from Glasgow and Reykjavik to
Archangel in convoy PQ 8 with a cargo of
military stores.
20.1.1942: Towed into Archangel.
13.9.1942: Sailed for the UK after
temporary repairs in convoy QP.14.

4.12.1944: Transferred to J. and C.
Harrison Ltd., London.
24.9.1951: Sold to Wheelock, Marden and
Co. Ltd., Hong Kong.
27.9.1951: Renamed CHOKO.
5.1952: Sold to Sanko Kisen K.K.,
Amagasaki, Japan and renamed CHOKO
MARU.
31.5.1952: Register closed.
1955: Sold to Hakodate Kokai Gyogyo
K.K., Hakodate, Japan.
1960: Converted to a motor ship.
11.4.1964: Breaking up commenced at
Shodoshima, Kagawa Prefecture.

71. HARTINGTON (2) 1932-1942
O.N. 162716 5,496g 3,243n
425.5 x 56.3 x 26.0 feet
Q.4-cyl. by Central Marine Engine
Works (William Gray and Co. Ltd.), West
Hartlepool (20/25½/41½/61 x 48 inches);
470 NHP, 2,410 IHP, 11 knots.
21.4.1932: Launched by William Gray and
Co. Ltd., West Hartlepool (Yard No.1041)
for J. and C. Harrison Ltd., London.
2.6.1932: Registered at London (57/1932)
as HARTINGTON.
2.11.1942: Torpedoed and damaged by

the German submarine U 522 in the North
Atlantic in position 52.30 north, 45.30 west
while on a voyage from Halifax to Belfast
with a cargo of 8,000 tons of wheat and
six 30-ton tanks in convoy SC.107. Ship
subsequently torpedoed by U 438 then
torpedoed and sunk by U 521. Of the crew
of 47, 24 were lost.
19.5.1943: Register closed.

72. HARMANTEH 1932-1938
O.N. 162723 5,415g 3,243n
428.0 x 56.3 x 26.0 feet
T.3-cyl. by David Rowan and Co. Ltd.,
Glasgow (25/43/72 x 48 inches); 502 NHP,
2,200 IHP, 11 knots.
24.5.1932: Launched by Lithgows Ltd.,
Port Glasgow (Yard No.854) for J. and C.
Harrison, London.
18.6.1932: Registered at London (67/1932)
in the ownership of the Willis Steamship Co.
Ltd. (J. and C. Harrison Ltd., managers),
London as HARMANTEH.
22.5.1938: Wrecked on Zealous Island,
Messier Channel in the Gulf of Penas,
Chile while on a voyage from Santos to San
Francisco in ballast.
29.7.1938: Register closed.

73. HARLESDEN (2) 1932-1941
O.N. 162738 5,483g 3,219n
427.7 x 56.3 x 26.4 feet
T.3-cyl. by North Eastern Marine
Engineering Co. Ltd., Wallsend-on-Tyne
(23.5/40/68 x 48 inches); 408 NHP, 2,200
IHP, 10½ knots.
2.6.1932: Launched by R. and W. Hawthorn
Leslie Co. Ltd., Hebburn-on-Tyne (Yard
No.586) for J. and C. Harrison Ltd.,
London.
19.7.1932: Registered at London (83/1932)
as HARLESDEN.
22.2.1941: Shelled and sunk in the Central
Atlantic in position 47.12 north, 40.18 west
by the German battlecruiser GNEISENAU
while proceeding independently after
dispersal of convoy on a voyage from Hull,
Oban and Glasgow to New York in ballast.
Seven of her crew were lost and 34 taken as
prisoners of war.
13.10.1941: Register closed.

Harmatris (2) at a South African port. *[Ships in Focus]*

Top: *Hartington* (2), the flrsl Harrison ship with quadruple-expansion engines, docks at Avonmouth. *[J. and M. Clarkson]*

Harrison ships were frequent visitors to Vancouver in the 1930s, almost invariably loading timber. The photograph (middle) is an undated one of *Harmanteh* sailing, bottom is *Harlesden* (2) on 26th July 1933. *[J. and M. Clarkson (2)]*

Above: *Harborough* (1) in 1933. *[Ships in Focus]*.
Below: *Hartlepool*, which was fittingly built and engined at West Hartlepool. *[Russell Priest]*.

74. HARBOROUGH (1) 1932-1942

O.N. 162745 5,415g 3,205n
428.0 x 56.3 x 26.0 feet
T.3-cyl. by David Rowan and Co. Ltd.,
Glasgow (25/43/72 x 48 inches); 502 NHP,
2,200 IHP, 11 knots
22.6.1932: Launched by Lithgows Ltd.,
Port Glasgow (Yard No.856) for J. and C.
Harrison Ltd., London.
15.8.1932: Registered at London (90/1932)
in the ownership of the Willis Steamship Co.
Ltd. (J. and C. Harrison Ltd., managers),
London as HARBOROUGH.

6.11.1940: Bombed by German aircraft in
the North Sea in position 59.35 north, 02.53
west while on a voyage from Bahia Blanca
to Hull in convoy WN.31 with a cargo of
wheat in bulk. Abandoned on fire and towed
into Scapa Flow.
5.12.1940: Arrived on the Tyne for repairs.
14.9.1942: Shelled, torpedoed and sunk
by the German submarine U 515 60 miles
off Tobago in position 10.30 north, 60.20
west while on a voyage from Buenos Aires
and Rio de Janeiro to Trinidad and New
York with 8,000 tons of general cargo and

2,000 bags of mail. Five were lost from a
complement of 52, including one passenger.
1.4.1943: Register closed.

75. HARTLEPOOL 1932-1951

O.N. 162716 5,500g 3,262n
425.5 x 56.3 x 26.0 feet
Q.4-cyl. by Central Marine Engine
Works (William Gray and Co. Ltd.), West
Hartlepool (20/25½/41½/61 x 48 inches);
470 NHP, 2,410 IHP, 11 knots
1958: Oil engine 8-cyl. 4SCSA by Ito
Tekkosho, Shimizu, Japan (400 x 580 mm).
19.7.1932: Launched by William Gray and
Co. Ltd., West Hartlepool (Yard No.1054)
for J. and C. Harrison Ltd., London
9.9.1932: Registered at London (107/1932)
as HARTLEPOOL.
5.7.1940: Torpedoed by the German E-boat
S 26 16 miles south south west of Portland
Bill while on a voyage from the Tyne to
Sydney, Nova Scotia in ballast and beached
at Weymouth. Three members of the crew
were killed. Forepart refloated and towed to
Southampton; a new after-part fitted in 1941.
15.11.1951: Sold to Wheelock, Marden and
Co. Ltd., Hong Kong.
27.11.1951: Renamed ZUIKO.
1952: Sold to Sanko Kisen K.K.,
Amagasaki, Japan and renamed ZUIKO
MARU.
1958: Converted to a motor ship.
1961: Sold to Nippon Kisen K.K., Tokyo,
Japan.
1966: Sold to S. Maeda, Wakayama, Japan.
17.1.1968: Stranded off Yakeyama Saki,
Aomori while on a voyage from Toyama
to Nakhodka. The wreck was broken up in
situ.

76. HARLINGEN (4) 1933-1941

O.N. 163305 5,415g 3,205n
428.0 x 56.3 x 26.0 feet
T.3-cyl. by David Rowan and Co. Ltd.,
Glasgow (25/43/72 x 48 inches); 502 NHP,
2.200 IHP, 11 knots.

In another superb pictorial view, *Harlingen* (4) sails from Vancouver. Unlike previous ships named *Harlingen*, she was not sold on the stocks. *[J. and M. Clarkson]*

Hartismere (1) loading timber in Vancouver. *[Ships in Focus]*

17.11.1932: Launched by Lithgows Ltd., Port Glasgow (Yard No.857) for J. and C. Harrison Ltd., London.
2.1.1933: Registered at London (1/1933) in the ownership of the Willis Steam Ship Co. Ltd. (J. and C. Harrison Ltd., managers), London as HARLINGEN.
5.8.1941: Torpedoed and sunk by the German submarine U 75 in position 53.26 north, 15.40 west while on a voyage from Lagos and Freetown to Liverpool with a cargo of 8,000 tons of West African produce in convoy SL.81. Two were lost from her crew of 44.
28.10.1941: Register closed.

77. HARTISMERE (1) 1933-1942
O.N. 162716 5,498g 3,260n
425.5 x 56.3 x 26.0 feet
Q. 4-cyl. by Central Marine Engine Works (William Gray and Co. Ltd.), West Hartlepool (20/25½/41½/61 x 48 inches); 470 NHP, 2,410 IHP, 11 knots.
30.11.1932: Launched by William Gray and Co. Ltd., West Hartlepool (Yard No.1055) for J. and C. Harrison Ltd., London.
13.1.1933: Registered at London (5/1933) as HARTISMERE.
27.8.1940: Torpedoed and damaged by the German submarine U 100 in the North Atlantic in position 56.04 north, 12.0 west while on a voyage from Hull to Trois Rivieres in ballast in convoy OA.204. *31.8.1940:* Arrived in the Clyde under her own power.
8.7.1942: Torpedoed, shelled and sunk by the Japanese submarine I-10 in the Indian Ocean in position 18.00 south, 41.22 east while on a voyage from Philadelphia and Lourenco Marques to Alexandria with 8,000 tons of general cargo. Her entire crew of 47 was saved.
17.10.1942: Register closed.

78. HARDINGHAM (1) 1933-1940
O.N. 163310 5,415g 3,208n
428.0 x 56.3 x 26.0 feet
T.3-cyl. by David Rowan and Co. Ltd., Glasgow (25/43/72 x 48 inches); 502 NHP, 2,200 IHP, 11 knots.
15.12.1932: Launched by Lithgows Ltd., Port Glasgow (Yard No.858) for J. and C. Harrison Ltd., London.
24.1.1933: Registered at London (8/1933) in the ownership of the Willis Steamship Co. Ltd. (J. and C. Harrison Ltd., managers), London as HARDINGHAM.
8.6.1940: Mined off the Thames Estuary in position 51.34 north, 01.37 east and subsequently sunk at 51.59 north, 01.40 east while on a voyage from Blyth to Villa Constitucion with a cargo of 7,375 tons of coal. Two were lost from a crew of 38.
13.6.1940: Register closed.

A fine view of *Hardingham* (1) at Beira in January 1939. *[Ships in Focus]*

79. HARBLEDOWN 1933-1941
O.N. 163310 5,414g 3,207n
428.0 x 56.3 x 26.0 feet
T.3-cyl. by David Rowan and Co. Ltd.,
Glasgow (25/43/72 x 48 inches); 502 NHP,
2,200 IHP, 11 knots.
27.3.1933: Launched by Lithgows Ltd.,
Port Glasgow (Yard No.861) for J. and C.
Harrison Ltd., London.
24.4.1933: Registered at London
(42/1933) in the ownership of the
National Steamship Co. Ltd. (J. and C.
Harrison Ltd., managers), London as
HARBLEDOWN.
4.4.1941: Torpedoed and sunk by the
German submarine U 94 in the North
Atlantic in position 58.30 north, 23.20
west while on a voyage from Portland,
Maine to London with a cargo of 94,157
bushels of wheat in convoy SC.26. 16
members of her crew of 39 were lost.
1.5.1941: Register closed.

80. HARBURY (4) 1933-1943
O.N. 163399 5,081g 3,033n
418.0 x 56.3 x 24.6 feet
T.3-cyl. by David Rowan and Co. Ltd.,
Glasgow (22½/36/65 x 48 inches); 444 NHP,
2,000 IHP, 11 knots.
18.9.1933: Launched by Lithgows Ltd., Port
Glasgow (Yard No.862) for J. and C. Harrison
Ltd., London.
21.10.1933: Registered at London (123/1933)
in the ownership of the National Steamship
Co. Ltd. (J. and C. Harrison Ltd., managers),
London as HARBURY.
29.10.1942: Transferred to J. and C. Harrison
Ltd., London.
5.5.1943: Torpedoed and damaged by the
German submarine U 628 in the North
Atlantic in position 55.10 north, 42.59 west
after straggling from convoy ONS.5 while on
a voyage from Swansea and Milford Haven
to St. John, New Brunswick with a cargo
of 6,129 tons of coal. The abandoned and

derelict ship was subsequently torpedoed and
sunk by U 264. Seven members of her crew
of 50 were lost.
16.6.1943: Register closed.

81. HARCALO (3) 1933-1940
O.N. 163410 5,081g 3,033n
418.0 x 56.3 x 24.6 feet
T.3-cyl. by David Rowan and Co. Ltd.,
Glasgow (22½/36/65 x 48 inches); 444 NHP,
2,000 IHP, 11 knots
18.10.1933: Launched by Lithgows Ltd., Port
Glasgow (Yard No.863) for J. and C. Harrison
Ltd., London.
15.11.1933: Registered at London (136/1933)
in the ownership of the National Steamship
Co. Ltd. (J. and C. Harrison Ltd., managers),
London as HARCALO.
6.6.1940: Mined in the Thames Estuary while
on a voyage from Benisaf to London with
a cargo of 7,500 tons of iron ore. She was
beached three cables north west of the Gull

Above: *Harbledown* sails from Cape Town. *[Ships in Focus]*
Bottom: Also photographed at the Cape is *Harbury* (4). *[Ships in Focus]*

other Indian produce. Six were lost from a crew of 39.

24.9.1942: Register closed.

83. HARTLEBURY 1934-1942

O.N. 163443 5,082g 3,036n

418.0 x 56.3 x 24.6 feet

T.3-cyl. by David Rowan and Co. Ltd., Glasgow (22½/36/65 x 48 inches); 444 NHP, 2,000 IHP, 11 knots.

30.1.1934: Launched by Lithgows Ltd., Port Glasgow (Yard No.865) for J. and C. Harrison Ltd., London.

26.2.1934: Registered at London (17/1934) in the ownership of the National Steamship Co. Ltd. (J. and C. Harrison Ltd., managers), London as HARTLEBURY.

6.7.1942: Torpedoed and sunk by the German submarine U 355 in the Arctic Sea 17 miles south of Britwin Lighthouse, Nova Zembla in position 70.17 north, 56.10 east after dispersing from convoy PQ 17 while on a voyage from Sunderland and Reykjavik to North Russia with a cargo of 3,200 tons of military stores. 38 of her crew of 56 were lost.

25.11.1942: Register closed.

Buoy in position 51.19 north, 1.30 east and broke in two. The wreck was subsequently dispersed. Three were lost from a crew of 39.

13.6.1940: Register closed.

82. HARPASA 1934-1942

O.N. 163434 5,082g 3,036n

418.0 x 56.3 x 24.6 feet

T.3-cyl. by David Rowan and Co. Ltd., Glasgow (22½/36/65 x 48 inches); 444 NHP, 2,000 IHP, 11 knots.

5.12.1933: Launched by Lithgows Ltd., Port Glasgow (Yard No.864) for J. and C. Harrison Ltd., London.

12.1.1934: Registered at London (5/1934) in the ownership of the National Steamship Co. Ltd. (J. and C. Harrison Ltd., managers), London as HARPASA.

5.4.1942: Bombed and sunk by B5N bombers from the Imperial Japanese aircraft carrier RYUJO in the Indian Ocean in position 19.19 north, 85.46 east while on a voyage from Calcutta to Mombasa with 7,240 tons of general cargo, including gunnies, rice and

Top: Harcalo (3). [A. Hardwicke/Kevin O'Donoghue collection]

Above: Harpasa in the Mersey. [Basil Feilden/J. and M. Clarkson]

Right: Hartlebury approaching Avonmouth. [J. and M. Clarkson]

84. HARPAGON (1) 1935-1942

O.N. 163488 5,719g 3,378n
428.0 x 58.3 x 26.1 feet
T.3-cyl. by David Rowan and Co. Ltd.,
Glasgow (23½/37½/68 x 48 inches); 475
NHP, 2,120 IHP, 11 knots.
22.4.1935: Launched by Lithgows Ltd.,
Port Glasgow (Yard No.874) for J. and C.
Harrison Ltd., London.
6.6.1935: Registered at London (95/1935)
in the ownership of the National Steamship
Co. Ltd. (J. and C. Harrison Ltd., managers),
London as HARPAGON.
22.4.1937: Transferred to the Gowland
Steamship Co. Ltd. (J. and C. Harrison Ltd.,
managers), London.
20.4.1942: Torpedoed and sunk by the
German submarine U 109 150 miles north
north west of Bermuda in position 34.35
north, 65.50 west while on a voyage from
New York to Table Bay and Bombay with
a cargo of 2,602 tons of explosives and
5,415 tons general cargo including tanks and
aircraft. 41 were lost from a crew of 49.
18.11.1942: Register closed.

85. HARMALA 1935-1943

O.N. 164536 5,730g 3,382n
433.2 x 58.3 x 26.1 feet
T.3-cyl. by David Rowan and Co. Ltd.,
Glasgow (23/37½/68 x 48 inches); 475 NHP,
2,120 IHP, 11 knots.
15.8.1935: Launched by Lithgows Ltd.,
Port Glasgow (Yard No.875) for J. and C.
Harrison Ltd., London.
20.9.1935: Registered at London (154/1935)
the Gowland Steamship Co. Ltd. (J. and
C. Harrison Ltd., managers), London as
HARMALA.
7.2.1943: Torpedoed and sunk by the
German submarine U 614 in the North
Atlantic in position 55.14 north, 26.37
west while on a voyage from Rio de
Janeiro, Trinidad, New York and Halifax to

With *Harpagon* (1) the time-honoured long-bridge-deck design was abandoned.
[Ships in Focus]

Middlesbrough with a cargo of 8,500 tons
of iron ore in convoy SC 118. 40 were lost
from her crew of 53.
10.4.1943: Register closed.

86. HARPALYCUS (1) 1935-1956

O.N. 164552 5,629g 3,344n
434.6 x 58.3 x 26.0 feet
T.3-cyl. by North Eastern Marine
Engineering Co. Ltd., Wallsend-on-Tyne
(23½/40/68 x 48 inches); 471 NHP, 1,800
IHP, 10½ knots.
26.9.1935: Launched by R. and W.
Hawthorn Leslie Co. Ltd., Hebburn-on-Tyne
(Yard No.597) for J. and C. Harrison Ltd.,
London.
9.11.1935: Registered at London (173/1935)
in the ownership of the Gowland Steamship
Co. Ltd. (J. and C. Harrison Ltd., managers),
London as HARPALYCUS.
30.9.1936: Transferred to the National
Steamship Co. Ltd. (J. and C. Harrison Ltd.,
managers), London.
12.3.1942: Transferred back to the Gowland
Steamship Co. Ltd. (J. and C. Harrison Ltd.,
managers), London.
2.1956: Sold to Salamis Shipping Co.

Ltd. (Tsavliris (Hellas) Maritime Co. Ltd.,
managers), Piraeus, Greece and renamed
GEORGIOS TSAVLIRIS.
23.2.1956: Register closed.
1964: Transferred to Trafalgar Shipping Co.
Ltd. (Tsavliris Shipping Ltd., managers),
London and renamed NEWMEADOW.
1965: Transferred to Kantara Shipping Ltd.,
Famagusta, Cyprus (Tsavliris Shipping Ltd.,
London, managers).
22.11.1966: Sprang a leak while on a voyage
from Haifa to Sibenik with a cargo of
phosphates and foundered the next day about
18 miles from Kassos Island in position
35.07 north, 27.18 east.

87. HARPAGUS (4) 1940-1941

O.N. 167421 5,173g 2,980n
437.0 x 58.5 x 25.1 feet
T.3-cyl. by North Eastern Marine Engineering
Co. Ltd., Sunderland (23½/38/66 x 45
inches); 470 NHP, 2,150 IHP, 10½ knots.
27.11.1939: Launched by Bartram and Sons
Ltd., Sunderland (Yard No.282) for J. and C.
Harrison Ltd., London.
3.4.1940: Registered at London (61/1940) as
HARPAGUS.

Harmala. [Ships in Focus]

Harpalycus (1) at Cape Town in 1955 (above) and at Durban (below). *[Ships in Focus; J. and M. Clarkson collection]*

20.5.1941: Torpedoed and sunk by the German submarine U 109 south east of Cape Farewell in position 56.47 north, 40.55 west while on a voyage from Baltimore and Halifax to Barry Roads with a cargo of 8,250 tons of grain in convoy HX.126. A total of 58 lives were lost from her complement of 76, which included three passengers and 26 survivors from the NORMAN MONARCH (4,718/1937).

27.10.1941: Register closed.

88. HARPALYCE (4) 1940
O.N. 167592 5,169g 2,977n
437.0 x 58.5 x 25.1 feet
T.3-cyl. by North Eastern Marine Engineering Co. Ltd., Sunderland (23½/38/66 x 45 inches); 470 NHP, 2,150 IHP, 10½ knots.
22.3.1940: Launched by Bartram and Sons Ltd., Sunderland (Yard No.283) for J. and C. Harrison Ltd., London.
19.6.1940: Registered at London (268/1940) as HARPALYCE.
25.8.1940: Torpedoed and sunk by the German submarine U 124 north west of the Orkney Islands in position 58.52 north, 06.34 west while on a voyage from Baltimore and Halifax to Hull with a cargo of 8,000 tons of steel in convoy HX. 65A. From her crew of 47, 37 lives were lost

The short-lived Harpalyce (4) completing at Sunderland. *[J. and M. Clarkson collection]*

19.10.1940: Register closed.

89. HARDINGHAM (2) 1942-1944
O.N.168314 7,269g 5,041n
428.8 x 56.5 x 35.5 feet
Oil engine 3-cyl. 2SCDA by William Doxford and Sons Ltd., Pallion, Sunderland (600mm x 2,320mm); 2,500 BHP, 12 knots.
1.6.1942: Launched by William Doxford and Sons Ltd., Pallion, Sunderland (Yard No.692) for J. and C. Harrison Ltd., London.
9.9.1942: Registered at London (94/1942) in the ownership of the Willis Steamship Co.

Hardingham (2) was completed in 1942, but sold in 1944. She is seen in Liverpool. *[National Maritime Museum G3895]*

Ltd. (J. and C. Harrison Ltd., managers), London as HARDINGHAM.

13.12.1944: Sold to the Hain Steamship Co. Ltd., London.

5.4.1945: Caught fire and abandoned in Colombo Outer Anchorage after an accident re-lighting donkey boilers while on a voyage from New York to Calcutta with a cargo of explosives and general. Blew up and sank in position 06.59 north, 79.49 east.

22.6.1945: Register closed.

90. HARPALYCE (5) 1942-1944

O.N.168334 7,269g 5,042n
428.8 x 56.5 x 35.5 feet
Oil engine 3-cyl. 2SCDA by William Doxford and Sons Ltd., Pallion, Sunderland (600mm x 2,320mm); 2,500 BHP, 12 knots.

30.6.1942: Launched by William Doxford and Sons Ltd., Pallion, Sunderland (Yard No.694) for J. and C. Harrison Ltd., London.

23.10.1942: Registered at London (123/1942) in the ownership of the National Steamship Co. Ltd. (J. and C. Harrison Ltd., managers), London as HARPALYCE.

30.11.1944: Sold to the Hain Steamship Co. Ltd., London.

18.7.1946: Renamed TREWELLARD.

17.12.1956: Transferred to the Peninsular and Oriental Steam Navigation Company, London.

6.2.1958: Transferred to the Hain Steamship Co. Ltd., London.

10.1962: Sold to Santa Marina Compania Maritima S.A. (N.E. Vernicos Shipping Company, managers), Piraeus, Greece and renamed ARTEMON.

15.10.1962: Register closed.

1.11.1965: Caught fire off Piraeus while on a voyage from Cebu to Rotterdam with a cargo of copra.

6.11.1965: Beached in Ambelaki Bay.

8.11.1965: Fire extinguished. Later abandoned to the underwriters as a constructive total loss.

8.10.1866: Arrived in tow at Valencia to be broken up by Desguaces Incolesa.

12.1966: Demolition began.

91. HARPAGUS (5) 1942-1944

O.N.168347 7,269g 5,042n
428.8 x 56.5 x 35.5 feet
Oil engine 3-cyl. 2SCDA by William Doxford and Sons Ltd., Pallion, Sunderland (600mm x 2,320mm); 2,500 BHP, 12 knots

28.8.1942: Launched by William Doxford and Sons Ltd., Pallion, Sunderland (Yard No.695) for J. and C. Harrison Ltd., London.

25.11.1942: Registered at London (140/1942) in the ownership of the National Steamship Co. Ltd. (J. and C. Harrison Ltd, managers), London as HARPAGUS.

15.5.1944: Sold to the Hain Steamship Co. Ltd., London.

19.8.1944: Mined one and a half miles north of the West Breakwater, Arromanches, Normandy while on a voyage from Southend to Arromanches with a cargo of military stores. The forepart sank, but the afterpart was towed to Southampton for discharge.

Harpalyce (5), above in war rig, was sold in 1944, to become Hain's *Trewellard*, seen below in peacetime colours. *[Nigel Farrell collection; Fotoflite incorporating Skyfotos 6090]*

Under Hain's ownership *Harpagus* is seen (above) at Southampton after being mined near Arromanches. Repaired, she was renamed *Treworlas* in 1946 (below). *[J. and M. Clarkson collection (2)]*

Her master died but the remaining crew of 62 was saved.

1.12.1944: Arrived on the Tyne in tow after grounding on West Barrow Sand and then being beached off Sheerness for removal of overhanging wreckage.

5.1946: New forepart launched and joined to the vessel.

13.9.1946: Renamed TREWORLAS.

30.11.1956: Transferred to the Peninsular and Oriental Steam Navigation Company, London.

12.2.1958: Transferred to the Hain Steamship Co. Ltd., London.

21.9.1960: Arrived at Briton Ferry to be broken up by Thomas W. Ward Ltd.

26.6.1961: Register closed.

92. HARLESDEN (3) 1943-1944
O.N.168406 7,273g 5,339n
428.8 x 56.5 x 35.5 feet
Oil engine 3-cyl. 2SCDA by William Doxford and Sons Ltd., Pallion, Sunderland (600mm x 2,320mm); 2,500 BHP, 12 knots.

23.10.1942: Launched by William Doxford and Sons Ltd., Pallion, Sunderland (Yard No.699) for J. and C. Harrison Ltd., London.

9.3.1943: Registered at London (41/1943) as HARLESDEN.

18.2.1944: Sold to the Hain Steamship Co. Ltd., London.

17.11.1945: Renamed TREWIDDEN.

21.4.1959: Sold to the Black Star Line Ltd., Accra, Ghana.

21.4.1959: Register closed; vessel re-registered at Takoradi as ANKOBRA RIVER.

1964: Sold to the Tenes Shipping Co. S.A. Panama (G.C. Calafatis and Co., Piraeus, Greece, managers) and renamed ELAND under the Liberian flag.

29.10.1968: Arrived at Kaohsiung to be broken up by Tien Cheng Manufacturing Co. Ltd.

Harlesden (3) in wartime (above) and following sale to Hains and renaming *Trewidden* (below). *[Nigel Farrell collection; Fotoflite incorporating Skyfotos 7865]*

93. HARTINGTON (3) 1945-1962
O.N.180756 7,325g 4,755n
429.0 x 56.5 x 35.5 feet
Oil engine 3-cyl. 2SCDA by William Doxford and Sons Ltd., Pallion, Sunderland (600mm x 2,320mm); 2,500 BHP, 12 knots.

29.3.1945: Launched by William Doxford and Sons Ltd., Pallion, Sunderland (Yard No.731) for J. and C. Harrison Ltd., London.

29.10.1945: Registered at London (326/1945) in the ownership of the Willis Steamship Co. Ltd. (J. and C. Harrison Ltd., managers), London as HARTINGTON.

14.3.1946: Transferred to the National Steamship Co. Ltd. (J and C Harrison Ltd, managers), London.

9.2.1962: Sold to Stuart Navigation Co. (Bahamas) Ltd., Nassau, Bermuda (W. Wei-Yung Lee, London, manager).

Hartington (3) was launched during the war but not completed until October 1945. *[Kevin O'Donoghue collection]*

Harpalion (4) (above) and in later life as *Almar* (below) on the New Waterway in May 1972. *[J. and M. Clarkson; World Ship Society Ltd.]*

20.2.1962: Renamed ABACO.
22.8.1962: Register closed.
1962: Sold to the Sycamore Steamship Co. Ltd. (World-Wide (Shipping) Ltd., managers), Hong Kong.
1963: Renamed FUNABASHI.
16.2.1966: Damaged in collision with the Liberian steamship WHITE MOUNTAIN (7,178/1943), which capsized and sank, off Singapore in position 01.19 north, 104.18 east. Subsequently laid up unrepaired at Singapore.
6.1967: Breaking up commenced by Hong Huat Hardware Co. Ltd., Singapore.

94. HARPALION (4) 1947-1962

O.N.181623 5441g 3,34n
445.1 x 59.5 x 24.6 feet
Oil engine 3-cyl. 2SCDA by William Doxford and Sons Ltd., Pallion, Sunderland (600mm x 2,320mm); 3,300 BHP, 12 ½ knots
9.12.1946: Launched by Burntisland Shipbuilding Co. Ltd., Burntisland (Yard No. 309) for J. and C. Harrison Ltd., London.
8.5.1947: Registered at London (143/1947) in the ownership of the National Steamship Co. Ltd. (J. and C. Harrison Ltd., managers), London as HARPALION.
6.1962: Sold to Marveras Compania Naviera S.A., Piraeus, Greece and renamed ALMAR.
3.7.1962: Register closed.
1976: Sold to Compania Kos International (Kos International (Belgium) S.A., managers), Panama and renamed IJESHA LION.
14.6.1977: Damaged by an engine room fire while at Abidjan with a cargo of sugar. Abandoned to the underwriters as a constructive total loss and sold to Recuperaciones Submarinas S.A., Santander to be broken up.
4.6.1979: Arrived in tow at Santander having been renamed HALLI for delivery.
28.6.1979: Breaking up commenced.

95. HARPAGON (2) 1947-1958

O.N.180024 7,219g 4,380n
422.8 x 57.0 x 34.1 feet
1947: 7,280g 4,490n

423.9 x 57.0 x 34.9 feet
T.3-cyl. by the General Machinery Corporation, Hamilton, Ontario, Canada (24 ½/37/70 x 48 inches); 2,500 IHP, 11 knots.
3.1944: Launched by the New England Shipbuilding Corporation, South Portland, Maine, USA (Yard No.3009) for the United States Maritime Commission as SAMDERRY and bare-boat chartered to the Ministry of War Transport (J. and C. Harrison Ltd., managers), London.
1.12.1944: Registered at London (365/1944).
8.5.1947: Register closed pending return to the United States Maritime Commission; vessel sold instead to J. and C. Harrison Ltd., London and renamed HARPAGON.
12.5.1947: Re-registered at London (150/1947).
5.1958: Sold to Parpanta Compania Naviera S.A., Monrovia, Liberia and renamed MARIA XILAS.
20.5.1958: Register closed.
1960: Transferred to the Greek flag and registered at Piraeus.
9.6.1967: Arrived at Hirao, Japan to be broken up by Matsukura Kaiji K.K.

96. HARPERLEY (4) 1947-1955

O.N.168954 7,058g 4,855n
431.5 x 56.2 x 35.2 feet

T.3-cyl. by the Central Marine Engineering Works, West Hartlepool (24½/39/70 x 48 inches); 510 NHP, 2,500 IHP, 11½ knots.
6.2.1943: Launched by William Gray and Co. Ltd., West Hartlepool (Yard No.1142) for the Ministry of War Transport, London (J.E. Murrell and Son, West Hartlepool, managers) as EMPIRE PROWESS.
4.1943: Registered at West Hartlepool (4/1943).
5.1947: Acquired by the National Steamship Co. Ltd. (J. and C. Harrison Ltd., managers), London and renamed HARPERLEY.
30.5.1947: Registered at London (178/1947).
27.7.1955: Sold to J.A. Billmeir and Co. Ltd., London.
20.8.1955: Renamed ELSTEAD.
22.10.1959: Arrived at Nagasaki, Japan for breaking up by Nippon Sangyo Kaihatsu K.K.
23.10.1959: Register closed.

97. HARPATHIAN (3) 1947-1956

O.N.169891 7,255g 4,372n
422.8 x 57.0 x 34.3 feet
1947: 7,280g 4,453n
423.9 x 57.0 x 34.9 feet
T.3-cyl. by the General Machinery Corporation, Hamilton, Ontario, Canada (24½/37/70 x 48 inches); 2,500 IHP, 11 knots.
5.1944: Launched by J.A. Jones Construction Co., Brunswick, Georgia,

Top: The Liberty *Harpagon* (2) at Cape Town in October 1950. *[Ships in Focus]*

Middle: A fine study of the war-built *Harperley* (4) dated 19th July 1953. *[John McRoberts/J. and M. Clarkson]*

Bottom: The Liberty *Harpathian* (3) also at Cape Town in 1949. *[Ships in Focus]*

Hartismere (2). [Fotoflite incorporating Skyfotos]

USA (Yard No.141) for the United States Maritime Commission and bare-boat chartered to the Ministry of War Transport (J. and C. Harrison Ltd., managers), London as SAMAUSTRAL.

22.6.1944: Registered at London (209/1944).

24.6.1947: Register closed pending return to the United States Maritime Commission but acquired by J. and C. Harrison Ltd., London.

25.6.1947: Re-registered at London (222/1947) as HARPATHIAN.

11.1956: Sold to Tito Campanella Navigazione S.p.A., Genoa, Italy and renamed SUNCAMPANELLA.

28.11.1956: Register closed.

1963: Sold to Marpotente Compania Naviera S.A. Monrovia, Liberia (Angelos Ltd., London, managers) and renamed CALIOPI A.

1966: Sold to Seawave Shipping Co., Monrovia (Overland Trust Bank, Lugano, Switzerland) and renamed MARACH.

29.6.1971: Arrived at Bilbao, Spain to be broken up by Alfonso Garcia.

98. HARTISMERE (2) 1947-1962
O.N.181665 5,719g 3,279n
444.5 x 59.5 x 26.2 feet
Oil engine 4-cyl. 2SCSA by William Doxford and Sons Ltd., Pallion, Sunderland (600mm x 2,320mm); 3,300 BHP, 12¾ knots.

6.3.1947: Launched by William Doxford and Sons Ltd., Pallion, Sunderland (Yard No.742) for J. and C. Harrison Ltd., London.

30.6.1947: Registered at London (235/1947) in the ownership of the National Steamship Co. Ltd. (J. and C. Harrison Ltd., managers), London as HARTISMERE.

27.2.1962: Sold to Dell Enterprises Ltd., Hamilton, Bermuda (James W. Elwell and Co. Inc., New York) and renamed RECIFE.

10.1963: Sold to Maritime and Industrial Corporation, Monrovia, Liberia (S.A. Enchimar, Brussels, Belgium) and renamed CAROLINA.

25.10.1963: Register closed.

1965: Sold to Saint Spyridon Maritime Co. Ltd. (E.A. Karavias, manager), Monrovia and renamed TARSEUS.

25.4.1973: Arrived at Faslane for breaking up by Shipbreaking Industries Ltd.

99. HARBOROUGH (2) 1956-1959
O.N.187512 6,671g 3,503n
465.5 x 62.1 x 26.4 feet
Oil engine 4-cyl. 2SCSA by North Eastern Marine Engineering Co. Ltd., Wallsend-on-Tyne (700mm x 2,320mm); 4,800 BHP, 14 knots.

4.9.1956: Launched by Blyth Dry Docks and Shipbuilding Co. Ltd., Blyth (Yard No.365) for J. and C. Harrison Ltd., London.

3.12.1956: Registered at London (189/1956) in the ownership of the National Steamship Co. Ltd. (J. and C. Harrison Ltd., managers), London as HARBOROUGH.

18.4.1959: Sank in the Weser Estuary after striking the wreck of the USSR steamer KHOLOMOGORY (2,332/1930) in thick fog while on a voyage from Gdynia to Buenos Aires.

18.4.1959: Register closed.

100. HARPAGUS (6) 1958-1973
O.N.187701 6,803g 3,542n
466.3 x 62.3 x 26.8 feet
1968: 10,118g 6,108n
521.2 x 62.3 x 27.9 feet
Oil engine 4-cyl. 2SCSA by William Doxford and Sons Ltd., Pallion, Sunderland (700mm x 2,320mm); 4,800 BHP, 13½ knots.

24.9.1957: Launched by William Doxford and Sons Ltd., Pallion, Sunderland (Yard

Harborough (2) fitting out at Blyth on 13th October 1956 (above) and in service (opposite page top). [P.A. Vicary; Ships in Focus]

No.823) for J. and C. Harrison Ltd.,
London.
7.1.1958: Registered at London (4/1958)
as HARPAGUS.
7.5.1968: Re-registered at London
(191/1968) after lengthening by the
Netherlands Dock and Shipbuilding Co.
Ltd., Amsterdam.
10.1973: Sold to Irinikos Shipping
Corporation, Monrovia, Liberia
(Mavrakis Shipping S.A., Piraeus,
Greece, managers) and renamed
IRINIKOS.
3.10.1973: Register closed.
1978: Management transferred to
Mayamar Marine Enterprises, Piraeus.
1980: Sold to Far Eastern Express
Shipping Corporation, Monrovia, Liberia
(Intermarine Shipping Ltd., London,
managers) and renamed VICTORY FIVE.
6.8.1982: Arrived at Kaohsiung for breaking
up.

Harpagus (6) as built in charterer's colours off Tilbury in January 1962 (above) and after
lengthening (below). *[Roy Fenton collection; J. and M. Clarkson collection].*

Harpalyce (6) as built (above) and in 1961 after lengthening (below). *[Fotoflite incorporating Skyfotos; Ships in Focus]*

101. HARPALYCE (6) 1958-1972
O.N.187732 6,803g 3,542n
466.3 x 62.3 x 26.8 feet
1967: 10,296g 6,437n
521.2 x 62.3 x 27.9 feet
Oil engine 4-cyl. 2SCSA by William
Doxford and Sons Ltd., Pallion, Sunderland
(700mm x 2,320mm); 4,800 BHP, 13½
knots.
21.11.1957: Launched by William Doxford
and Sons Ltd., Pallion, Sunderland (Yard
No.824) for J. and C. Harrison Ltd., London.
10.3.1958: Registered at London (42/1958)
as HARPALYCE.
2.11.1967: Re-registered at London
(429/1967) after lengthening by the
Netherlands Dock and Shipbuilding Co.
Ltd., Amsterdam, Netherlands.
2.1972: Sold to Compania Navegadora
Tropica S.A., Panama (Victoria Steamship

Co. Ltd., London, managers) and renamed
PATAGONIA.
24.2.1972: Register closed.
1974: Renamed EFCHARIS.
1977: Management transferred to Demetrios
Margaronis, Piraeus.
1982: Sold to Intra Trophy Shipping Co.
Ltd., Maldives (Global Shipping Co.
(Private) Ltd., Dubai, managers) and
renamed INTRA TROPHY.
14.1.1983: Arrived at Vlissingen for repairs
to grounding damage but subsequently sold
to Indian breakers.
12.4.1983: Arrived at Cochin and then
proceeded to Bhavnagar for breaking up.

102. HARMATTAN (4) 1959-1971
O.N.300835 9,236g 5,200n
470.0 x 62.5 x 26.8 feet
1968: 10,411g 6,280n

530.0 x 62.5 x 28.3 feet
Oil engine 5-cyl. 2SCSA by John G.
Kincaid and Co. Ltd., Greenock (620mm x
2,870mm); 4,800 BHP, 13½ knots.
15.4.1958: Launched by Lithgows Ltd.,
Port Glasgow (Yard No.1119) for J. and C.
Harrison Ltd., London.
13.2.1959: Registered at London (27/1959)
in the ownership of the Gowland Steamship
Co. Ltd. (J. and C. Harrison Ltd., managers),
London as HARMATTAN.
12.7.1968: Re-registered at London
(316/1968) after lengthening by the
Netherlands Dock and Shipbuilding Co.
Ltd., Amsterdam, Netherlands.
18.12.1971: Heavily damaged by Indian
naval missile fire while lying off Karachi.
Subsequently sold locally for breaking up.
5.1972: Broken up at Karachi.
4.9.1973: Register closed.

Harmattan (4) in original condition on 1st June 1959. *[Fotoflite incorporating Skyfotos BW672239]*

103. HARPALYCUS (2) 1959-1975

O.N.300860 6,800g 3,540n
465.5 x 62.1 x 26.4 feet
1968: 10,212g 6,293n
528.0 x 62.4 x 27.5 feet
Oil engine 4-cyl. 2SCSA by North Eastern Marine Engineering Co. Ltd., Wallsend-on-Tyne (700mm x 2,320mm); 4,800 BHP, 14 knots.
20.11.1958: Launched by Blyth Dry Docks and Shipbuilding Co. Ltd., Blyth (Yard No.369) for J. and C. Harrison Ltd., London.
6.4.1959: Registered at London (62/1959) in the ownership of the National Steamship Co. Ltd. (J. and C. Harrison Ltd., managers), London as HARPALYCUS.
10.9.1968: Re-registered at London (396/1968) after lengthening by the Netherlands Dock and Shipbuilding Co. Ltd., Amsterdam, Netherlands.
8.1975: Sold to Filiikos Shipping Corporation, Monrovia, Liberia (Mavrakis

The fine view above in New Zealand waters shows *Harpalycus* (2) as she was built. She is seen below after lengthening in 1968. *[Ships in Focus; Nigel Farrell collection]*

Shipping S.A., Piraeus, Greece, managers), and renamed FILIKOS.
28.8.1975: Register closed.
1978: Management transferred to Mayamar Marine Enterprises, Piraeus.

1980: Sold to Pan World Shipping Corporation, Monrovia, Liberia (Intermarine Shipping Ltd., London, managers) and renamed SABRINA.
7.5.1982: Arrived at Bombay for breaking up.

The bulk carrier *Harfleet* in Macmillan Bloudel colours. *[M.R. Dippy/Nigel Farrell collection]*

104. HARFLEET 1973-1979

O.N.360656 16,715g 11,400n
545.8 x 83.7 x 41.9 feet
Oil engine 6-cyl. 2SCDA by Harland and
Wolff Ltd., Belfast (740mm x 1,600mm);
11,600 BHP, 15 knots.
6.3.1973: Launched by Upper Clyde
Shipbuilders Ltd., Scotstoun Division (Yard
No.125) for J. and C. Harrison Ltd., London.
6.6.1973: Registered at London (244/1973)
in the ownership of the Gowland Steamship
Co. Ltd. (J. and C. Harrison Ltd., managers),
London as HARFLEET.
4.1979: Sold to Chi Grace Navigation Inc.,
Monrovia, Liberia (Chi Yuen Navigation
Co. Ltd., Taipei, Taiwan) and renamed CHI
GRACE.
12.4.1979: Register closed.
1979: Renamed ATLAS.
1981: Transferred to Astarte Shipping
Company, Monrovia, Liberia (Chi Yuen

Navigation Co. Ltd., Taipei) and renamed
ANTACUS.
16.7.1984: Foundered in heavy weather after
water entered the engine room in position
40.00 north, 26.05 west while on a voyage
from Bremerhaven to New Orleans with a
cargo of steel coils and rails.

105. HARFLEUR (2) 1973-1979

O.N.360968 16,715g 11,400n
545.8 x 83.7 x 41.9 feet
Oil engine 6-cyl. 2SCDA by Harland and
Wolff Ltd., Belfast (740mm x 1,600mm);
11,600 BHP, 15 knots.
14.9.1973: Launched by Upper Clyde
Shipbuilders Ltd., Scotstoun Division (Yard
No.129) for J. and C. Harrison Ltd., London.
21.12.1973: Registered at London (661/1973)
as HARFLEUR.
2.1979: Sold to Chi Trust Navigation Inc.,
Monrovia, Liberia (Chi Yuen Navigation Co.

Ltd., Taipei, Taiwan) and renamed CHI TRUST.
12.2.1979: Register closed.
1980: Renamed ANDROMEDA.
1981: Transferred to Arion Navigation Inc.,
Monrovia (Chi Yuen Navigation Co. Ltd.,
Taipei).
1986: Sold to Staronset Shipping Co. Ltd.,
Limassol, Cyprus (G. Kalogeratos and Co.,
Piraeus, Greece) and renamed ARHON.
1990: Transferred to Evgeros Shipping Co.
Ltd., Ta'Xbiex, Malta (G. Kalogeratos and Co.,
Piraeus).
1994: Sold to Sea Star Union S.A., Panama
City, Panama (Starlady Marine Ltd., Piraeus,
Greece).
1995: Resold to Evgeros Shipping Co. Ltd.,
Ta'Xbiex, Malta (G. Kalogeratos and Co.,
Piraeus). There is some evidence that ultimate
owners were Starlady Marine Ltd.
18.11.1997: Arrived at Alang, India for
demolition.

The bulk carrier *Harfleur* at Melbourne, also in Macmillan Bloudel colours. *[Bill Volum/Russell Priest collection]*

Harcourt, Harrison's last and smallest ship, photographed on the New Waterway on 24th September 1977. *[Les Ring/World Ship Society Ltd. 67524]*

106. HARCOURT 1975-1979
O.N. 363447 443g 229n
174.8 x 30.8 x 9.1 feet
Oil engine 6-cyl. 4SCDA by Maschinenbau Augsburg-Nürnberg, Augsburg, West Germany (235mm x 330mm); 515 BHP, 10 knots.
16.8.1961: Launched by Deutsche Industrie-Werke A.G., Berlin-Spandau, West Germany (Yard No. 300025) for Schepers River See Linie, Duisborg-Ruhrort, West Germany as SPREE.
1.11.1961: Completed.
6.1974: Sold to Timber Carriers Ltd. (Torben Nielson, manager), London and renamed TIMBER QUEEN.
29.8.1974: Registered at London (387/1974).
14.2.1975: Acquired by J. and C. Harrison Ltd., London.
4.3.1975: Renamed HARCOURT.
18.7.1979: Sold to T. Hicks and Co., Lodelark Ltd. and Finekey Ltd., Saffron Walden, Essex.
7.9.1979: Renamed BARCOURT.
24.4.1981: Sold to Concord Leasing Ltd., Brentford (Nialed Shipping Co. Ltd., Gravesend, managers).
19.8.1981: Renamed KIMBLE.
1981: Leased to Naviera Jepa S. de R.L., San Lorenzo, Honduras (Nialed Shipping Co. Ltd., Gravesend, managers).
3.1982: Sold to Dynamic Steamship Inc., Antwerp, Belgium, renamed SABINE and registered in San Lorenzo, Honduras.
9.3.1982: Register closed.
1985: Sold to Tillamar Shipping Co. S.A., Panama.
1988: Renamed PAUL MARIE.
1990: Sold to Becks Shipping S. de R.L., San Lorenzo and renamed BECKS.
1993: Moved to Belize registry.
1994: Renamed CHRIST CAPABLE and registered in San Lorenzo, Honduras.
1995: Renamed VENANTE B.
22.10.1996: Scuttled to form an artificial reef off Boynton Beach, near Palm Beach, Florida. She had been in the Miami River since 1991 at least.

Managed ships

M1. WAR SPANIEL 1918-1919
O.N. 142475 5,298g 3,218n
400.3 x 52.4 x 28.5 feet
T.3-cyl. by North Eastern Marine Engineering Co. Ltd., Sunderland (27/44/73 x 48 inches); 517 NHP, 3,000 IHP, 11½ knots.
28.3.1918: Launched by Short Brothers Ltd., Sunderland (Yard No. 399) for the Shipping Controller (J. and C. Harrison Ltd., managers), London as WAR SPANIEL.
5.7.1918: Registered at London (252/1918).
29.1.1919: Sold to the Gulf Line Ltd. (Furness, Withy and Co. Ltd., managers), London.
11.6.1919: Renamed CASTELLANO.
4.1922: Sold to Yamashita Kisen Goshi Kaisha (Yamashita Kisen Kogyo K.K., managers), Dairen, Japan and renamed HOKKOH MARU.
10.4.1922: Register closed.
1938: Name re-styled HOKKO MARU.
28.11.1943: Torpedoed and sunk by the US submarine RATON 300 miles north west of the Admiralty Islands in position 01.40 north, 141.51 east.

M2. WAR MASTIFF 1918-1919
O.N. 142625 5,298g 3,218n
400.3 x 52.4 x 28.5 feet
T.3-cyl. by North Eastern Marine Engineering Co. Ltd., Sunderland (27/44/73 x 48 inches); 517 NHP, 3,000 IHP, 11½ knots.
30.5.1918: Launched by Short Brothers Ltd., Sunderland (Yard No.400) for the Shipping Controller (J and C. Harrison Ltd., managers), London.
27.8.1918: Registered at London (307/1918).
21.11.1919: Sold to the Liverpool, Brazil and River Plate Steam Navigation Co. Ltd., Liverpool.
26.11.1919: Registered at Liverpool (100/1919).
28.11.1919: Renamed BIELA.
28.6.1934: Owner renamed Lamport and Holt Line Ltd.
15.2.1942: Torpedoed and sunk by the German submarine U 98 in the North Atlantic in position 42.55 north, 45.40 west while on a voyage from Liverpool to Buenos Aires with general cargo. The entire crew of 49 were lost.
20.4.1942: Registered closed.

M3. OAKCREST 1940-1941
O.N. 171313 5,407g 3327n
403.0 x 52.5 x 27.5 feet
T.3-cyl. by John G. Kincaid and Co. Ltd., Greenock (27/44/73 x 48 inches); 512 NHP, 10 knots.
30.1.1929: Launched by Robert Duncan and Co. Ltd., Port Glasgow (Yard No.387) for Prekomorska Plovidba D.D., Susak, Yugoslavia as KORANA.
2.3.1940: Transferred to the British flag and registered at London (44/1940) in the ownership of the Crest Shipping Co. Ltd., London.
22.3.1940: J. and C. Harrison Ltd. appointed managers.
23.3.1940: Renamed OAKCREST.
22.11.1940: Torpedoed and sunk by the German submarine U 123 in the North Atlantic in approximate position 53 north, 17 west while on a voyage from Liverpool to New York in convoy OB.244 in ballast. 35 were lost from a crew of 41.
12.8.1941: Register closed.

Lamport and Holt's *Biela* was briefly managed by Harrisons when built as *War Mastiff*. *[Basil Feilden/J. and M. Clarkson]*

M4. FIRCREST 1940

O.N. 146204 5,394g 3,371n
420.5 x 54.5 x 27.9 feet
Q. 4-cyl. by Bremer Vulkan Schiffbau
and Machinenfabrik, Vegesack, Germany
(24/34½/50/62 x 53½): 519 NHP, 2,500 IHP,
10 knots.
3.1904: Launched by Bremer Vulkan
Schiffbau and Machinenfabrik, Vegesack
(Yard No.499) for Roland Linie A.G.,
Bremen, Germany as RIOL.
8.1914: Laid up at Valparaiso at the
beginning of the First World War.
1918: Machinery damaged by the crew
before the vessel could be taken over by the
Allied Powers.
8.1920: Towed back to Bremerhaven and
repaired; allocated to Great Britain.
3.12.1921: Registered at London (676/1921)
in the ownership of the Shipping Controller.
3.12.1921: Sold to Douglas Smith, Cardiff.
11.12.1921: Registered at Bideford
(11/1921). Smith remained the beneficial
owner, but the vessel operated as part of the
fleet of Leeds Shipping Co. Ltd. (Sir W.R.
Smith and Sons Ltd., managers), Cardiff.
3.1927: Sold to Jugoslovensko-
Amerikaniska Plovidba A.D., Split,
Yugoslavia and renamed PRERADOVIC.
18.3.1927: Register closed.
1928: Owner renamed Jugoslavenski Lloyd
D.D., Split, Yugoslavia.
23.4.1940: Transferred to the British flag
and registered at London (77/1940) in the
ownership of the Crest Shipping Co. Ltd. (J.
and C. Harrison Ltd., managers), London as
FIRCREST.
25.8.1940: Torpedoed and sunk by the
German submarine U 124 in the North
Atlantic in position 58.52 north, 06.34 west
while on a voyage from Wabana to the Tees
with a cargo of 7,900 tons of iron ore in
convoy HX.65A. The entire crew of 40 was
lost.
21.12.1940: Register closed.

M5. HAMPTON LODGE 1941-1943

O.N. 132608 3,645g 2,241n
348.5 x 60.3 x 23.6 feet
T.3-cyl. by Rankine and Blackmore,
Greenock (25/41/67 x 45 inches); 362 NHP,
1,650 IHP, 10½ knots.
31.8.1911: Launched by the Greenock and
Grangemouth Dockyard Co. Ltd., Greenock
(Yard No.333) for H. Meldrum and Co.,
London.
21.9.1911: Registered at London (126/1911)
in the ownership of the Essex Steamship
Co. Ltd. (H. Meldrum and Co., managers),
London as ESSEX ABBEY.
30.10.1916: Sold to Grahams and Co.
(Cooper and Moncreif, managers), London.
3.11.1916: Renamed PANAYIOTIS.
6.1.1920: Sold to the Loyal Line Ltd., Cardiff
(Carpenter and Tuck, London, managers).
31.1.1920: Registered at Cardiff (4/1920) as
LOYAL DEVONIAN.
6.1932: Sold to Captain S.N. Vlassopol,
Braila, Romania and renamed INGINER N.
VLASSOPOL.
24.6.1932: Register closed.
2.1941: Requisitioned while under repair at
London.
15.2.1941: Registered at London (23/1941) in
the ownership of the Ministry of Shipping (J.
and C. Harrison Ltd., managers), London as
HAMPTON LODGE.
20.12.1941: Register closed (presumably
in anticipation of a subsequently cancelled
disposal to an Allied Power).

23.12.1941: Re-registered at London
(203/1941).
20.1.1943: Bombed by a German Ju-88 north
west of Algiers in position 36.44 north, 01.50
east while on a ballast voyage from Algiers
to Oran and Benisaf in convoy KMS.6. The
vessel was abandoned and entire crew saved
by the rescue tug ST. DAY. The derelict
foundered the following morning.
17.2.1943: Register closed.

M6. EMPIRE STOUR 1941-1946

See 65. HARPENDEN (3)

M7. RADHURST 1941-1943

O.N. 168237 3,454g 2,125n
331.4 x 46.3 x 20.9 feet
T.3-cyl. by David Rowan and Co., Glasgow
(23/38/62 x 42 inches); 282 NHP, 9 knots.
4.1916: Launched by Cantieri Navale
Triestino, Montefalcone, Italy (Yard No.15)
for T. Cossovich, Trieste as NEREIDE.
1920: Transferred to the Italian flag
with owning company renamed Societa
Anonimadi Navigazione a Vapor (T.
Cossovich, manager), Trieste, Italy.
1924: Sold to Navigazione Mercantile
Societa Anonima, Trieste, Italy.
1924: Sold to Brodarsko Akc Drustvo
'Oceania', Susak, Yugoslavia and renamed
SAVA.
29.3.1941: Time charted by the Ministry of
Shipping, London.
4.4.1941: Transferred to the British flag.
8.11.1941: Registered at London (214/1941)
in the ownership of the Ministry of
War Transport (J. and C. Harrison Ltd.,
managers), London as RADHURST.
20.2.1943: Torpedoed and sunk by the
German submarine U 525 in the North
Atlantic in approximate position 49.28 north,
44.50 west while on a voyage from the
Tyne via Loch Ewe and the Clyde to New
York in ballast after straggling from convoy
ONS.165S. The entire crew of 42 was lost.
23.3.1944: Register closed.

M8. RADPORT 1941-1946

O.N. 168552 5,355g 3,318n
420.6 x 54.7 x 25.0 feet
T.3-cyl. by Workman, Clark and Co. Ltd.,
Belfast (25½/42½/70 x 51 inches); 484 NHP,
1,800 IHP, 9½ knots.
28.1.1925: Launched by Workman, Clark and
Co. Ltd., Belfast (Yard No.481) for Dubrovacka
Parobrodska Plovidba, A.D., Dubrovnik,
Yugoslavia as FEDERIKO GLAVIC.
1938: Owner became Dubrovacka Plovidba, A.D.
12.6.1941: Requisitioned by the Ministry of
War Transport, London.
15.7.1941: Transferred to the British flag.
20.10.1941: Registered at Manchester
(2/1941) in the ownership of the Ministry
of War Transport (J. and C. Harrison Ltd.,
managers), London as RADPORT.
7.1946: Returned to Yugoslav ownership
with Jugoslavenska Slobodna Plovidba,
Dubrovnik, Yugoslavia and renamed
BEOGRAD.
15.7.1946: Register closed.

The former *Essex Abbey* was managed by Harrisons as *Hampton Lodge* from 1941
to 1943. *[Nigel Farrell collection]*
Radport at New York on 8th August 1942 (below). *[William Schell collection]*

1950: Owner renamed Jugoslavenska
Linijska Plovidba, Dubrovnik.
1957: Sold to Atlantska Plovidba, Dubrovnik.
5.3.1970: Arrived at Split to be broken up by
Brodospas.

M9. EMPIRE CAREY 1941-1942

O.N. 168934 2,866g 1,688n
315.4 x 46.6 x 23.0 feet
T.3-cyl. by William Gray and Co. Ltd., West
Hartlepool (20/31/55 x 39 inches); 269
NHP, 1,080 IHP, 10 knots.
20.10.1941: Launched by William Gray and
Co. Ltd., West Hartlepool (Yard No.1125)
for the Ministry of War Transport (J. and
C. Harrison Ltd., managers), London as
EMPIRE CAREY.
9.12.1941: Registered at West Hartlepool
(15/1941).
5.1942: Sold to the Norwegian Government
and renamed RAGNHILD; placed under the
management of the Norwegian Shipping and
Trade Mission, Oslo.
4.5.1942: British register closed
1946: Sold to John Wilson's Rederi A/S
(John Wilson and Søn, managers), Oslo,
Norway and renamed PENELOPE.
1949: Registered in Panama under the
ownership of John Wilson and Son, Panama.
1950: Sold to Rederi A/B Pandia (Arthur
Karlsson, manager), Mariehamn, Finland.
1955: Transferred to Ångfartygs A/B Alfa
(Fraenk Lundqvist, manager), Mariehamn,
Finland.
1972: Sold to Wohatz and Co, Göteborg,
Sweden, for conversion to a floating storage
vessel.

M10. EMPIRE BYRON 1941-1942

O.N. 169005 6,645g 4,796n
416.8 x 56.6 x 34.0 feet
T.3-cyl. by Bartram and Sons Ltd.,
Sunderland (27½/38/66 x 45 inches); 445
NHP, 2,000 IHP, 10½ knots.
6.10.1941: Launched by Bartram and
Sons Ltd., Sunderland (Yard No.289) for
the Ministry of War Transport (J. and C.
Harrison Ltd., London, managers), London
as EMPIRE BYRON.
20.12.1941: Registered at Sunderland
(91/1941).
5.7.1942: Torpedoed and sunk by the
German submarine U 703 in position 76.18
north, 33.30 east after dispersing from
convoy PQ.17 while on a voyage from Hull
and Reykjavik to North Russia with a cargo
of 3,500 tons of military stores. Eight of
the crew and one passenger were lost, and
one passenger taken prisoner from a total
complement of 65.
10.8.1942: Register closed.

M11. FORT MAUREPAS 1942-1947

O.N. 168386 7,133g 4,181n
424.6 x 57.2 x 34.9 feet
T.3-cyl. by Dominion Engineering Works
Ltd., Montreal, Quebec, Canada (24½/37/70
x 48 inches); 2,500 IHP, 10½ knots.
1.7.1942: Launched by West Coast
Shipbuilders Ltd., Vancouver, British

The Finnish *Penelope* had been managed by J. and C. Harrison Ltd. for the Ministry
of War Transport as *Empire Carey* in 1941 and 1942. *[J. and M. Clarkson]*

Columbia (Yard No.105) for the Ministry
of War Transport (J. and C. Harrison Ltd.,
managers), London as FORT MAUREPAS.
4.12.1942: Registered at London
(144/1942).
11.1947: Returned to the United States
Maritime Commission.
11.11.1947: Register closed.
1948: Sold to 'Corrado' Societa di
Navigazione, Genoa, Italy and renamed
ROSA CORRADO.
1963: Transferred to Sicilarma Societa di
Navigazione per Azioni (Corrado Societa di
Navigazione, managers), Palermo, Italy and
renamed TINDARI.
26.11.1965: Arrived at Vado Ligure to be
broken up by A.R.D.E.M.

M12. FORT LA MONTEE 1942-1943

O.N. 168386 7,134g 4,181n
424.6 x 57.2 x 34.9 feet
T.3-cyl. by Canadian Allis-Chalmers Ltd.,
Montreal, Quebec, Canada (24½/37/70 x 48
inches); 2,500 IHP, 10½ knots.
12.9.1942: Launched by North Vancouver
Ship Repairs Ltd., North Vancouver, British
Columbia (Yard No.111) for the Ministry
of War Transport (J. and C. Harrison Ltd.,
managers), London as FORT LA MONTEE.
26.1.1943: Registered at London (14/1943).
4.8.1943: Caught fire in Algiers harbour
following ignition of a part cargo of
detonators and phosphorus shells; towed
clear of the harbour but then blew up. The
ship broke in two, with the stern sinking
immediately, and the remains of the bow
section subsequently being scuttled by naval
gunfire. Of the crew of 56, 25 were killed.
15.9.1943: Register closed.

M13. OCEAN GYPSY 1942-1946

O.N. 169067 7,178g 4,352n
441.5 x 57.0 x 34.8 feet
T.3-cyl. by John Inglis and Co. Ltd.,
Toronto, Ontario, Canada (24½/39/70 x 48
inches); 342 NHP, 2,500 IHP, 11 knots
18.10.1942: Launched by the Todd-Bath Iron
Shipbuilding Corporation, South Portland,
Maine, USA (Yard No.29) for the Ministry
of War Transport (J. and C. Harrison Ltd.,

managers), London as OCEAN GYPSY.
7.11.1942: Delivered.
16.11.1942: Sailed from New York for the
United Kingdom.
1.11.1943: Registered at Manchester.
28.7.1946: Bareboat chartered to the Clan
Line Steamers Ltd. (Cayzer, Irvine and Co.
Ltd., managers), London.
31.12.1947: Sold to Clan Line Steamers Ltd.
(Cayzer, Irvine and Co. Ltd., managers),
London for £108,105 and renamed CLAN
MACBRIDE.
2.1950: Converted to burn oil fuel.
22.5.1958: Sold to Panamanian Oriental
Steamship Corporation, Panama (Wheelock,
Marden and Co. Ltd., Hong Kong,
managers) for £110,000 and renamed
ALICE.
1961: Sold to Valles Steamship Co. Ltd.,
Panama (C.S. Koo, Hong Kong, managers).
7.10.1966: Arrived at Hirao, Japan to be
broken up by Matsukuru Kaiji K.K.

M14. OCEAN GLORY 1942-1946

O.N. 169176 7,178g 4,352n
441.5 x 57.0 x 34.8 feet
T.3-cyl. by John Inglis and Co. Ltd.,
Toronto, Ontario, Canada (24½/39/70 x 48
inches): 342 NHP, 2,500 IHP, 11 knots.
18.10.1942: Launched by the Todd-Bath
Iron Shipbuilding Corporation, South
Portland, Maine, USA (Yard No.30) for
the Ministry of War Transport (J. and
C. Harrison Ltd., managers), London as
OCEAN GLORY.
18.11.1942: Delivered; sailed from New
York for the UK on 25.11.1942.
13.1.1943: Registered at Newcastle-upon-
Tyne.
1946: Bareboat chartered to the Clan Line
Steamers Ltd. (Cayzer, Irvine and Co. Ltd.,
managers), London.
31.12.1947: Sold to Clan Line Steamers Ltd.
(Cayzer, Irvine and Co. Ltd., managers),
London for £107,343 and renamed CLAN
MACBETH.
7.1950: Converted to burn oil fuel.
4.4.1959: Sold to Panamanian Oriental
Steamship Corporation, Panama (Wheelock,
Marden and Co. Ltd., Hong Kong,

managers) for £70,000 and renamed
MADONNA.
1961: Sold to Sincere Navigation
Corporation (V.K. Eddie Hsu, manager),
Taipeh, Taiwan and renamed SINCERE
TRADER.
15.10.1964: Left Osaka for Kaohsiung to be
broken up.
11.1964: Demolition began by the China
National Machinery Import and Export
Corporation, Kaohsiung.

M15. EMPIRE FLORIZEL 1943
O.N. 169503 7,056g 4,814n
432.7 x 56.2 x 34.3 feet
T.3-cyl. by John Brown and Co. Ltd.,
Clydebank (23½/37½/68 x 48 inches): 219
NHP, 2,100 IHP, 10½ knots
21.4.1943: Launched by Lithgows Ltd., Port
Glasgow (Yard No.990) for the Ministry
of War Transport (J. and C. Harrison Ltd.,
managers), London as EMPIRE FLORIZEL.
26.5.1943: Registered at Greenock (8/1943).
21.7.1943: Bombed and set on fire during
a combined German and Italian air attack
while in port at Augusta, Sicily with a cargo
of 4,000 tons of military and invasion stores.
The burning vessel was sunk by naval
gunfire after multiple explosions. Nine were
lost from a total complement of 83 including
14 passengers.
9.9.1943: Register closed.

M16. FORT ATHABASKA 1943
O.N. 168449 7,132g 4,181n
424.6 x 57.2 x 34.9 feet
T.3-cyl. by John Inglis Co. Ltd., Toronto,
Ontario (24½/39/70 x 48 inches); 2,500 IHP,
10½ knots.
4.4.1943: Launched by Burrard Dry
Dock Co. Ltd., North Vancouver, British
Columbia (Yard No.175) for the Ministry
of War Transport (J. and C. Harrison Ltd.,
managers), London as FORT ATHABASKA.
30.7.1943: Registered at London
(178/1943).
2.12.1943: Blew up and sank in Bari harbour
after catching fire due to the explosion of
the United States steamer JOHN HARVEY
(7,177/1943) which had been bombed by
German aircraft during an air raid on the
port. Of the crew of 56, two were killed and
44 reported missing.
19.1.1944: Register closed.

M17. FORT FRONTENAC 1943-1946
O.N. 169646 7,148g 4228n
424.7 x 57.2 x 34.9 feet
T.3-cyl. by Dominion Engineering Works
Ltd., Montreal, Quebec, Canada (24½/37/70
x 48 inches); 2,500 IHP, 10½ knots.
25.8.1943: Launched by Marine Industries
Ltd., Sorel, Quebec (Yard No.120) for
the Ministry of War Transport (J. and C.
Harrison Ltd., managers), London as FORT
FRONTENAC.
24.11.1943: Registered at London (280/1943).
1946: Transferred to the Ministry of
Transport (South American Saint Line Ltd.,
managers), London.

Ocean Glory, previously managed by Harrisons, was bareboat chartered to Clan
Line from 1946. Photographed leaving Cape Town, she is still clearly still a coal
burner. *[World Ship Society Ltd.]*

A United States Coast Guard photograph of the *Fort Athabaska* taken on 5th July
1943. *[J. and M. Clarkson collection]*

Laurentian Valley had been managed by Harrisons as *Fort Frontenac*. *[J.K. Byass/
World Ship Society Ltd.]*

1950: Sold to Laurentian Marine Co. Ltd.
(Fern Hill Steamship Co. Ltd., managers),
London and renamed LAURENTIAN
VALLEY.
10.1957: Sold to Corona Compania Naviera
S.A., Monrovia, Liberia and renamed
AEGEAN SEA.
19.10.1957: Register closed.
1958: Sold to 'Uzeda' Societa di
Navigazione S.p.A. (Matteo Scuderi),
Catania, Italy and renamed ACHILLE.
25.4.1968: Arrived at La Spezia to be broken
up by Cantiere Navale 'Santa Maria' S.p.A.

M18. FORT LENNOX 1943-1946
O.N. 169649 7,149g 4,228n
424.7 x 57.2 x 34.9 feet
T.3-cyl. by Dominion Engineering Works
Ltd., Montreal, Quebec, Canada (24½/37/70
x 48 inches); 2,500 IHP, 10½ knots.
18.9.1943: Launched by Marine Industries
Ltd., Sorel, Quebec (Yard No.121) for
the Ministry of War Transport (J. and C.
Harrison Ltd., managers), London as FORT
LENNOX.
1.12.1943: Registered at London
(283/1943).

1946: Transferred to the Ministry of Transport (Goulandris Brothers, managers), London.
11.1947: Sold to Vancouver Oriental Line Ltd., Montreal, Quebec and renamed CARIBOU COUNTY.
11.11.1947: Register closed.
1950: Renamed HARROW HILL and management transferred to Counties Ship Management Co. Ltd., London under the British flag.
1960: Sold to Empresa Naviera La Libertad S.A., Panama (C.S. Koo, Hong Kong), and renamed SILVER PEAK.
12.4.1967: Stranded in bad weather on rocks about 100 miles from Keelung in position 25.44 north, 123.30 east while on a voyage from Yawata to Hong Kong in ballast. Abandoned to the underwriters as a constructive total loss and sold locally for scrapping.

M19. EMPIRE CROWN 1943-1945
O.N. 169054 7,070g 4,905n
430.9 x 56.2 x 35.2 feet
T.3-cyl. by John Readhead and Sons Ltd., South Shields (24½/39/70 x 48 inches); 342 NHP, 2,500 IHP, 11 knots.
16.10.1943: Launched by John Readhead and Sons Ltd., South Shields (Yard No.537) for the Ministry of War Transport (J. and C. Harrison Ltd., managers), London as EMPIRE CROWN.
23.12.1943: Registered at South Shields (5/1943).
8.1945: Handed over to the French Government, renamed CAPITAINE G LACOLEY and operated by the Ministere de la Marine Marchande (Heuzey and Chastellain, managers), Rouen, France.
24.8.1945: Register closed.
1948: Sold to Compagnie des Transports Maritimes et Fluviaux (J. Chastellain et Compagnie, managers), Rouen, France.
1961: Sold to Mparmpapetros Shipping Co. S.A., Panama (Pateras Shipbrokers Ltd., London, managers) and renamed MPARMPA PETROS.
21.5.1963: Stranded at Porto de Pedras, 40 miles north of Maceio, while on a voyage from Buenos Aires to Naples with a cargo of grain. Subsequently abandoned to the underwriters as a constructive total loss.

M20. FORT PIC 1943-1948
O.N. 169729 7,150g 4,228n
424.7 x 57.2 x 34.9 feet
T.3-cyl. by Dominion Engineering Works Ltd., Montreal, Quebec, Canada (24½/37/70 x 48 inches); 2,500 IHP, 10½ knots.
7.11.1943: Launched by Marine Industries Ltd., Sorel, Quebec (Yard No.125) for the Ministry of War Transport (J. and C. Harrison Ltd., managers), London as FORT PIC.
13.1.1944: Registered at London (18/1944).
1948: Sold to Acadia Overseas Freighters Halifax Ltd., Halifax, Nova Scotia and renamed HALIGONIAN BARON.
16.9.1948: Register closed.

Fort Lennox was managed by Harrisons from delivery in 1943 to 1946. *[Ships in Focus]*

Wembley Hill, of Counties Ship Management, had been in Harrison management as *Fort Pic. [Roy Fenton collection]*

1950: Renamed WEMBLEY HILL and management transferred to Counties Ship Management Co. Ltd., London.
1957: Sold to Transcontinental Oil Transportation Corporation, Monrovia, Liberia and renamed CASSIOPEIA.
1960: Sold to Transoceanic Finance and Trading Corporation, Piraeus, Greece.
1961: Sold to Oceania Industrial Corporation Ltd. (Wallem and Co., managers), Hong Kong and renamed SHAUKIWAN.

1965: Sold to Keh Kok S.A., Monrovia (Asia Shipping Enterprises, Ltd, Hong Kong) and renamed ASIA ENTERPRISES.
18.4.1967: Arrived at Yokosuka to be broken up by Amakasu Sangyo Kisen K.K.

M21. SAMAUSTRAL 1944-1947
See No. 95. HARPATHIAN (3)

M22. SAMDERRY 1944-1947
See No. 93. HARPAGON (2)

Samderry at Leith in June 1946, with the Icelandic steamer *Reykjafoss* (1,657/1911) alongside. *[Roy Fenton collection]*

M23. EDDYSTONE 1974-1978

O.N. 341958 444g 250n 600d
51.82 x 8.26 x 3.32 metres
Oil engine 6-cyl. 4SCSA by Appingedammer
Brons Motorenfabriek, Appingedam,
Netherlands; 396 BHP, 10 knots.
30.8.1954: Launched by E.J. Smit en
Zoon's Scheepwerven N.V., Westerbroek,
Netherlands (Yard No. 733).
26.10.1954: Completed for H. Schothorst
(N.V. 'Carebeka', managers), Groningen,
Netherlands as EDDYSTONE.
2.1972: Sold to Captain G.V. Blake, Ipswich
and registered in Guernsey.
5.1974: Acquired by Remodene Ltd.,
Southend-on-Sea (J. and C. Harrison Ltd.,
London, managers).
1978: Sold to Conrad Shipping Ltd., Guernsey.
11.1980: Sold to Pelham Dale and Partners
Ltd., Fakenham, Norfolk and renamed
CARRICK.
1987: Sold to Edward E. Seaman, Diss,
Norfolk
1987: Sold to Fieldfalcon Ltd., Beccles,
Suffolk (G.F. Sully Shipping, Great
Yarmouth, managers).
31.1.1988: Arrived at Milton Creek,
Sittingbourne for demolition by Liguria
Maritime Ltd.
3.1988: Demolition completed.

M24. GEMSTONE 1975-1979

O.N. 358897 499g 297n 864d
56.65 x 9.1 x 3.56 metres
Oil engine 8-cyl. 4SCSA by N.V.
Motorenfabriek 'De Industrie', Alphen a/d
Rijn, Netherlands; 466 HP, 9 knots.
1.1959: Completed by N.V.
Scheepsbouwwerft v/h de Groot & van
Vliet, Bolnes, Netherlands (Yard No. 323)
for Schellen Scheepvaart & Bevrachting
N.V., Rotterdam, Netherlands as JUVALTA.
1973: Sold to Mrs. N.V. Williamson and
Mrs. Y. Andrew (Fife Shipping Co. Ltd.,
London) and renamed JOINTYN.
1975: Acquired by Remodene Ltd.,
Southend-on-Sea (J. and C. Harrison
Ltd., London, managers) and renamed
GEMSTONE.
1979: Sold to Thomas J. Allsworth
(Alsworth Shipping Co. Ltd., managers),
Queenborough, Kent.
1983: Sold Bondminster Ltd. and N.
Watson, Southsea, Hampshire.
20.6.1994: Deleted from 'Lloyd's Register'.
27.7.2001: British registry closed.

M25. PATTREE 1975-1977/1979

O.N. 363308 438g 241n 699d
51.14 x 8.95 x 3.41 metres
Oil engine 6-cyl. 4SCSA by Klockner-
Humboldt-Deutz A.G., Koln, West Germany.
1957: Completed by J.J. Sietas Schiffswerft,
Hamburg, West Germany (Yard No. 405) for
Partenreederei ms 'Barbara' (Gerda Janka,
manager), Hamburg as BARBARA.
1966: Sold to Hans Shirren, Hamburg,
1968: Sold to Partenreederei m.s. 'Barbara'
(Hans Shirren, manager), Hamburg.
1974: Sold to Ensign Freight Services Ltd.,

One of a number of former Dutch motor coasters managed by J. and C. Harrison Ltd. for various owners in the 1970s was *Eddystone,* seen above laid-up in Holland on 28th July 1980, a few months before her sale to British buyers. *[World Ship Society Ltd.]*

Managed on behalf of Remodene Ltd. was *Gemstone.* Her eventual fate is unknown, although she was recorded at Georgetown, Demerara in 1984. *[FotoFlite incorporating Skyfotos, 338394]*

In the funnel colours of Ensign Freight Services Ltd. is the Harrison-managed, German-built *Pattree.* There is evidence that she briefly returned to management by J. and C. Harrison Ltd. in 1979 when she was owned by Concord Credit Ltd. of Brentford. *[J. and M. Clarkson]*

London and renamed PATTREE.

1975: Managers became J. and C. Harrison Ltd.

1977: Sold to Concord Credit Ltd., Brentford (Whitbury Shipping Co. Ltd., Sheerness, managers).

1979: Managers became J. and C. Harrison Ltd.

1979: Managers became Whitbury Shipping Co. Ltd., Sheerness.

1983: Sold to Whitbury Shipping Co. Ltd., Sheerness.

1984: Sold to Cassco Ltd. Cayman Islands (A. Hasselqvist, manager), and registered in Kingstown, St.Vincent and the Grenadines.

1996: Sold to Francis Bynoe, Kingstown, St.Vincent and the Grenadines.

1998: Sold to unknown owners.

2005: Renamed PATRI.

10.2011: Still listed by Equasis.

M26. BENLOW VIKING 1975

O.N. 366110 496g 275n 750d
56.70 x 9.05 x 3.53 metres
Oil engine 8-cyl. 4SCSA by Appingedammer Brons Motorenfabriek, Appingedam, Netherlands; 500 BHP, 10 knots.

19.2.1958: Launched by N.V. Scheepswerf 'Foxhol' v/h Gebr Muller, Foxhol, Netherlands (Yard No. 103).

17.5.1958: Completed for Rederij m.s. 'Wijmers' (J. Bont) (N.V. 'Carebeka' managers), Groningen, Netherlands as WIJMERS.

11.1973: Renamed VLIESTROOM.

3.1974: Sold to N.V. Poromoka & J.C. Moerman (B.V. Spedico, managers), Rotterdam, Netherlands.

6.1974: Sold to Rederij Viking C.V.O.A., Schiedam, Netherlands.

1.1975: Sold to Kustvaartbedrijf Moerman, Rotterdam and renamed VIKING.

1975: Sold to Benlow Shipping Company (J. and C. Harrison Ltd., managers), London and renamed BENLOW VIKING.

1975: Sold to St. Swithins Shipping Co. Ltd. (Clark, A.L. Clifford and Partners Ltd., managers), London

5.1976: Sold to N.C. Tibbles, D.J.O. Graham and M.M. Sharp, London.

1976: Sold to Marine Management Corporation, London (Marico Shipping Ltd., London and Haifa, managers), renamed LEK VIKING and registered in Singapore.

1979: Renamed VIKING and registered in Panama.

1984: Sold to Warrior Shipping Inc. (Marimed Shipping Ltd., London, managers) and registered in Panama.

17.3.1984: Arrested off Stromboli, Italy by the Italian Coastguard for alleged gun running and taken to Messina where she was laid up.

4.1992: Sold for demolition whilst lying at Messina.

2.1994: Demolition began.

26.7.1994: Demolition complete.

M27. BENLOW TRADER 1975

O.N. 360150 480g 289n 625d
51.54 x 8.44 x 3.106 metres
Oil engine 6-cyl. 4SCSA by Appingedammer Brons Motorenfabriek, Appingedam, Netherlands; 375 BHP, 10 knots.

11.1952: Completed by N.V. Martenshoekster Scheepsbouw, Martenshoek, Netherlands (Yard No. 77) for H. Liberg (Scheepvaart Kantoor 'Liberg'), Raamsdonkveer, Netherlands as OLIVIER VAN NOORT.

1970: Sold to Rederij Viking C.v.o.A. (Rotterdamse Bevrachtings Scheepvaart Maatschappij N.V.), Rotterdam and renamed CAPRICORN.

1972: Sold to Bulk Cargo Handling Services Ltd., Liverpool and renamed SEAFORTH TRADER.

1975: Sold to Benlow Shipping Company (J. and C. Harrison Ltd., managers), London and renamed BENLOW TRADER.

1975: Sold to St. Swithins Shipping Co. Ltd. (Clark, A.L. Clifford and Partners Ltd., managers), London.

1977: Renamed ARGUS PROGRESS.

1978: Sold to Marine Management Corporation (Arcom Shipping Management Ltd.), London, renamed LEK UNITY and registered in Singapore.

1979: Renamed UNITY and registered in Panama.

1985: Broken up in Israel.

M28. BORELLY 1979

O.N. 362314 430g 203n 508d
50.98 x 8.08 x 2.85 metres
Oil engine 6-cyl. 4SCSA by Maschinenbau Kiel A.G., Kiel, West Germany.

1956: Completed by Scheepswerf Janssen N.V., Druten, Netherlands (Yard No. J.141) for Eltje M. Hut (Wijnne & Barends N.V., managers), Delfzijl, Netherlands as BORELLY.

1975: Sold to Concord Leasing Ltd.,

In 1975 Benlow Shipping Company of St. Swithins Lane, London entrusted Harrisons with the management of two of their coasters, including the *Benlow Viking*. [FotoFlite incorporating Skyfotos/David Whiteside collection]

Sailing from Yarmouth in the summer of 1975 is the oldest of the group of six coasters managed by Harrisons, the now gearless *Benlow Trader*, built in the Netherlands in 1952. [J. and M. Clarkson]

Brentford (Whitbury Shipping Co. Ltd., Sheerness, managers).

1979: Managers J. and C. Harrison Ltd., London.

1979: Managers became Whitbury Shipping Co. Ltd., Sheerness.

1982: Sold to Valley Commercial Company, Road Bay, Anguilla and renamed MIRABELLE.

1982: Sold to Transportes Maritimos Interoceanica Ltda., Bogota, Colombia, renamed SAN LUIS I and registered at Isla de San Andres, Colombia.

7.2003: Sold to Aldo Papilla Lopez and Marlon Valencia Fernandez, Isla de San Andres, Colombia

16.12.2011: Deleted from 'Lloyd's Register' as continuing existence in doubt.

Last coaster to come into Harrisons' management was another former Dutch veteran, the *Borelly* of Concord Leasing Ltd., Brentford, briefly managed in 1979. *[J. and M. Clarkson]*

Acknowledgements

I owe a particularly deep debt of gratitude to Peter Harrison-Sleap for his whole-hearted support of this project and for providing me with copies of his family's collection of documents and photographs on the Harrison shipping venture. I am equally grateful to Roy Fenton for suggesting I attempt a history of J. and C. Harrison, and for giving me all the assistance and encouragement an author could ever hope for from his publisher. In addition, I would like to thank the following for their contributions to my research and their contributions to a collection of photographs both larger and wider than I thought possible at the beginning of the project: John Clarkson, Pauline Cowen, Captain David Davies, Mike Day, Ian Farquhar, Nigel Farrell, John Lingwood, Malcolm Mackenzie, the National Maritime Museum (David Hodge and Bob Todd), the National Museum of Wales (David Jenkins), Peter Newell, Kevin O'Donoghue, Bill Schell, Stuart Smith, Rob Stuart, Alastair Sutherland, John Wharton, and the World Ship Society (Jim McFaul, Tony Smith and David Whiteside).

Nomenclature

Harrisons quickly adopted the scheme of giving their ships names beginning with 'Har'. As the fleet expanded, more and more were needed until a total of 46 had been used. Place names featured prominently, some differing only in one letter; e.g. Harlington, Harrington and Hartington. There were some family names, a number from Greek history and mythology, and some truly obscure or antiquarian, such as Harcalo and Harmala. The owners had their own preferences, leading to Harpalyce and Harpagus being each used six times. Names whose provenance has been found are listed below.

Harberton	A village near Totnes in Devon.
Harbledown	A suburb of Canterbury.
Harborne	A district of Birmingham.
Harborough	The villages of Harborough Parva and Harborough Magna are in Warwickshire. There is also Market Harborough in Leicestershire
Harbury	A vllage in Warwickshire.
Harcalo	A person knowledgable about poisons derived from plants and animals.
Harcourt	Probably a family name, features in the village of Stanton Harcourt near Eynsham in Oxfordshire.
Harcroft	A family name.
Harden	Occurs as a place name at least four times in England, including a village near Bingley in West Yorkshire.
Hardingham	A village in Norfolk.
Hardy	A family name, used early and only once.
Harfield	There is a Harfield Village near Cape Town.
Harfleet, Harflete	Family names.
Harfleur	A town near Le Havre in France.
Harford	A village in Devon.
Harlech	A small town on the coast of Gwynedd.
Harlesden	A borough in west London.
Harley	There are villages of this name in Shropshire and Yorkshire.
Harlingen	A Dutch town on the Ijsselmeer, which gave its name to a town in southern Texas. One of only two foreign place names used, but seemingly chosen mainly for ships which were sold on the stocks.
Harlington	Villages in Bedfordshire and south Yorkshire and a district in Hillingdon, west London.
Harlow	A town in Essex.
Harlyn	Place name near Padstow, Cornwall.
Harmala	A type of drug produced by plants of the rue family
Harmattan	A hot, dry wind which blows south from the Sahara.
Harmonic	A musical term derived from harmony.
Harmony	A term for things which are in agreement.
Harpagon	Principle character in Moliere's play 'La'Avare', ('The Miser').
Harpagus	A general of the Medes in the Sixth Century BC.
Harpalion	A Trojan warrior mentioned in the Aeneid.
Harpalus	A contemporary of Alexander the Great in the Fourth Century BC.
Harpalyce	The daughter of Harpalycus.
Harpalycus	A king of Thrace.
Harpasa	An ancient town in Turkey, now Arpaz.
Harpenden	A town in Hertfordshire.
Harperley	A place name from County Durham.
Harport	Loch Harport is on the Isle of Skye.
Harrington	Villages in Northamptonshire and Lincolnshire, and a district of Workington.
Hartington	A small town in Derbyshire.
Hartismere	A district of Suffolk
Hartlebury	A village in Worcestershire.
Hartlepool	An industrial town near the mouth of the River Tees. Surprisingly used just once, but at least on one of many locally-built Harrison ships.

Most Harrison ships were given place names, which varied from well known ones such as *Harlingen*, the fourth of the name seen above left at Vancouver in 1935, to the obscure, as in *Harperley*, a location in Durham. The latter was used for the fourth and last time for a Second World War-built steamer, right. *[R. Moffat Scott/Roy Fenton collection; J. and M. Clarkson]*

Other names were more exotic, if often downright obscure. The fourth and last *Harpalion* (left, in 1954) was named after a Trojan who fell in the Trojan Wars, whilst the origin of *Harpathian* - used for the third time for this Liberty (right) - cannot be traced. *[Ships in Focus; J.Y. Freeman]*